Caring
for Old
Houses

D0317932

Caring for Old Houses

Pamela Cunnington
edited by Alison Henry

Marston House

First published in 1984 as *Care for Old Houses*
This revised paperback edition
published 2002 by Marston House,
Marston Magna, Yeovil, Somerset BA22 8DH, UK

British Cataloguing-in-Publication Data
A catalogue record for this book
is available from the British Library

ISBN 1 899296 17 4

Most photographs and line drawings are by the author.
The photograph by Tim Woodcock on the cover of the book
shows pargetting on houses at Saffron Walden, Essex.

Printed in China by Regent Publishing Services Ltd.

Contents

Acknowledgements

The author thanked all those who have helped her with material for this book, especially the following people who provided information for the case studies: Mr John Sell, of Sell, Wade, Postins: Messrs Truscott, Bullen and Brown of the Department of Technical Services, Chester City Council: Mr G. Lane of Norwich City Planning Department; Mr and Mrs M. Gooch; Mr C. Kenyon; Mr S. Bateman, of the City of Bradford Metropolitan Council Technical Services Directorate; Mr R. J. Taigel, of Anthony Short and Partners; Messrs M. Pearce and K. Stubbs, of the Planning Department, Hampshire County Council; and Mr I. Trowbridge.

Information on other buildings has been given by the Borough Planning Officer, Newcastle under Lyme, Staffordshire; the City Planning Officer, Exeter City Council; the Norwich Preservation Trust; Mr N. Taylor, of Fisher, Hollingsworth and Partners; the Director of Environmental Services, City of Stoke on Trent; The Lincoln Civic Trust Ltd; the Planning Officer, West Lindsey District Council, Lincolnshire; Mr A. Dobby, Lincoln City Council; the Director of Technical Services, Scarborough Borough Council, and the Planning Officer, Mendip District Council. She expressed her gratitude to all these people for their time and trouble in answering her queries.

The following building owners who supplied photographs or allowed photographs of the interiors of their houses to be included are acknowledged: Mr. O. Rowlands; Mr and Mrs C. D. Womersley; Mr and Mrs K. Percival: Mr R. Scott; Mr and Mrs R. Harvey; Mrs Hayward; Mr Lefort; Mr H. Van Manen. Also, the Incumbents of churches at Shobdon, Bibury, Walpole Saint Peter, Kings Lynn, and Wootton Wawen, for similar permission to use interior photographs. Pentracide Ltd, Bournemouth, kindly supplied the pictures of dry rot.

The photograph of Saint Mary's Almshouses, Glastonbury, is reproduced by permission of the Trustees of Saint Benedict's Church Council. The photograph of Stranger's Hall, Norwich, is reproduced by permission of the Norwich Museums Service. The photograph of the Merchant's House, The Rows, Great Yarmouth, is by permission of the Historic Buildings and Monuments Commission for England.

Finally, the publishers would like to thank Alison Henry for her diligent work in updating the text for the 2002 edition, bearing in mind the changes in legislation and attitudes to conservation which have developed over the last two decades, and Tim Woodcock for making available his fine collection of photographs of vernacular buildings.

Introduction

It is probably true that more people are interested in the care and preservation of historic buildings today than at any time in the past. Conservation might almost be described as a 'growth' industry. This interest and concern manifests itself in several ways. Almost any proposal to demolish a well-known building will arouse protests, often from people who have until then taken the building for granted and shown little interest in it. Civic societies and similar organisations, and building preservation trusts are being formed in more and more towns and villages. More local authorities are conscious of their responsibilities in this field, and some are offering financial aid to owners of historic buildings, as well as sometimes taking more account of the historic environment when preparing or approving development schemes. On a more personal level, many people dream of finding, buying and rehabilitating an old house and, in spite of the problems which can arise if and when the dream becomes reality, find more satisfaction from this than they would in building a new house, or buying one ready-made.

This book is intended to encourage and help all those who are trying to preserve our historic buildings, whether as members of a local 'pressure group' trying to influence decisions in a constructive way, or as private individuals concerned with repairing and adapting an old house for their own use. In many cases they will, of course, be the same people.

In the first part of the book I have looked at the general aspects of historic buildings conservation, the historical background, the current legal position, and the main threats likely to affect different types of building. The second section will I hope be helpful to those who propose to rescue and repair an old house for themselves, while in the final section I have given some examples of historic buildings which have been saved, by private individuals, building preservation trusts, or local authorities. I hope that these will encourage others to do the same, and to realise that very few buildings cannot be rescued if the will to do so is there.

Ightham Mote, Kent, a medieval court-yard house, has been little altered since the sixteenth century. Soon after the Second World War there were fears for its future when, in need of repair, it was put up for sale, at a time when the historic buildings legislation was at an early stage of development, and a number of country houses were demolished. Fortunately, Ightham Mote found a sympathetic purchaser and now belongs to the National Trust.

Part I. *The Framework of Conservation*

1 Preserving the past: the historical background

If we were to ask a sample of people why they felt old buildings should be preserved, I imagine that we should receive some of the following answers: 'Old buildings are beautiful, and add to the character of our towns and villages.' 'They are a tourist attraction; people do not come here to see supermarkets and tower blocks.' 'Many modern buildings are ugly, mechanical-looking, and impersonal.' 'Redevelopment is making all our towns look alike.' 'Old buildings contain fine craftsmanship which we do not seem able to copy today.'

Underlying these answers is another, which might not be put into words: that old buildings, and streets, can give us a sense of continuity, stability and security, which is lost when our surroundings are suddenly and drastically changed, and familiar landmarks disappear. This is not something to be taken lightly by planners and others who have to decide on these matters.

In addition to these sentiments, there is another reason why old buildings are important; they can provide valuable information, complementary to written evidence, about our history, and how our ancestors lived and worked. This was brought home to me some years ago, when I was concerned with repairs to a medieval church in Kent. Apart from some nineteenth-century restoration the building appeared to date from the fourteenth century, and the surviving documentary evidence indicated that it had been completely rebuilt by the lord of the manor at that time. Although the name of the settlement indicated a probable Saxon origin, there was no mention of a church in the Domesday Book. During the repairs, however, we uncovered what could only have been a small Saxon window, which must have formed part of the original construction of the west gable wall. Clearly, the fourteenth-century work was a remodelling of a much earlier church, not a complete new building. Discoveries of this kind, which are not unusual, indicate the care needed when carrying out work on old buildings—a subject to which I return later.

We must of course remember that the reasons for wanting to preserve an old building today may be quite unconnected with its original function. Edward I's Welsh castles, for instance, were intended to subdue a conquered race—very different from their role today as a major tourist attraction.

Preserving the past: the historical background

It is often said that we cannot preserve everything. This is true, although it may too often be used as an excuse for not preserving enough. It is important, though, to see that the right buildings are saved and to get our priorities straight. This does not mean concentrating only on the stately homes and other major buildings, important as these are. History does not consist simply of the lives and actions of famous people. The smaller houses, homes of ordinary people, the village churches where they worshipped, even their workplaces, can often be just as important in their way. Far too often these humbler buildings have been regarded simply as sub-standard property, and they have been demolished or had their character obliterated by insensitive modernisation, with no appreciation of their significance. I think that the preservation of a historic town or village may be compared with the performance of a fine piece of music. First class soloists are invaluable, but no more so than a good choir and orchestra.

Often, old buildings have to be adapted to suit present day needs, but the way this is done is important. To be able to modernise an old house without destroying most of its historic value we must understand its original design. Simply maintaining a superficial prettiness is not enough. I think we need to be more careful in these matters than ever before because we have the technical means to be so much more destructive, by carrying out drastic alterations, in the way that modern deep ploughing is so much more destructive of field monuments than was the old shallow ploughing of the past.

It is sometimes said that the failure of much new building to appeal to us is due to shortage of money—because we cannot afford anything better—but I doubt if this is always the case. Many of the old houses we so admire were built by people with a far lower standard of living, and less technical knowledge than we enjoy today. Perhaps we just prefer to spend our money on other things.

Is the present concern for historic buildings really something new—peculiar to our own age? Before looking at the problems of today let us see how our attitude to old buildings has developed over the centuries. There is little evidence, for instance, that the Roman invaders were much concerned with preserving what were, to them, the primitive structures of the native peoples of Britain. In Dorchester, Dorset, a Neolithic henge monument, probably of some local religious significance, was converted by the Romans into an amphitheatre for their new town. This may have secured its preservation, but the motive must have been purely utilitarian. The Romans themselves built substantially, and evidence of their buildings, towns and roads, is still being revealed by archaeology, although little remains standing in Britain. Structures such as the Baths at Wroxeter, the Jewry Wall at Leicester, and the Roman Arch at Lincoln are exceptional, generally owing their survival to their having been incorporated in later structures on the site. The Saxons who followed the Romans generally showed scant appreciation of their work. Roman buildings

Saint Peter's Church, Bradwell on Sea, Essex. A Saxon church built on the site of a Roman fort, and incorporating some Roman material.

Saint Laurence's Chapel, Bradford on Avon, Wiltshire. After use as a cottage for several centuries this Saxon church is now restored to its original use.

Saint Peter's Church, Wootton Wawen, Warwickshire. The Saxon tower arch of a cruciform church has survived, but the rest of the building was rebuilt at various stages during the Middle Ages.

were either deliberately destroyed, left to decay, or robbed of their materials. Re-used Roman bricks and other materials may be found in many Saxon and medieval buildings, such as the Saxon church at Bradwell on Sea, Essex, and Escombe in County Durham, where a complete stone arch from a nearby Roman fort forms the chancel arch of the church.

If the Saxons showed little respect for the work of the Romans, the same was true of the next invaders, the Normans, who rebuilt most of the Saxon churches. Those that have survived are generally in remote or unimportant places. The timber church at Greenstead, Essex, is a well-known example, as is Worth, in Sussex, in the Wealden forest, largely unaltered until the nineteenth-century tower was added. The Saxon church at Bradford-on-Avon, Wilts, in the centre of a town, owes its survival to the fact that the Normans did not rebuild, but abandoned it for a new building nearby. The old church was converted to secular uses, and was only discovered in the nineteenth century. In contrast to these survivals, the Saxon church at Wootton Wawen, Warwickshire, was almost entirely rebuilt in stages during the middle ages, only the central tower surviving. Throughout the medieval period both churches and houses were repeatedly rebuilt, enlarged and altered in the 'modern' style of their day, with little apparent regard for the work they replaced.

To our way of thinking, perhaps a most surprising example of this attitude was the rebuilding of Westminster Abbey by Henry III. The Abbey had been founded and built by Edward the Confessor who, throughout the middle ages, was venerated as a saint, being regarded as Patron of England before Saint George became popular. We might have expected the great church he had built to be treasured and preserved in his memory, but Henry presumably thought he was doing the saint a greater honour by rebuilding his church on a more magnificent scale. Only a small part of the crypt of the Confessor's

Saint Mary's Church, Bibury, Gloucestershire. This Saxon church was enlarged during the Middle Ages. The jambs of the original chancel arch survive, but the arch itself was rebuilt in the Gothic style.

Walpole Saint Peter Church, Norfolk. A splendid, unspoilt, late medieval church, retaining many early furnishings.

church was allowed to remain. On the other hand, Westminster Abbey does provide an example of an exception to this rule. Henry III did not complete the rebuilding of the nave, and the western part of Edward's church survived until the fifteenth century. When this was eventually rebuilt it followed, in its general lines, the style of Henry's work, which was by then two hundred years out of date.

As a general rule, however, rebuilding and alteration of older buildings was quite uncompromising. If the builders could not afford to rebuild completely—as was more often the case in the later middle ages—they might give an older building a face-lift. Examples of this may be seen at Gloucester and Winchester Cathedrals, and Sherborne Abbey, Dorset—all cases where Norman churches were remodelled in the Perpendicular style. Today I suppose we might call such work 'vandalism', and we must remember that the word 'Gothic', applied to medieval architecture was originally a term of abuse. The medieval builders were, however, supremely confident that what they were creating was an improvement on the original, and we can hardly say that their confidence was not justified when we look at an unspoiled church of that period.

In domestic building, the story was the same. The Norman and early medieval houses, designed partly for defence, with thick walls and small windows, did not appeal to the nobility and gentry of the fifteenth century. The great houses were rebuilt and altered to provide more comfort, as well as echoing their owners' wealth, and their example was followed by the yeomen and town merchants. Where, in towns, Norman and early medieval vaulted cellars survive under later superstructures this is probably because it would have been more trouble to reconstruct than to retain them.

The continuous process of rebuilding and beautifying churches came to an abrupt halt in the middle of the sixteenth century, with the Reformation and its accompanying political and social changes,

The Deanery, Winchester, Hampshire. Converted from monastic buildings after the Dissolution, this house shows a combination of medieval and eighteenth century work.

which coincided with the revival of classical learning and a renewed appreciation of the architecture of ancient Greece and Rome. Medieval buildings were now considered barbarous, and of no artistic merit. The dissolution of the monasteries heralded a new wave of destruction, but now with a difference. The monastic buildings were not demolished to be replaced with something finer. They were destroyed for the sake of their materials, or simply allowed to decay. A small proportion were adapted for other purposes, either as parish churches or for secular use. Alterations carried out for this reason began to reflect the newly popular classical style, producing a hybrid effect in many instances.

The later sixteenth century was a great period of house building, at all social levels. There was much re-use of materials from monastic buildings, but little respect for medieval work. In the following century the Civil War, and in particular the activities of Cromwell and his followers, has been blamed for the loss of many historic buildings. Some of this occurred as a direct result of the fighting, and both sides were probably equally to blame. Deliberate destruction was mainly confined to castles, fortified houses and other buildings of actual or potential military significance. There is little evidence of deliberate damage to the actual structure of churches, although their furnishings suffered considerably, from a combination of religious bigotry and plain vandalism. In a few cases churches were completely destroyed, as at Compton Wynyates, Warwickshire, where the church, in the grounds of a mansion belonging to a Royalist family, had to be rebuilt completely after the war. Here, the architectural style of the new church was still Gothic—survival rather than revival—perhaps an attempt to reproduce the old building, but the interior planning and furnishings were in the style of the day, designed for prayer book worship. Churches destroyed or badly damaged during the Second World War were often similarly treated.

Corfe Castle, Dorset. 'Slighted' after a siege in the Civil War, but still an impressive ruin.

Transformed yet protected by constant use, Vicar's Close, part of the Wells Cathedral precinct, was first const- ructed at the time of the Black Death, 1342. The chimney stacks date from the sixteenth century.

ABOVE *Saint Margaret's Church, Kings Lynn, Norfolk. The nave of this former priory church was rebuilt in a Gothic style after being destroyed in a storm in the eighteenth century.*

Stokesay Castle, Shropshire. a fortified manor of twelfth century origin. Most of the structure dates from the thirteenth centuy. After the Civil War the house was leased as a farm, and much of it used as workshops and stores. It thus escaped eighteenth and nineteenth century 'modernization'.

Preserving the past: the historical background

During the seventeenth and eighteenth centuries, repairs to medieval churches were generally carried out in a strictly utilitarian manner, with few concessions to their architectural character. Where money was available it was more often spent on building a new church, or remodelling the old one in the classical style, than on what we would call a sympathetic restoration of the old building. Churches were filled with box pews and galleries to accommodate the growing population, and to meet a desire for more comfort, with little regard for the architecture. The parish church at Whitby, North Yorkshire, is a noted example of this treatment. Today, though, we must admit that these buildings have an attraction of their own.

As at all times, there were exceptions. Sir Christopher Wren, generally acknowledged as a strict classicist, carried out careful repairs at such buildings as Salisbury Cathedral and Westminster Abbey. He even built a few new churches in a Gothic style, though this, one suspects, was probably the result of pressure from his clients rather than his own choice. The church at Staunton Harold, Leice- stershire, built during the Civil War, is Gothic in style, though its furnishings, like those at Compton Wynyates, are designed for reformed worship. In the eighteenth century the nave of Saint Margaret's Church, Kings Lynn, Norfolk, was rebuilt in quite a con- vincing Gothic style, after it had been destroyed in a storm. Throughout this period, too, medieval and Tudor houses were often rebuilt or remodelled in the new, fashionable, and probably more con- venient style of their day. Where we find a large medieval or Tudor house largely unaltered, as at Compton Wynyates, or Haddon Hall, Derbyshire, this was often because it had come down in the world, and was no longer the principal residence of its owners. Even the smaller houses were often given face-lifts, and additions to houses of all types were generally in the style of the day.

Shobdon Church, Herefordshire. Rebuilt in the eighteenth century in a fanciful 'Strawberry Hill' Gothic style.

By the early eighteenth century, however, there was a revival of interest in Gothic architecture, which was beginning to be admired for its picturesque qualities. Many of the surviving monastic ruins were now appreciated and preserved as landscape features, and were sometimes copied by the construction of mock ruins in the parks of large country houses. It is fair to say that many monastic remains owe their present survival to this fashion, although they were sometimes altered to make them even more picturesque with little regard for historical accuracy.

With the nineteenth century came a complete change of attitude. Medieval buildings were now studied seriously, and came to be regarded with respect. Following the writings of Augustus Welby Pugin, Gothic was considered to be the only true christian architecture, and 'restoration' became the order of the day. Unfortunately, much of this work was itself as damaging as the unashamed destruction of the previous centuries. The Victorians did not aim to replace

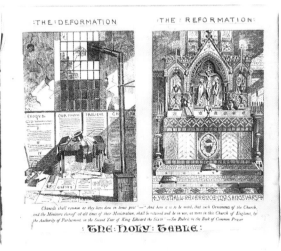

'The Deformation and the Reformation', a book published by Mowbrays in the mid-nineteenth century with illustrations, probably inspired by Pugin's 'Contrasts'. These show vividly the Victorian attitude to church design, furnishing and ceremonial.

genuine medieval work with work in the style of their day, but with what they believed was a more 'correct' medieval style. Paradoxically, such work now strikes us as typically Victorian. In this process, late medieval architecture, which was considered 'debased' when compared with that of the thirteenth and early fourteenth centuries, suffered badly. Work of the seventeenth and eighteenth centuries, regarded as 'pagan', received even worse treatment.

A few voices were raised in protest. John Ruskin, one of the first nineteenth-century writers to show a real interest in medieval art, hit out at this insensitive treatment. In *The Seven Lamps of Architecture* he says of 'restoration': 'It means the most total destruction which a building can suffer; a destruction out of which no remnants can be gathered, a destruction accompanied with a false description of the thing destroyed.' Strong words indeed! Ruskin goes on to suggest that if an old building reaches the stage when 'restoration' becomes necessary it would be better to demolish it—an extreme view which would rarely be accepted by most conservationists today. Everyone faced with the problem of preserving an old building has to decide how far repair should be taken—at what stage does 'pleasing decay' become unpleasing dereliction. We must, though, have great sympathy for Ruskin when we look at such work as that of Lord Grimthorpe at St Alban's Cathedral. Ruskin goes on to make a very important point. 'Take proper care of your monuments, and you will not need to restore them. A few sheets of lead put in time upon the roof, a few dead leaves and sticks swept in time out of a watercourse will save both roof and wall from ruin. Watch an old building with anxious care, guard it as best you may, and at any cost, from every influence of dilapidation.' Few would argue with these sentiments.

On the whole, however, Ruskin's protests went unheeded, although his enthusiasm for Venetian Gothic had a considerable influence on the design of new buildings. 'Restoration' (in the nineteenth-century sense of the word) was too fashionable among the clergy and other building owners, and too profitable for architects and builders engaged in the work. In fairness we must admit that many of our cathedrals and churches needed repair, and the Victorian architects such as Sir Gilbert Scott and George Edmund Street may well have saved them from collapse; but with a different approach some of the results could have been happier.

Still, the voice of protest was growing, together with a truer insight into the nature of medieval architecture. To the words of Ruskin were added those of such people as Thomas Carlyle and William Morris. The Society for the Protection of Ancient Buildings, nicknamed the 'Anti-scrape' Society was founded by Morris in 1877, and in spite of much early opposition its ideas were gradually accepted. The Society's principles were based on simple repair, without attempting to make a building more 'correct', and avoiding unnecessary renewal of old work. If additions had to be made to an old building they should be simple and unobtrusive, without actually copying the old work

A house at Sidmouth, Devon, built with material salvaged from the adjoining church when this was rebuilt in the nineteenth century.

or attempting to mislead future historians. (This is sometimes more easily said than done.)

Throughout the nineteenth century Renaissance buildings were most at risk, now that they had in their turn become unfashionable. Several of Wren's London churches were demolished with few objections. Others were altered in imitation of Gothic or Romanesque design. Georgian country houses were now given Gothic revival face-lifts. In view of the current popularity of Georgian architecture it is important to remember that this dates only from the twentieth century, and only in quite recent years has anyone had anything good to say about Victorian architecture. The second fifty years in the life of a building are probably its most dangerous. It is old enough to be out of date but not yet old enough to be considered 'historic'. Today we are just beginning to look objectively at the buildings of the 1920s to 1950s, and to realise that the best of them merit preservation.

By the end of the nineteenth century we find a growing belief that historic buildings and monuments should be preserved, if necessary, by the State. The first Ancient Monuments Act was passed in 1882, and this enabled certain scheduled monuments to be taken into official guardianship. At this stage action was mainly confined to pre-historic monuments. The Act did nothing to protect the great number of monuments and buildings which did not qualify for scheduling. Successive Acts widened the scope of the Act of 1882, but churches and inhabited houses were specifically excluded from this protection.

Churches, at least those belonging to the Church of England, were given some protection by the faculty system—the need to obtain approval from the chancellor of the diocese before a church could be demolished, rebuilt or altered, but I am afraid that this could sometimes be circumvented by a wealthy and autocratic incumbent or patron of the living, who was often the local landowner. The foundation of the Council for the Care of Churches, and of the Diocesan Advisory Committees in the 1920s (a lasting memorial to Dr Francis Eeles) has, however, done much to secure more sympathetic treatment for churches.

The destruction of many historic buildings during the Second World War strengthened the public demand for more effective measures for protection, and it was only in the Town and Country Planning Act of 1947 that this was given to inhabited houses and similar buildings by their inclusion in the statutory Lists of Buildings of Special Architectural or Historic Interest. Successive Acts have strengthened this protection, which will be described in more detail in the next chapter, but their successful operation depends largely upon the local authorities, backed by public opinion.

Recently there has been a change of emphasis, in that not only individual buildings, but whole streets and towns and buildings of comparatively recent date, including industrial monuments, may now be considered worthy of, and given, legal protection. We are even seeing such relics of World War II as pill boxes and tank traps

East Compton Church, Dorset. All but the tower of this church was demolished when a new church was built in the nineteenth century on a different site. The old tower has now been repaired by the Society for the Protection of Ancient Buildings.

being scheduled as Ancient Monuments—the successors after all to the medieval castle.

All this legislation, however, does not mean that historic buildings are no longer at risk. Although the consent of the Secretary of State for the Environment has to be obtained before a listed building can be demolished, pressures for demolition are still strong in many areas, especially where financial interests are involved. Still, if our own age has seen an acceleration of the process of giving historic buildings legal protection, it has also seen a corresponding acceptance of the idea that public money may have to be spent to achieve this. Both central and local government may offer financial help to owners of historic buildings. Details of this and of the work of voluntary societies in this field will be given in a later chapter.

We have come a long way from those Saxon invaders who cared so little for Roman buildings, and from the medieval builders who so confidently destroyed older work, believing they were creating something finer. Some might say that the pendulum has swung too far in the opposite direction, and that preoccupation with the past shows a lack of confidence in ourselves. There may be some truth in this, but I prefer to think that perhaps we have become humbler and less arrogant, more ready to appreciate the work of our predecessors. But if we are to continue to take a strong line in preserving the past, I think it is probably just as important to see that the buildings and towns we are creating today will be worthy of equal care by our successors.

A signal box on a closed railway line in Derbyshire. The line has been made into a 'trail' for walkers, and the signal box is used as an information centre in connection with this.

Monuments to two nineteenth century developments in transport. A railway bridge over the Worcester and Birmingham Canal.

2 The current legal position

I have outlined the historical background to the present concern for our historic buildings. Let us now look in more detail at the position today. Government policy relating to planning and the historic environment in England is set out in Planning Policy Guidance 15, known as PPG15, published in 1994. This provides useful advice about the interpretation of the relevant planning acts and local authorities must take this advice into account when dealing with historic buildings and areas. It is therefore helpful for owners of historic buildings and other interested parties to be familiar with the contents of PPG15. Whilst the situation in Wales, Scotland, Northern Ireland and even Greater London varies in some details the overall effect of the legislation is similar to that for England.

So what protection do old buildings really enjoy? We have probably all heard of listed buildings but there is still a good deal of misunderstanding about what this means. First, what is a listed building? Legally, it is simply a building included in a List of Buildings of Special Architectural or Historic Interest prepared or approved by the Secretary of State for Culture, Media and Sport or one of her predecessor ministers.

As we have seen, the preparation of the lists of historic buildings originated in the Town and Country Planning Act of 1947. This required the then Minister of Town and Country Planning to compile such lists in every borough, urban and rural district in Britain and a specialist team of investigators was appointed for the purpose. The lists described the selected buildings and graded them in descending order of importance. Grade I buildings were those considered to be of national importance and Grade II buildings of regional importance. A few Grade II buildings of particular merit were listed as Grade II*. A supplementary list of buildings of local interest, or Grade III buildings, was also prepared but this list had no legal force so Grade III buildings had no legal protection. In Scotland buildings are graded A, B and C whilst in Northern Ireland the grades are A, B+ and B.

We can well appreciate that owing to the size and complexity of the task of preparing the lists and the need to cover the whole country as quickly as possible there were omissions and inaccuracies in the original lists. For instance there was no general inspection of the interiors of buildings, and the fact that the surveys were carried out while petrol rationing was in force meant that many rural buildings away from the main village centres were not visited. Almost as soon as the lists had been completed therefore, in the 1960s, it was appreciated that they would have to be revised in a more thorough manner and in 1968 the first resurvey began. The resurvey of England is now complete and in the rest of the country the process is nearing completion.

The resurvey was carried out by teams of inspectors employed by English Heritage, Cadw, Historic Scotland or by the Department of the Environment in Northern Ireland. The inspectors consulted with the local planning authorities and any local historical societies, who often provided useful local information. Then, using local maps and the original list as a guide, the new survey was undertaken. A draft list was prepared and circulated to the local authority for comment or correction. The draft list was always inspected by an inspector from the Department of the Environment (or latterly the Department for Culture, Media and Sport) so that no building was listed on the recommendation of one person. This helped to avoid the risk of personal bias or individual taste influencing the listing. The lists were then confirmed by the Secretary of State and the buildings included in it were thenceforward listed.

The listings were compiled in volumes containing a written description of each building. Each volume may contain the buildings for just one parish, if it is a large parish, or for several smaller parishes. The volumes have green covers and have thus come to be known as 'greenbacks'. Maps were also issued showing the location of the buildings listed, but it is the greenback entry which is the statutory part of the listing.

Once a statutory list had been issued it was made available for public inspection at council offices. The owners and occupiers were notified and the listing was registered as a land charge on the property (except in Scotland). This means that it is, or should be, revealed by a search when the property changes hands, but one still hears the excuse 'I didn't know it was listed' when unauthorised work has been carried out.

The result of the resurvey was a fourfold increase in the number of listed buildings. Most of the old Grade III buildings on the supplementary lists were upgraded and included in the new statutory lists, unless they had been badly mutilated. Several types of buildings were included on the lists for the first time: Victorian, and even later buildings, particularly those designed by well know architects; more of the simpler vernacular buildings, cottages and small town houses, and early agricultural and industrial buildings whose value is more appreciated now; and more buildings of group value were included, as were such items as walls, railings and gates and street furniture.

Buildings are still being added to the lists, in one of two main ways; firstly as a result of systematic survey of buildings of a particular type

Pre-1700 buildings in contrasting styles. RIGHT *A cruck cottage at Styal, Cheshire,* BELOW *A dated stone house at Hawes, Yorkshire.*

which are known or thought to be under-represented in the lists, for example textile mills in south west England or airfield buildings, or secondly, following proposals by local authorities, amenity societies or individuals that particular buildings should be added to the list, or 'spot listed'. Anyone can request the Secretary of State to list a building. Requests should be accompanied by a justification for listing the building, a location plan, such as an Ordnance Survey map extract, showing, if possible, the location of other listed buildings nearby, clear, up-to-date photographic prints of the main elevations of the building and any other information about the building such as the date of its construction, details of any specialised functions it may have performed, any historical associations, the name of its architect if known, its group value in the street scene and details of any interior features of interest.

In deciding whether to list a building the Secretary of State will take into account definite criteria, originally drawn up by the Historic Buildings Council (the forerunner of English Heritage). These criteria are described in PPG15, paragraphs 6.10 to 6.16, and are as follows:

1. **Architectural interest:** the lists are meant to include all buildings which are of importance to the nation for the interest of their architectural design, decoration and craftsmanship. This also includes important examples of particular building types and techniques, for example buildings displaying technological innovation or virtuosity such as the early use of cast iron or reinforced concrete, and buildings displaying significant plan forms.

The current legal position

An eighteenth century terrace of small stone houses at Bath, Avon.

2. **Historic interest:** this includes buildings which illustrate important aspects of the nation's social, economic, cultural or military history, for instance factories, warehouses, railway buildings, schools, theatres and cinemas, pill boxes, almshouses and hospitals, prisons and lock-ups, markets, mills and farm buildings.

3. **Close historical associations:** with nationally important people or events, such as the birthplace of a famous person or the place where an important scientific discovery was made. In such cases the Secretary of State normally takes the view that the building itself should also be of some architectural merit or historic

LEFT *An eighteenth century brick house at Stratford on Avon, Warwickshire. Houses of this five-bay plan, built for merchants, professional men and prosperous farmers were common throughout the century.* BELOW *Eighteenth century vernacular Dorset farmhouse in cob and thatch.*

Nineteenth century estate cottages showing the influence of the Gothic Revival.

An early nineteenth century lodge in 'cottage orné' style.

Hill Close, Studland, Dorset, by C.A.Voysey, 1896. The Arts and Crafts Movement influenced domestic design until well into the twentieth century.

interest, and the association with a famous person or event may justify a higher grading, or tip the balance in favour of listing a building which would otherwise be borderline.

4. **Group value:** this includes buildings which may, on their own, be of limited architectural interest but which, together with other historic buildings, form part of an important architectural group or example of town planning such as squares, terraces or model villages, or form part of a historic street scene.

The age and rarity of a building are factors contributing to its historic interest. The older a building is, and the fewer of its kind survive, the more likely it is to have historic interest and to be listed. Thus the following buildings are, or should be, listed:

The current legal position

Canal workers' houses along the Leeds and Liverpool Canal, near Bingley, Yorkshire.

1. all buildings built before 1700 which survive in anything like their original condition;

2. most buildings built between 1700 and 1840, although some selection is necessary;

3. between 1840 and 1914 only buildings of definite quality and character, including the best examples of particular building types;

4. after 1914 selected buildings of high quality, including the major works of major architects.

5. buildings between ten and thirty years old which are of outstanding quality and under threat.

Building less than ten years old are not listed.

ABOVE A row of medieval almshouses at Glastonbury, Somerset. These are at present used only as stores, illustrating the difficulty in bringing such buildings up to modern standards without destroying their character. RIGHT Colston Almshouses, Bristol. These late seventeenth century almshouses are still in use, and well maintained.

Although anyone can ask for a building to be considered for listing, the final responsibility rests with the Secretary of State, and there is no appeal against the decision either way. This has sometimes led to criticism from local authorities, building owners and others who may feel that they should be more fully consulted. I am sure, though, that it is right that the final decision on listing a building should be taken by someone who has no financial or other vested interest in its preservation or its destruction. If the listing were to be left to those who had such an interest, the value of the lists as impartial assessments of buildings would be seriously in doubt. The Secretary of State has made it clear that in considering a building for listing only its architectural or historic interest, either individually or as part of a group, will be taken into account. Factors such as its condition, the wishes of the owner, or any plans the local authority may have for redevelopment or road proposals which may affect the building will not have any bearing on the decision to list it. At a later stage, if and when an application is made to demolish or alter the building, these other factors may well have to be considered.

As I am afraid there is still a good deal of misunderstanding about the meaning and effects of listing I think it might be useful to try to clarify some of them. First, listed buildings are not all large and imposing buildings or ones with strong historical connections. As we have seen, they include a wide range of building types of different dates. Next, listing does not cover only the exterior of the building - a very frequent misconception - even if, as is quite common, there is no mention of the interior of the building in the list description. If we really think about it this would be absurd. In many buildings internal features such as fireplaces, staircases, panelling and sometimes the actual plan form, are just as important as the exterior. It must be remembered that the purpose of the list description is simply to aid identification of the building; it is not a statement of what is or is not important about the building. Indeed, the list description may well refer to modern features such as a flat roofed extension or a twentieth century door, but this does not mean that such features are deemed to be of historic interest. Furthermore the listing includes all buildings or structures attached to the listed building or forming part of the curtilage of the building since before June 1948. This means that, for instance, a boundary wall attached to a listed building or an outbuilding in the grounds of a listed house is protected, even if it is not specifically mentioned in the list description.

However, listing does not mean that all these buildings and structures have complete and permanent protection and cannot be demolished or altered in any way at any time. Opponents of listing sometimes actually complain that listing is 'sterilising' a building or the area. Listing of course does not mean this: what is does mean is that there can be no harmful alteration or demolition of a listed building without the local authority first having the chance to consider alternative solutions. It is not always appreciated that

The current legal position

demolition is not the only danger to an historic building. Alterations of a kind which could well be permitted development for an unlisted building, and therefore not needing planning permission, can often be almost as disastrous. I am thinking of such things as a complete change of roofing material, alterations to doors and windows, in particular their replacement with uPVC, the insertion of large picture windows or large flat roofed dormers, painting over brick or stonework, or the stripping of plaster from walls never meant to be exposed. All these things can have a drastic effect on the character, not only of the building concerned but also on the whole group of which it forms a part.

Anyone wanting to demolish a listed building or to alter or extend it in any way which would affect its character as a building of special architectural or historic interest has to submit an application for listed building consent to the local planning authority. This is in addition to any planning or building regulations approval which may be required.

PPG 15 states that 'applicants for listed building consent must be able to justify their proposals. They will need to show why works which would affect the character of a listed building are desirable or necessary. They should provide the local authority with full information to enable them to assess the likely impact of their proposals on the special architectural or historic interest of the building.' At the very least, drawings of the building as existing and as proposed will be required together with details of the materials and finishes intended. However, in many cases more detailed information will be needed. This will vary for each case depending on the type of building and the scale of the works but will often include documentary evidence about the building or the results of a historical survey of the building fabric. If all this seems unnecessarily onerous we should remember that it is often the small details of historic buildings, such as the pattern of brickwork coursing, the subtle colour and texture of limewashed render or the profile of glazing bars, which give them their special character, and such details are easily harmed through ignorance or carelessness.

Most local planning authorities employ specialist conservation officers to advise on works to listed buildings. They are usually happy to visit the building and discuss ideas for alterations or extensions at an early stage, before full plans are drawn up. In this way owners may avoid wasting money on architects' fees for schemes which are unlikely to meet the required criteria for approval.

When the council receives an application it is required to advertise it, by a notice on or near the building, where it can be seen by the public, and in a local newspaper. English Heritage should be notified about any application relating to a Grade I or II* building, and about applications for total or partial demolition to a Grade II building. In addition to this, if total or partial demolition is involved, certain national amenity societies have to be notified. The local authority is required to take account of any representations received as a result of

ABOVE *Simple artisan cottages at Stratford on Avon, Warwickshire, which have escaped alteration and retained their character.*

RIGHT *A 1930s modern house in Dorchester, Dorset; architect C. W. Pike.* BELOW *Estate cottages at Bryantspuddle, Dorset, built c.1930, in Garden City style, designed by Halsey Ricardo and Macdonald Gill.*

these advertisements and notifications before determining the application. It is therefore important that all those who are concerned about these matters, such as local amenity societies, should study the advertisements in the press or on the site and should be prepared to comment constructively on the application. It is no use simply complaining after the decision has been made.

If the local authority decides to approve an application for alterations, not involving demolition, to a Grade II building it may determine the application itself. However, if it decides to grant consent for any work to a Grade I or II* building or for work of total or partial demolition of a Grade II building it must forward the application, with drawings and copies of any representations received, to the Secretary of State. Within twenty eight days the Secretary of State must either agree that consent should be granted or call in the application and hold a public enquiry. At these enquiries, all individuals and organisations who have made representations may attend and give evidence. This is another reason why it is important for local organisations and interested individuals to send in representations, as this entitles them to attend and speak at the enquiry.

If on the other hand the local authority decides to refuse an application it may do so without reference to the Secretary of State. The applicant has the right to appeal in these cases and this also may lead to a public enquiry.

It is an offence to demolish or alter a listed building without consent, and the penalty may be imprisonment or a fine, the amount of the fine taking into consideration any increase in the value of the building or site as a result of the unauthorised work. It is also an offence to carry out work which would damage a listed building, in order to expedite the granting of consent for demolition, e.g. by encouraging deterioration by removing part of the roof. The council may also issue an enforcement notice, requiring the reinstatement of the building to its state before the unauthorised work was carried out. This course is normally applicable to cases of unauthorised alterations, where reinstatement is practicable. It is only in exceptional circumstances that a council would be likely to enforce the reconstruction of a demolished building.

Although these measures seem quite strong there is a weakness in the law which can result in listed buildings being lost. It is, as we have seen, an offence to carry out works of alteration to a listed building without consent, but if proceedings are brought it is a defence for the owner if he can prove that the works were urgently necessary in the interests of safety or health and notice in writing of the need for the work was given to the local authority as soon as was reasonably possible. The purpose of the notice is presumably to give the council officers the opportunity to inspect the building, but an unscrupulous owner might move in quickly and destroy the evidence.

In addition, if a local authority considers that a building has become so ruinous or dilapidated as to be dangerous it may serve a

Spa Bridge, Scarborough, Yorkshire. Originally a toll bridge, this is a fine example of early nineteenth century engineering.

The current legal position

dangerous structures notice on the owner under the Building Act, requiring him to either make the building safe or to demolish all or part of it. The service of such a notice does not remove the obligation of the owner to obtain listed building consent or, in an emergency, to serve notice on the council that he intends to carry out the work as set out above. If, however, the owner were to demolish the building in these circumstances he might well have a valid defence in any proceedings brought by the council, since he could produce the notice served on him by the council, stating that the building was dangerous.

However, in most cases the local authority will wish to see buildings retained and repaired rather than demolished. If the owner of a listed building fails to keep it in repair there are two courses open to the local authority. Firstly it may serve an urgent repairs notice on a building which is unoccupied, or on the unoccupied parts of a partially occupied building. This specifies works urgently necessary to prevent further deterioration of the building and gives seven days notice of the council's intention to carry out the work. If, after seven days, the owner has not done the repairs himself, the council can get the work done and claim the cost from the owner. Secondly, the council may serve a full repairs notice. This specifies all the works considered necessary for the proper preservation of the building and can include full restoration. If, after at least two months from the date of the notice the owner has failed to put these works in hand, the council may start compulsory purchase proceedings. Both these courses of action could involve the authority in some financial risk since they may be unable to recover the cost of emergency work if the owner is on a low income, or they may be unable to sell a building which they have purchased compulsorily. So, there is often a reluctance, particularly amongst elected members, to put these measures into effect. However, very often the threat of such action is sufficient to prompt an owner to undertake work himself, and so these provisions can be effective in dealing with neglected listed buildings.

Of course, if an owner genuinely wants to preserve his building but simply cannot afford to, the planning authority has the power to offer grants and loans to assist in this work. This power is entirely discretionary, and it is up to individual councils to decide whether or not to make use of it. Unfortunately, most councils' budget for this type of work is very small. There is no doubt, however, that councils who do offer assistance are in a stronger position, morally if not legally, when it comes to dealing with listed building applications, or with cases of wilful neglect. In the case of buildings of outstanding importance, normally those Graded I or II*, assistance may be available from English Heritage or the equivalent body in Wales, Scotland or Northern Ireland. Sometimes assistance may be available from both sources either individually or for whole towns or areas under one of the partnership schemes. Further details of financial aid are given in a later chapter.

Certain categories of listed building are exempt from the normal legal provisions. First, *Scheduled Ancient Monuments*: a number of listed buildings are also scheduled ancient monuments; they are normally uninhabited buildings such as tithe barns, or structures such as bridges or market crosses. In these cases, if the owner wishes to demolish or alter the monument he does not apply to the local authority, but directly to the Secretary of State, who determines the application.

Second, some *ecclesiastical buildings*: churches belonging to denominations which have their own effective system of control to deal with proposals for alterations, extension and demolition are exempt from the need for listed building consent. These denominations are the Church of England, the Church in Wales, the Roman Catholic Church, the Methodist Church, the United Reformed Church and the Baptist Union. The exemption only applies to churches which are for the time being in use for ecclesiastical purposes. It follows therefore that a redundant church belonging to one of the above denominations cannot be demolished without listed building consent since it is no longer in ecclesiastical use and therefore no longer benefits from ecclesiastical exemption. There is an exception to this rule for the Church of England where proposals for demolition of redundant churches are dealt with under the Pastoral Measure. Ecclesiastical exemption only extends to listed building consent. Exempt churches are still subject to planning permission. Churches of all other denominations are subject to listed building control in the normal way.

Third, *Crown property*: although Crown buildings may be listed, they are exempt from listed building control. As well as buildings owned by the monarch and the Dukes of Lancaster and Cornwall, Crown land also includes land owned or held in trust for a Government department. Government departments are, however, expected to consult the planning authority if they wish to alter or demolish a listed building.

The 1967 Civic Amenities Act empowered local authorities to designate areas in towns and villages as 'conservation areas'. This meant that the whole area was considered worthy of conservation and enhancement, quite apart from the protection given to individual listed buildings in the area. It must be admitted, though, that protection given to the area as a result of designation is not as great as is sometimes imagined; indeed until the passing of the Town and Country Amenities Act 1974, it really gave no additional protection, apart from that afforded by normal planning control. Since the passing of the 1974 Act, however, consent has been needed for the demolition of any building, whether listed or not, in a designated conservation area. A few categories of building are exempt from this provision, including very small buildings such as garden sheds, some boundary walls and fences and post-1914 agricultural buildings. The procedure for obtaining conservation area consent is the same as that for listed building consent, except that the application does not have to be referred to English Heritage (except for buidlings in London) or to

The current legal position

Unfortunately conservation area designation provides very little protection from many of the alterations and extensions which can be so damaging to the character of historic buildings, and to their settings. Under the General Development Order certain types of work to houses are permitted development, needing no planning permission, even in a conservation area. Thus there is normally no control over such things as the replacement of traditional timber windows and doors with uPVC, the replacement of a natural slate roof with artificial slates or the painting of brickwork. Legislation does exist to enable local authorities to remove permitted development rights in conservation areas in relation to some of these works, such as the painting of a previously unpainted building, by the making of an 'Article 4 direction'. In practice however, the removal of permitted development rights is often politically unpopular and Article 4 directions are only usually made in exceptionally sensitive conservation areas.

Although the resurvey started in 1968 was thorough, we occasionally come across a building which was overlooked by the inspectors; often an early building with a good interior or medieval roof structure but with perhaps an unassuming nineteenth century frontage of little interest. Such buildings often come to light when the planning authority is notified of plans to demolish or alter them. In these cases the authority may consider that the building should be listed but feel that the imminent threat to the building does not allow time to apply to the Secretary of State for spot listing. In such cases the authority may serve a building preservation notice. This has the effect of immediately listing the building, and lasts for six months, or until the Secretary of State decides to confirm it. If it is confirmed the building is added to the statutory list. If, however, the notice is not confirmed, the owner may make a claim for compensation if he has suffered loss as a result of the notice, and this may deter some councils from taking this action.

A building preservation notice or unexpected spot listing can cause great inconvenience and possible hardship for a building owner who finds his building suddenly and unexpectedly listed just as he is about to start work on it. Legislation therefore allows anyone, although usually an owner or prospective purchaser, to apply for a certificate of immunity from listing, provided that an application for planning permission has been submitted. If granted, this means that the building cannot be listed for five years from the date of the certificate. Since, however, the building will first be assessed by an inspector from the Listing Branch, it will in fact be spot listed if found to be of listable quality. This may not be the outcome hoped for by the owner but at least in such a case he will know where he stands.

I hope it will now be clear that although historic buildings do not enjoy complete protection, the present legistlation, if conscientiously applied, should mean that no listed building is demolished or harm-

Eighteenth century house near Gravesend, Kent. although listed, it was demolished about 1960.

fully altered without very careful consideration and adequate opportunity for the public to know what is happening and to express their views. We must remember, though, that if the planning authorities are to take a strong line in these matters, public vigilance and support are essential, particularly where public expenditure is concerned. There is a limit to the extent to which the law can keep ahead of public opinion in this as in many other matters. In the end it is probably true that we get the architecture - and the environment - we deserve.

Adjoining buildings of different periods and construction, in different materials, often give group value, in Dorset, RIGHT, *and Powys,* BELOW.

31

3 Buildings at risk

More historic buildings are protected by listing today than at any time in the past and more people seem to appreciate the contribution that old buildings make to our towns, villages and countryside. Consequently fewer old buildings are demolished to make way for new developments than was the case perhaps twenty years ago. But many potentially useful buildings are still at risk of deterioration through neglect. This often occurs when, for whatever reason, a building is no longer needed or suitable for its original use. Once a building becomes redundant there is usually great reluctance on the part of the owner to spend money on maintaining a useless structure. Blocked gutters or slipped slates soon lead to water penetration and timber decay. An overgrown building encourages vandalism — windows might be smashed and, at worst, the building might go up in flames. Theft of building materials and architectural features such as fireplaces is all too common from an empty building. The cost of repairing the building in order to bring it back into use starts to mount up and it becomes increasingly difficult to find a new owner.

As we have seen, local authorities have powers to take legal action against owners who neglect listed buildings, but the procedures are time consuming and can be costly. For many buildings a change of ownership is the key to securing their future. Save Britain's Heritage was one of the first organisations to publish a register of buildings at risk and this initiative has been followed by English Heritage and many local authorities. The aim of the registers is to raise awareness of problem buildings and encourage potential new owners to come forward. English Heritage grant aid, and that of many local authorities, is now targeted at bringing buildings at risk back into use.

Let us look at some of the buildings which may be most at risk today, and the problems of their preservation.

The larger country house

Eighteenth century house in the Trinity area of Frome, Somerset. This area had become derelict, and was threatened with wholesale clearance, but was saved and rehabilitated by the Frome Historic Buildings Trust.

The threats to the continued existence of the larger country houses have received considerable publicity in recent years, following the demolition of many of them in the 1950s and 1960s. The rate of destruction has now decreased, due to increased public concern, and

33

Hengrave Hall, Suffolk. A large sixteenth century house, now used as a conference centre.

greater availability of financial aid, but there is no cause for complacency. Many country houses still face problems, and their future is uncertain.

The term 'country house' covers a wide variety of buildings, ranging from 'palaces' such as Blenheim and Castle Howard to more modest manor houses, but I suppose it is fair to say that most of them were built for a way of life that has largely died out. They were the centres of landed estates, providing employment for large numbers of indoor and outdoor servants and forming, with their owners, self-supporting communities. Even when these houses remain in the ownership and occupation of a private family this no longer applies to the same extent: certainly large indoor staffs are rare today.

The reasons for this change are well known. Taxation, in particular Estate Duty and its successor Inheritance Tax, has resulted in selling off much of the land which previously supported the houses: increasing maintenance costs and lack of staff have made it uneconomic for the whole house to continue in occupation. In some cases houses have been reduced in size by partial demolition: in others the whole building has gradually deteriorated. However, while it is easy enough to see the reason for the problems facing these houses and their owners, the solution is less obvious.

A late-nineteenth century house by Alfred Waterhouse, at Iwerne Minster, Dorset, now a public school.

Much depends on the size and situation of the house. In the case of the 'palaces' it will probably be increasingly difficult for them to remain as private family houses. Opening to the public on a frankly commercial basis — going into the 'stately homes' business — may be the answer in some cases, but can involve massive problems of security, and the resultant commercial exploitation of the house and its setting inevitably changes its character. Acquisition by the National Trust, with the owner continuing to occupy part of the house, may be the most acceptable alternative. Certainly the Trust will eschew the more blatant forms of commercialism, and will

A large country house, converted for educational use. Although this has preserved the building it was not enhanced by the addition of prefabricated units.

make sure that visitors' cars and coaches are parked discreetly out of sight of the house. Unfortunately, however, the Trust can now only accept a house if there is a sufficient endowment to maintain it, and increasing inflation is making this more difficult every year. The problem is often exacerbated by the fact that by the time a house is offered to the Trust it may well need extensive repair.

A third alternative may be some form of new use, a conference centre, college, residential or nursing home, offices for a firm seeking prestige premises, or luxury flats. These uses may be successful, but we should not underrate the problems they can cause. First, adaptation for any use of this kind is bound to involve internal alterations. It is not simply a question of what the new users may want to do to the house, but what they will be compelled to do to satisfy the requirements of the Building Regulations. These works can be very damaging, involving screening off staircases, inserting extra doors and lobbies, covering fine panelling and panelled doors with fire-resisting boarding, or replacing them with flush doors, and erection of external fire escape staircases. While it is sometimes possible to obtain relaxation of some aspects of the Building Regulations to avoid spoiling a historic building, this is less likely for aspects relating to health and safety such as fire precautions. In addition, if a licence is being sought, as for a hotel, the requirements may be even more stringent.

Furthermore, a use of this kind will probably generate a need to provide space for large numbers of vehicles, resulting in alterations to entrances and access drives and construction of large parking areas, all of which can affect the environment of the house. More seriously, if the new use prospers and expands, there may be a demand for additional accommodation. However well designed it will have some impact on the house and, in practice, such accommodation too often takes the form of system-built units quite unworthy of their setting.

When we consider the rather smaller houses, those of 'manor

house' class and style, the future looks more promising. Even today many of them still function as private family homes, and this should surely be encouraged in every way, by appropriate tax reliefs and other financial aid if necessary. Government grants are often conditional on some degree of public access, and this is most desirable. I am sure that the more people can see these houses, and appreciate the beauty of their architecture, their furnishings and their settings, the more likely they are to support measures for their preservation, even if this does involve the use of public funds.

As with the larger houses, a smaller manor house may be acquired by the National Trust: indeed some of the Trust's most attractive properties are in this category. Because of financial restrictions, though, the Trust will probably be able to accept smaller houses only if they are of exceptional architectural or historic interest, and would otherwise be unlikely to survive unspoiled. If these houses are converted to new uses, the same problems are likely to be encountered as we have seen facing the larger houses, but it is sometimes practicable to convert a medium sized country house into two or more units — houses rather than flats — without being involved in so many difficulties with Building Regulations.

To sum up, it is probably best for as many country houses as possible to remain in private hands, with assistance from central and local government funds. In most of cases this is likely to be more economical and satisfactory than taking them into public ownership.

A complex of medieval buildings, including two first-floor halls, at Cheney Longbridge, Shropshire, now used as farm buildings.

Farmhouses and cottages

In recent decades the fate of these humbler houses has often been linked with that of the larger houses. This may seem surprising, until we realise that until quite recently most farmhouses and cottages belonged to large estates. While the estate prospered, the farms and their buildings were generally well maintained, and the main danger to the older houses, especially cottages, was that a conscientious landlord might be more inclined to build new rather than to repair the old ones.

The increased taxation and inflation which took their toll of the larger houses in the twentieth century also affected the farmhouses and cottages. Small farms were sometimes combined to form more economic units and the thus-redundant farmhouses were either

A farmhouse of sixteenth century origin, near Wimborne, Dorset. Derelict for many years it is now being repaired by new owners, and no longer part of a farm.

demolished, divided up to form cottages or even used as farm buildings. Cottages, especially those in outlying areas, were allowed to fall into decay as new farming methods required fewer workers. The low controlled rents at which many cottages were let did not cover the cost of repairs, and the general standard of maintenance declined. As we have seen, land was often sold off to help meet Estate Duty, and the new owners did not always want all the buldings.

This process of decay was only halted when, thanks to the increase in car ownership, the countryside became more accessible and people began to move out from the towns. Old farmhouses and cottages became popular with commuters, retired people, and as weekend and holiday homes. This has given many of them a new lease of life, and we might think that these buildings are no longer at risk. However, if we look at the situation more closely there are still problems.

First, although redundant farmhouses and cottages can now fetch

ABOVE *Small isolated cottages may be at risk if no longer needed for agricultural use.*

Cottages let at low, controlled rents often suffer from neglect, particularly if their sites have potential development value. These cottages at Herne, Kent, have been repaired since this photograph was taken.

Even when cottages are rescued and repaired, the work is not always carried out in a very sympathetic manner. Standard modern windows destroy the scale of the façade.

very high prices on the open market, they are not always offered for sale. If a farmhouse is in the centre of a farm unit the owner may not want to sell, and to risk the inconvenience, or worse, of another owner in the middle of his land. Generally, only houses on the edges of farm holdings become available; others are still left to decay. Next, it must be admitted that the renovation of these smaller houses has not always been particularly sympathetic. This may be due to ignorance of their historic value and of the local building tradition, often combined with a rigid interpretation of the Building and Public Health Regulations, all leading in many cases to over-drastic remodelling. It is no exaggeration to say that in dealing with small houses and cottages it is possible to do as much harm by spending too much money as by spending too little.

A rather specialised type of small house which may be at risk today is the almshouse. These have played an important social role in the

RIGHT *A nineteenth century almshouse at Bridport, Dorset, still in use. The accommodation has been improved, and new extensions built at the rear, leaving the original block largely unaltered.*

Almshouses at Corfe Castle, Dorset, well adapted to provide improved accommodation.

past, before the days of the welfare state. Groups of almshouses, often attractively designed, form important elements in many towns and villages. Many of them, though, provide accommodation which is not acceptable by today's standards: the units are often very small and lack modern amenities. The charities owning and running them have probably been hit by inflation and loss of value of their endowments whereas, in towns at least, the value of the almshouse sites will probably have increased very greatly. For this reason, many of the urban almshouses have been sold and the proceeds used to build modern accommodation on the outskirts of the towns, where land is cheaper and the environment probably more pleasant. In some cases the old almshouses have been converted to other uses, such as the Geffrye Museum in east London, and Napper's Mite in Dorchester, Dorset. More often, though, they have been demolished to make way for commercial developments and there is still a risk to others.

In rural areas there has not been this pressure to sell, and some almshouses have been well modernised, often by being converted into fewer, larger units. The National Association of Almshouses has done good work in advising trustees on schemes of improvement, and sources of financial aid. In some cases, however, it has not apparently been feasible to retain the buildings and they have been sold, sometimes becoming private houses, or used for community purposes.

Napper's Mite in Dorchester, once almshouses, now a shopping precinct.

A fine town house in Devizes, Wilts. The insertion of a modern shop front spoils the symmetry and scale of the design.

Town houses

Most of our old towns contain a number of early merchant's houses, many of them now converted to shops. In the process the ground floors have generally been gutted, and the insertion of modern shop fronts has not only changed their character but, in many cases, actually weakened their structure. The back gardens have often been built over, and as a result of all these changes the early origins of the houses are concealed and forgotten. Since fewer traders now live over the shop the upper floors tend either to be used simply for storage, or even left empty. This leads to lack of maintenance and decay in the roof structure, which may well be the oldest and least altered part of the building. All too often it is only during demolition, or further drastic alterations, that the true character of the house is discovered, and by then it may be too late to save it.

As we have seen, the Department for Culture, Media and Sport lists, particularly the early ones, were made on the basis of an external inspection only, and thus many early town houses were not included.

The splendid façade of these town houses in Blandford, Dorset, designed by John Bastard, is marred by the shop fronts at street level.

A Georgian house in Worcester, converted into flats by a Housing Association.

This sixteenth century timber-framed house in Exeter, Devon, was moved on rollers to its present site to make way for a new road.

The revised lists have improved the situation, but it is fair to say that in an old town it should never be assumed that a building is of the date suggested by the façade. Certainly before any such building, whether listed or not, is demolished or altered, there should be a full survey by someone with a knowledge of historic buildings, as many early town houses still remain to be found.

Quite apart from the danger that early town houses may be lost through ignorance, they are often at risk from commercial pressures for redevelopment, and from urban road proposals. Even if the drastic comprehensive developments popular in the 1960s and 1970s are now less common it is still usual for several adjoining buildings in a town street to be acquired by a developer for rebuilding or converting into a single large shop unit. Many old town streets are made up of a series of narrow-fronted buildings, derived from the old burgage plots, creating a definite vertical rhythm. This can be badly disrupted if a new building with strong horizontal lines, taking up two or more of the old narrow plots, is inserted. This is now generally appreciated by planning authorities, who may insist that the old façade is retained, or rebuilt in replica, but who may apparently be quite happy to see everything behind the façade rebuilt, regardless of what early structures may be lost in the process.

If towns are to prosper it may not be possible to resist all proposals for redevelopment or alterations. It is therefore most important to decide which buildings, streets and areas should be preserved for their historic interest, and proper surveys should be carried out at an early stage, before any development plans are prepared. It may sometimes be possible for a local authority to enlist the help of a local historical society in this work. The importance of early town houses is at last being more generally appreciated, and some societies have produced excellent reports on streets and areas of their towns. It is tragic that much of this work still has to be done keeping just ahead of the bulldozer, rather than as a preliminary stage in the planning process.

The former market hall in Exeter, Devon, has been preserved and incorporated in a modern shopping precinct.

The Old Dispensary in Warwick, still in use as a medical centre.

Public buildings

Town halls, guildhalls, market halls, schools, theatres and cinemas and other public buildings are often of considerable intrinsic architectural value, and play an important part in the town or village scene. Many of them are at risk today, either because their original purpose has disappeared or because it has changed and expanded to such an extent that the old building is no longer suitable. Often, too, these buildings occupy sites of high potential development value.

Another problem for conservationists is that many of these buildings are of comparatively recent date, and built in a style which is now unfashionable but not yet generally accepted as 'historic'. It is only in the last few decades that Victorian and Edwardian buildings have achieved wider appreciation and protection. To many people, the buildings of the 1920s and 1930s are still considered of little merit. However, tastes are changing in this respect and some buildings of this period have been listed by the DCMS. Some buildings dating from the 1960s and 1970s have also been listed, often to the incredulity of the press and general public.

It is easy for us to say that these buildings should be saved, that their disappearance will rob the town of much of its character, that we shall reach a stage when all towns will look alike. This is undoubtedly true, but the remedy is less easy. Buildings in this group, often large and distinctive in character, can only be saved if a viable use can be found for them. Some quite imaginative conversion schemes have been carried out, but it must be admitted that these often prove very costly, because of the nature and construction of the building. If it is of real merit, every effort should be made to find a new use, possibly by asking SAVE, The Society for the Protection of Ancient Buildings or the local authority to help find a purchaser. These buildings are often familiar landmarks, and there may be a desire to preserve them for this reason, rather than for their actual architectural merit. For a local amenity society this is dangerous ground on which to fight. If the demolition of such a building is to be opposed it will be wise to have an independent architectural opinion.

The Railway Museum at Swindon, Wiltshire, converted from a redundant chapel.

Churches and chapels

Both in towns and villages, the parish church is often the most prominent and indeed the oldest surviving building. Many churches are of medieval origin, and contain substantial ancient work. Apart from their structures, they also often contain fine fittings and monuments, stained glass and furnishings. Many eighteenth- and nineteenth-century churches, too, are of considerable architectural merit, and a number of fine churches and chapels of denominations other than the Church of England survive from later periods. Most of these churches have probably passed through phases when they were loved and cared for, some when they underwent substantial rebuilding and alterations, and others when they were neglected, even disused. When we look back at the chequered history of the Church in Britain it is perhaps surprising that so many old churches have survived. Indeed, we may take this survival for granted and assume that it will continue. What are the threats to churches today?

Many old churches were either rebuilt or restored (often too substantially) during the nineteenth century. Today there is generally a better understanding of the way an old church should be treated, but far less money may be available for the work. Costs have risen, and there are fewer wealthy patrons and clergy to finance church repairs. On the other hand, most appeals for funds for this purpose meet with an amazingly generous response, often from people who do not normally attend church. Assistance may be available from other sources. Sometimes the diocese (or other denominational authority) can help with a grant or loan. The Historic Churches Preservation Trust, the Incorporated Church Building Society, local county church trusts and some other charities may give grants, and churches of all denominations may qualify for state aid if they are of sufficient historic or architectural interest.

Shortage of funds for repairs is often a serious problem, but on its own it is rarely a threat to the survival of a church, provided that the congregation and the church authorities want it to survive. When churches are closed, it is generally because the population has shrunk, or moved away from the church. This is most common with town churches, but it also occurs in rural areas, and is resulting in churches being declared redundant. The procedure for dealing with redundant churches, in the Church of England, is laid down in the Pastoral Measure of 1983, modified by the Pastoral (Amendment) Measure 1993.

The first step is the preparation of a pastoral scheme, providing for the church to be made redundant, often as the result of the amalgamation of livings or parishes. The planning authority is asked for its comments on the proposal, but has no power to prevent it. If the scheme is approved, the future of the church building has to be considered by the Church Commissioners, who are first required to consult the Advisory Board for Redundant Churches on the architectural importance of the church. Once a church has been made redundant there are only three alternatives for its future. If it is of real architectural or historic importance, and in particular if the interior and fittings are of so much value that conversion to another use would be damaging, it may be vested in the Churches Conservation Trust. This is a body set up specifically to hold and care for such churches, and it receives finance both from the Church and the State.

If the building does not qualify for vesting in the Trust, it becomes the duty of the diocesan authorities to try to find a suitable alternative use for it, and this involves full discussions with the local people. If the church is listed, any alterations needed for the new use will need listed building consent. Problems which have to be faced in these cases include the treatment of the churchyard and the disposal of monuments and fittings. In most cases the latter are moved to other churches. The question of the churchyard, especially if it has been used for recent burials, can present real problems, as strong local feelings may be aroused. It is no exaggeration to say that in many cases there is as much local concern about the graves as about the church itself.

Following the declaration of redundancy, there is a waiting period of up to three years for a use to be found for the church. At the end of that time, if the church has not been vested in the Trust, and if no use has been found for it, the Church Commissioners can order the demolition of the church, even if it is listed, without the need to obtain listed building consent. As we have seen, this exemption from the historic buildings legislation is enjoyed only by the Church of England. Other denominations must follow the normal listed buildings procedure. This is an anomaly, but I think there are signs that it may be modified, if not ended. As part of the arrangement by which state aid may be available for historic churches in use, it has been agreed by the Church Commissioners that before any listed church is demolished the Department of the Evironment will be informed, and if there is opposition to the proposal from the advisory board for redundant churches, or from the planning authority, and in certain other circumstances a non-statutory public inquiry will be held. This is an important development, although it is only fair to say that the cases of churches being demolished in the face of strong opposition from informed sources have been comparatively few.

Apart from the danger of demolition, or alterations resulting from a new use, what are the other threats to churches today? One which must not be overlooked is the growing incidence of vandalism and theft. More and more churches are having to be kept locked, not only in large towns where this trouble might be expected, but in rural and apparently 'respectable' residential areas. Opinions may vary on the reason for this, but it is an unfortunate fact of present day life.

Another factor which can affect churches is the desire for internal alterations to suit current liturgical fashions. There is a growing tendency to experiment with new forms of worship, which may

A small medieval church at Exeter, Devon, preserved in the centre of a new shopping precinct.

Buildings at risk

involve moving, or removing, certain fittings and furnishings. This of course is not new—drastic alterations of this kind followed the Reformation in the sixteenth century—and again in the nineteenth century when an attempt was made to restore what were considered to be the pre-Reformation arrangements. As a result, much of value was lost; screens, stone altars, stained glass and sculpture after the Reformation, and box pews, three-decker pulpits and galleries in the nineteenth century. While change cannot always be resisted it is, I think, important that superseded fittings should not be destroyed. Ecclesiastical fashions can change quite quickly, and the next generation may be eager to restore the very things we are now so busily removing.

It is sometimes suggested that churches, particularly those of greatest architectural and historic importance, should be taken over by the State, as ancient monuments, thus freeing the Church from the responsibility for their maintenance. This might be desirable in a few special cases but, as with country houses, I feel that it is best for them to remain in their present ownership, with state aid available as necessary, subject to control over the quality of work, and public access. Whatever the popularity of the Church as an institution today, there is undoubtedly a great deal of public support for the repair of church buildings, as evidenced by the splendid responses to appeals for this purpose. This would almost certainly vanish if churches were to be taken over by the State.

Farm buildings

Old farm buildings play an important part in the rural scene. Sometimes they are situated in the villages—a relic of pre-enclosure farming. Other groups or isolated buildings are found in open country, dating either from early enclosure of woodland and heath, or from the later Parliamentary Enclosures of the open fields and commons. Occasionally we find medieval or Tudor buildings, mainly barns and dovecotes, but most surviving farm buildings date from the eighteenth and nineteenth centuries, a period of agricultural expansion. Today, many of these buildings are at risk, and although more of them are now being included in the historic buildings list, they are likely to present increasing problems of preservation.

Farming today is an industry, and industry demands efficient buildings. Most old farm buildings were constructed for a system of agriculture very different from that practised now. Farm buildings at risk may be divided into two groups. First, those that are in the wrong place. Re-organisation of farming, with the consequent frequent amalgamation of small farms into larger units often calls for the resiting of the farm buildings. This applies particularly to the old 'village street' farms. They may have survived the Parliamentary Enclosures, but they are not conveniently placed for modern farming, and most of them are being abandoned. Farm buildings which become

Use as a saddlery has preserved this small granary without any disfiguring alterations.

46

Many old farm buildings, not needed for modern agriculture, are allowed to decay and eventually disappear. In contrast, the picture below shows a thatched barn in Dorset, well repaired and retained for agricultural use.

redundant for this reason are sometimes offered for sale for conversion to new uses, including housing. This may well be their best chance of survival, but any conversion work needs the greatest care if their essential character is not to be lost. Over-domestication — inserting cottage style windows and doors, and breaking up the roof slope with many dormers—is all too common. There have been some very good schemes, but it must be accepted that these are rarely compatible with the creation of a conventional style house. Sometimes the 'conversion' amounts to a substantial rebuilding, and one feels that the old building has simply been used as an excuse to obtain planning

permission for a new house in an area where it would not otherwise have been granted. It is sometimes better to try to find a use other than housing, which does not involve such drastic alteration.

Redundant farm buildings may not always be in the wrong place, they may simply be of the wrong type, unsuited for modern farming methods and large machinery. In these cases preservation is far more difficult; the farmer simply wants to replace the old buildings with modern ones on the same site. In these circumstances he is unlikely to be prepared to sell the old buildings, and in any case it would be difficult to find a purchaser for a group of buildings which, however attractive in themselves, are surrounded or overshadowed by modern farm buildings in use. The position is made more difficult by the fact that it seems easier for farmers to obtain grants from the DEFRA for putting up new farm buildings than for repairing old ones, although some grants are now available for repairs to traditional farm buildings using traditional methods. Consent to demolish listed farm buildings may be refused by the planning authority, but the erection of new farm buildings does not always need planning consent, and many fine listed barns, stables etc, are now hidden behind modern structures, with the consequent loss of much of their value. This may not be the end of the story. A farmer who has been refused consent to demolish old buildings he does not want is unlikely to spend money on their maintenance, and they may be left to decay—a process which may not be noticed by the public if the buildings are largely hidden by modern ones. Even if the planning authority realises what is happening it will be unlikely to serve a repairs notice on buildings in the middle of a farm complex, since the only real sanction, compulsory purchase, would rarely be practicable in this case.

Isolated farm buildings, such as the post-Enclosure field barns, also present problems, even when their owners are prepared to sell. It is less easy to find new uses for these than for those in or on the outskirts of villages. Many local authorities do not encourage housing conversions in these situations. In Derbyshire, some have found a new use as simple ramblers' hostels, or 'camping barns', in this way avoiding the need for drastic alterations to comply with the public health and safety regulations for normal hostels, and this initiative has been followed in the Lake District, Yorkshire Dales and on Dartmoor.

With farm buildings, we must consider similar buildings associated with rural industries, such as mills and maltings, and those typical of particular areas, such as the Kentish oast houses. Mills in particular are popular subjects for domestic conversion, but this often means that they are gutted, and their machinery lost. There is a renewed interest in milling today, and where a mill survives with most of its machinery intact the aim should always be to preserve it in working order. Maltings are particularly difficult subjects for conversion, because of the low headrooms nearly always found on the various floors. Altering these, and consequent changes in fenestration not only cause structural disturbance, but change the character of the

building. The effect of this must be anticipated when considering changes of use.

In view of the large numbers of these rural industrial buildings which are likely to become redundant it will probably be necessary to make a careful selection of the best examples for preservation. If possible this should be done at an early stage over an area as a whole, rather than on an ad hoc basis as individual buildings or groups are threatened. In some areas, particularly good groups of farm buildings have been preserved as agricultural museums. There is clearly a limit to the number of potential museums, but it is not unreasonable to hope that at least one could be established in each county, either by the local authorities or by voluntary societies.

Urban industrial buildings

These are of many types — factories, mills, warehouses, breweries and small workshops — dating mainly from the eighteenth century onwards. They vary a great deal in their character, and their architectural interest. Some are typical of particular regions, such as the bottle kilns of the Potteries, and the large textile mills of Yorkshire and Lancashire. Sometimes they are found directly associated with the industrial workers' housing, and these groups are of particular interest, to the social historian as well as to the industrial archaeologist.

Like the old farm buildings, they may be at risk for various reasons. The original use may have ceased or, conversely, it may have changed

The brewing industry has produced some interesting buildings in the past, often now redundant because of changed manufacturing processes. ABOVE *A nineteenth century former brewery at Gillingham, Dorset, in Italianate style.* LEFT *Oast houses near Ashurst, Kent.* BELOW *Maltings at Stowmarket, Suffolk.*

and grown to such an extent that the old buildings are no longer suitable. They may also be threatened by schemes of urban redevelopment and slum clearance. In many of these schemes, industries are encouraged to move out of town centres, on to suburban trading estates, especially if what was originally a small 'craft' industry has expanded, creating problems of noise and generating increased traffic. Most firms are quite happy to move out in these cases; they may be given financial assistance to do this by the local authority, and their old town centre sites will probably fetch a good price for redevelopment as shops or offices.

When this happens it is often difficult to look at these old industrial buildings objectively. To some people, especially those of the generation that grew up in their vicinity and perhaps worked in them, they are simply a reminder of a grim past they would prefer to forget. To others, whose main experience of early industrial Britain has been through the paintings of L. S. Lowry, they have acquired a romantic, nostalgic character. 'Coketown', with all its faults, is considered to be less inhuman than the concrete and glass of today's new towns.

These conflicting attitudes will present problems if we are faced with the decision whether or not to propose demolition of an old industrial building, and to put forward positive proposals for its preservation, In an attempt to adopt an objective viewpoint I would suggest that we ask ourselves the following questions:

First, is the building a good example of its type, and in particular, is it of local historic interest, i.e. built for a particular local industry? Second, to what extent has it survived unaltered, and does it contain any original or early machinery, whether water or steam powered? Third, is it of architectural significance in the town, as, for instance, the warehouses found on the quaysides of many ports? The age of the building is also important. In some towns, medieval warehouses have survived; these, and any buildings dating from before the Industrial Revolution are strong candidates for preservation, as also are any groups including contemporary industrial housing, especially if this remains in a reasonably unaltered state.

If the building is to be saved, it will of course be necessary to find a new use for it. With the growing interest in industrial archaeology, industrial museums are being set up in many towns, but as with farm buildings there is a limit to this possibility. Early industrial buildings have been converted to a variety of uses, including flats, offices, small craft workshops, or for some community purpose. Fortunately, most of them are solidly built, and the headrooms on each floor are generally reasonable, facilitating conversion, although it may be necessary to obtain relaxation of the Building Regulations in some cases.

I think it is important that any conversion work should respect the rather austere character of most of these buildings. Inserting cottage style or 'Georgian' bow windows in an attempt to humanise an industrial building is rarely successful. If the building contains early machinery this should if possible be retained in situ. If this cannot be done it should not be destroyed, but offered to a local museum.

Transport buildings

Buildings and other structures associated with transport are of many kinds, and may well be at risk today, simply because of the demands of modern transport systems. Let us look at them under three headings—roads, canals and railways.

An old stone bridge at Hebden Bridge, Yorkshire, has been saved from damage by heavy traffic by restricting it to pedestrian use.

ROADS The most important structures connected with road transport are, of course, bridges. Many medieval bridges survive, massive stone structures, spanning a river in a series of narrow arches carried on heavy piers and cutwaters, the parapets often incorporating a series of pedestrian refuges. Next came the rather lighter bridges of the seventeenth and eighteenth centuries, of stone or brick, sometimes with graceful balustraded parapets and fewer, wider arches. Finally, with the turnpike age, we have the work of engineers such as Telford and Rennie, making use of new techniques like that of the suspension bridge, to span a river with a single arch, with no cutwaters to obstruct the waterway.

All these may be at risk today, with the increase in traffic weight, density and speed. Old bridges suffer physical damage from heavy lorries, and even when this does not happen there can be pressure for their removal or drastic alteration to avoid restricting the traffic flow. In some cases it is possible to widen a bridge without destroying its character, although some very clumsy widening has been carried out in the past. In other cases it may be necessary to by-pass the bridge by constructing a new one beside it. In these cases the siting and design of the new bridge will need great care.

Most early bridges are now scheduled as ancient monuments, which means that the ancient monuments section of the Department for Culture, Media and Sport must approve any work of alterations. However, local opinion is still important, and any published plans for road improvements should be carefully studied to determine their effect on any important bridges.

Toll-houses, often of distinctive design, are often at risk from road-widening schemes.

Another category of building, associated with roads, which is often at risk is the tollhouse, a product of the turnpike system when tolls were collected at intervals along the road. These little houses are often of a distinctive character, the various Turnpike Trusts having their own styles. In order that the gatekeeper could see the approaching traffic and control the gate the houses were sited at the ede of the road, which of course makes them very vulnerable to road widening schemes. If they are of particularly good design it may be possible, and justifiable, to move them back to a new position. This can now sometimes be done by moving them intact, on rollers, rather than by demolishing and rebuilding.

Also, still linked to road transport, we have the roadside inns built to serve travellers. These range from the medieval hostels for pilgrims and other travellers to the coaching innns of the eighteenth and early nineteenth centuries. Occasionally they may be threatened by road widening schemes, though they are less vulnerable than the toll-houses, being generally set back further from the edge of the road. In rural areas some may be closed for economic resons, but when this happens they are more likely to be sold than demolished. The main danger to old inns is perhaps less obvious: they may suffer from being too successful and popular. When this happens we find them being enlarged to such an extent that the original small building is dominated by the new additions, even though these may be in a pseudo-'period' style. Equally damaging are the internal alterations often carried out - the pulling out of internal walls, and even chimney stacks containing early fireplaces, to create a single large bar in place of the original small rooms. Many early features are lost in this way, all too often to be replaced by mock Tudor or Georgian details made up in plastic or fibreglass.

CANALS The construction of the canal system in the eighteenth and early nineteenth centuries brought with it a range of interesting structures, the bridges, locks, aqueducts and tunnels, lock-keepers' and toll collectors' houses, stables and inns. With the decline of the canals in this century many of these structures fell into decay and were lost. In the last twenty years or so, however, the canals have experienced a great revival, and more and more of them are being restored for pleasure cruising and amenity use. This has meant that the canal buildings too are being repaired and brought back into use. Much good work has been done, both by the British Waterways Board and by volunteer groups.

Even so, we still find derelict buildings along canals, particularly lock-keepers' houses, since few locks are now manned. Some of these houses have been sold to private owners, and their restoration has not always been carried out in a particularly sympathetic manner. The bridges carrying roads and footpaths over the canals are often of simple but attractive design, in brick or a local stone. Some are well maintained, but others are deteriorating. Those carrying roads are, like other early bridges, suffering from the effects of heavy traffic, and are sometimes demolished, to be replaced by new structures, few of which are as attractive as their predecessors. Many canal bridges, however, do not carry roads, or even public footpaths. They were constructed to link fields when a canal passed through a farm, and are used only by animals. Due to later changes in land ownership or organisation they may no longer be necessary, and when in need of repair may simply be removed.

After a period of decline, the canalside inns are enjoying a new lease of life. As with the roadside inns, the main danger now is that they may be enlarged and gutted, with consequent loss of character.

This canal house at Chester has been well repaired, but its setting is not enhanced by the adjacent modern road bridge.

RAILWAYS As with the canals they succeeded, the construction of the railways in the nineteenth century brought with it a great number of buildings—stations, engine sheds and workshops, bridges, signal boxes — and of course railway housing and railway inns and hotels. With so many lines now closed, many of these became at risk.

Like the canals, the railways have their suporters, and where a redundant line has been taken over by a private company or trust the buildings are generally loving restored. Some redundant stations have been sold for other uses, including domestic conversion, commercial or industrial use.

The other danger to early railway buildings is that where lines are retained and modernised the old structures may be replaced with more efficient new ones, or may be given rather drastic face-lifts. There is some evidence, though, that the merits of Victorian railway architecture are now being appreciated, and that the 'image' of Railtrack is not necessarily enhanced by pulling it all down in favour of concrete and glass structures. The outcry over the demolition of the Euston Arch in the 1960s may not have prevented all further acts of vandalism, but it has probably made them less likely.

Conclusion

It will now be clear that nearly every type of old building may be at risk at some time, and we cannot take their safety for granted. A sympathetic owner may die, or sell, and when a real threat materialises much will depend on the attitude of the local authority. Most local authorities today profess a concern for historic buildings - it would be bad publicity to do otherwise—but they vary greatly in their ability and willingness to take effective action. Perhaps the best indication of local authorities' real concern for these matters is the way they look after their own historic buildings, not simply the few showpieces perhaps deliberately acquired for preservation and having some tourist value, but their 'everyday old buildings—early Victorian schools, old houses used as residential homes, farms and smallholdings, and similar buildings. A council which really believes in conservation will set an example to other owners—actions speak louder than words.

As can be seen from this example in Stratford on Avon, Warwickshire, conversion of an old coaching inn to shop use need not involve the insertion of standard shopfronts and facias, even for a multiple firm with a national image.

Thoresby College, Kings Lynn, Norfolk. An early sixteenth century College of Chantry Priests, which had suffered many changes during the succeeding centuries. By the 1960s part was divided into tenements, and part used as a warehouse, and its future seemed uncertain. Acquired by a local preservation trust it has been repaired and converted to new uses, with the aid of grants from the Historic Buildings Council, local authorities, and private trusts.

4 Financial aid

If we are to trying to save old buildings one of the main problems we shall have to face is that of the cost. This is equally true whether we are trying to save a threatened building in our town or village, or concerned mainly with our own old houses. It is therefore important to know of the various sources of financial help which may be available, and how to make the best use of the them.

Grant schemes change from time to time and it is inevitable that any information about availability of grant aid will become out of date almost as soon as it is written. Your local conservation officer should be able to give you up to date advice on possible sources of funding. Currently there are four basic sources of aid: central government, local government, the Heritage Lottery Fund and private trusts, and these sources may be combined in certain circumstances.

Central Government

Central government aid for historic buildings is administered through English Heritage and the corresponding bodies in Wales, Scotland and Northern Ireland. Assistance is normally only available for buildings or ancient monuments considered to be of national importance, and in practice is generally restricted to Grade I and Grade II* buildings. Occasionally assistance may be offered to a Grade II building, particularly if its true significance was not appreciated at the time of its listing, in which case it will usually be up-graded to II*, thus giving the Secretary of State control over any future alterations.

Because central government funds for these types of grants are limited, not every Grade I or II* building or ancient monument in need of repair will receive help. For secular buildings resources are targeted, for the time being at least, towards buildings and structural monuments at risk included in the English Heritage Register of Buildings at Risk, some country houses, and repair projects with significant social or economic regeneration benefits. (A separate grant scheme exists for places of worship, which is operated by English Heritage in conjunction with the Heritage Lottery Fund and is known as the Joint Churches Grant Scheme.)

For secular buildings an application for assistance is made directly

Financial aid

to English Heritage or the corresponding body in Wales, Scotland or Northern Ireland. The application will be dealt with by the appropriate regional office. If the application is considered eligible you will be expected to appoint a professional advisor experienced in specifying and supervising the type of work involved. This will normally be a registered architect or an RICS conservation accredited building surveyor. An architect or other specialist from English Heritage will visit the property to meet the owner and his professional advisor, to agree on the necessary work and the estimated cost. Grants are intended for major structural repairs, not for routine maintenance, works of alteration, conversion, improvement or demolition. It will be expected that work will be carried out to a high standard using traditional methods and materials, with the emphasis being on 'conservative repair'. It is important that no work should be put in hand until the specification has been agreed and the grant offered, as this would lead to automatic loss of the grant. Grants are normally offered as a percentage of the total cost of eligible works including professional fees and VAT. The percentage is not fixed and therefore varies to suit individual circumstances. However, grants are not normally offered for work to buildings whose owners are judged capable of affording the work without help from public funds.

If a grant is offered the English Heritage (or equivalent) architect may make periodic inspections to ensure that the work is being carried out as approved. No changes should be made to the agreed specification without his consent or the grant may be withdrawn.

It is normally a condition of the grant that there should be some provision for public access to the building. It may have to be open on a certain number of days in the year or by written arrangement with the owner. If the building has few interior features of interest access may only be required to the exterior. Grants must normally be repaid if the building is sold within ten years of the date of payment of the grant.

It will be apparent that the numbers of buildings eligible for grant aid under this scheme are relatively small, in relation to the total number of listed buildings. There is, however, one way in which central government aid may be available for Grade II and even, in some cases, unlisted buildings. This is through the Heritage Economic Regeneration Scheme, or HERS. These schemes are managed in partnership with local authorities and are targeted on small commercial and industrial premises in conservation areas where repair and refurbishment will make a significant contribution to economic and social regeneration. Local authorities have to submit a bid to English Heritage, justifying the need for a HERS scheme in a particular part of a town or city. Following a successful bid a schedule of buildings to be included in the scheme is drawn up and agreed. The list will normally include the listed buildings in the area but may also include unlisted buildings of group value. Generally the local authority (or authorities) and English Heritage share the funding. The range of work which may be eligible under a HERS is wider than for the Historic Buildings Grant Scheme and can include reinstatement of traditional shop fronts. In most cases a leaflet explaining the scheme, and showing the eligible buildings on a map, is prepared by the council and distributed to the building owners. Your local conservation officer will be able to advise of any HERS operating in your area.

Nearly twenty buildings in the main street of Langport, in Somerset, were identified for refurbishment under a HERS scheeme, and two years after the award was received several renovations had been completed, including the Langport Arms and the adjoining ex-bank. The owners of the Old Bookshop BELOW had undertaken its conversion from a motorcycle saleroom. The HERS scheme helped to renovate the shop front.

Financial aid

Local government

Assistance may be available from local government in two main ways, apart from HERS. Firstly, under the Planning (Listed Buildings and Conservation Areas) Act 1990 local authorities may offer grants or loans towards the repair of historic buildings. As well as listed

The Pennine village of Wycoller, Lancashire, had become derelict, following the decline of the weaving industry in the area. In the last few years it has been sensitively repaired, as shown RIGHT and BELOW, and revived as a community by the county council.

buildings unlisted ones may be eligible if the council consider them to be of sufficient historic interest, for instance, in a conservation area where unlisted buildings may be of group value. These grants and loans are entirely at the council's discretion. Some councils do not offer them at all and those that do so vary considerably in the amounts available and the conditions attached. Loans may be at any rate of interest, or interest-free, and the councils may decide on any period of repayment.

These schemes may well be the only source of grant aid for Grade II buildings outside a HERS area. As with English Heritage grants, most authorities will not offer assistance if work is started before approval is given, and the standard of work will have to be appropriate to the building. Any grant, or the balance of any loan, will probably have to be repaid if the building is sold within a specified period after it has been paid.

The second possible source of local authority grant aid is available for older houses, regardless of their historic value, under the Housing Acts. Such grants are normally administered by local authority Environmental Health Departments and they are intended to cover basic repairs and improvements in order to bring a building up to

Well reconditioned buildings in Wycoller, showing a feeling for the local tradition.

satisfactory health and safety standards. There are several different types of grant but all are discretionary and most of them are aimed at owners on a low income or in receipt of benefits.

If one of these grants is offered the council will normally require the house to be brought up to a satisfactory standard, which could mean carrying out work detrimental to the character of the house. In many old houses ceiling heights and window sizes may be below modern standards and could not be made to comply without spoiling the house. Also, some old staircases may not meet current Building Regulations, and some councils may insist on their replacement as a condition of grant. Councils have the power to modify the standard requirements in these cases but they are not bound to do so. Requirements under the Housing Act do not remove the need for an owner of a listed building to apply for consent for the alterations. Legislation is due to change shortly giving local authorities complete discretion in whether or not they continue to offer such improvement and repair grants, and it is likely that other schemes such as loans or

Local authority initiative. ABOVE New development combined with rehabilitation in Chester, the result of co-operation between the city council and a housing association. RIGHT Rehabilitation of the Railway Village, Swindon, Wiltshire, by the borough council.

Eighteenth century houses in Chester, acquired and repaired by a private trust, with the aid of grants from the Historic Buildings Council and the city council. The adjoining new buildings, by a housing association, have been designed to harmonise with the older buildings without copying their style.

Another interesting combination of renovation and new infil by a local authority, at Stratford on Avon, Warwickshire.

Financial aid

equity release schemes may be introduced. It is best to contact your local environmental health officer for information about the schemes available in your area.

Heritage Lottery Fund

As well as contributing, with English Heritage, to the Joint Churches Grant Scheme, the Heritage Lottery Fund (HLF) operates several other schemes which might provide funding for historic buildings. The Townscape Heritage Initiative (or THI) provides grants for the repair and regeneration of the historic environment in towns and cities across the UK. The main aim of the scheme is to make possible the continued viable use of the buildings which make up the character of historic urban areas, giving highest priority to the repair of historic buildings and to bringing derelict and under-used historic buildings back into use.

Local partnerships, usually led by the local authority, bid for funding from the HLF. If successful a grant is paid into a common fund, managed by the partner organisation(s), which must normally contribute an equal amount. Grants for individual projects, which can include the repair of buildings in private ownership, are then distributed from the common fund. The scope of eligible work can be wide, including reinstatement of lost features such as shop fronts. The emphasis is on bringing vacant space into beneficial use and making areas more attractive for business or tourism. Schemes normally operate for three years.

Charities and not-for-profit organisations may apply directly to the HLF for assistance under a range of heritage schemes designed for different types and sizes of project. The underpinning aims of these grants are to care for and protect our heritage, increase understanding and enjoyment of it, improve access to our heritage and to provide benefits to the community which will help to improve people's quality

Back-to-back houses at Bradford, Yorkshire, under repair by a private owner. At one time almost universally condemned as 'slums', houses of this traditional northern pattern are now sometimes being refurbished with the encouragement of the local authorities.

of life. Undoubtedly the HLF has made a significant contribution to many projects in which building conservation is an integral part. However, applications for large grants are complicated, time-consuming and may be costly, and there is little chance of success unless the objectives of the HLF, which may change from time to time to meet changing heritage needs, are fully understood. Further information and advice is available from the Heritage Lottery Fund.

Private and voluntary sources

There are a number of voluntary and private funds and trusts which may make grants for the repair of historic buildings. Some of these operate nationally, and will assist a wide range of buildings, while others are restricted to helping certain classes of building, such as churches; others again operate in a particular area. One very useful source of information about these funds is the *Directory of Grant-Making Trusts*, published annually by the Charities Aid Foundation. As well as listing the trusts under headings indicating the causes they may help, it gives useful advice on making an application for aid.

It will probably be found that it is easier to obtain help from private trusts for buildings which are used, or intended to be used, for some community purpose, rather than for private houses, or business premises. Some of the national amenity societies, such as the Society for the Protection of Ancient Buildings, may be able to advise on other voluntary funds and trusts.

Building preservation trusts

One of the most hopeful and positive developments in the field of building conservation in recent years has been the setting up of building preservation trusts in many parts of the country. The main purpose of these trusts is to acquire and repair historic buildings

61

Financial aid

King John's House, Romsey, Hampshire, a medieval building, repaired by the Romsey and District Preservation Trust.

Saint Mary's Guildhall, Lincoln, a building of early medieval date, under repair by the Lincoln Civic Trust Ltd.

which would otherwise be in danger of demolition or neglect. Trusts may be sponsored by a local authority, or be independent organisations. Some have developed from civic societies and similar bodies. They are generally based on a definite area, such as a county, a district or a town, and some of the most successful ones came into being as a result of a threat to a particular building.

Trusts may deal with their buildings, after repair, in two ways. Some trusts prefer to retain the buildings, letting them to suitable tenants and using the rent income for maintenance, and to help finance further work. Others prefer to recover their capital by selling the buildings, subject to covenants. Where the main purpose of a trust is to acquire and repair houses, retaining them for letting, it may be registered as a housing association under the Industrial and Provident Acts. Alternative constitutions may be as a trust registered as a charity, or a company limited by guarantee. All these have their advantages as well as their limitations, and legal and financial advice should be taken before deciding on the most appropriate form in the particular circumstances. If a group of individuals, or an existing amenity societ. are considering setting up a preservation trust, the Civic Trust will generally be able to give advice, and to send a speaker to address a meeting on the subject.

Preservation trusts may acquire their properties in various ways. They may be able to buy buildings themselves, or to accept them from a local authority which has bought them, possibly following the service of a repairs notice. When a trust is sponsored by a local authority the authority may make an initial capital grant, and/or

an annual contribution. All trusts may apply for assistance to the various sources of grant aid described earlier. Mortgages and loans may also be obtained, and those trusts which are registered as housing associations are often able to obtain finance on favourable terms.

One very useful source of help is the Architectural Heritage Fund. This fund can offer low interest loans to approved trusts to enable them to buy and repair property, the loan being repaid out of the proceeds of sale on completion of the work. Trusts may also accept individual subscriptions and donations, and may launch a public appeal.

One great advantage in having a preservation trust in a town is that it can provide a focus for conservation, to encourage financial

Nineteenth century houses in Winchester, Hampshire, once threatened with demolition, under repair by the Winchester City Preservation Trust.

BELOW *Specialised preservation. A weatherboarded watermill re-erected at the Museum of East Anglian Life, Stowmarket, Suffolk.*

support and arouse public interest. The sight of a building being repaired by a trust can result in private owners looking at their property in a new light. It also strengthens the hands of those opposed to the demolition of a historic building if there is a body able and willing to acquire and repair it. Example generally carries far more weight than mere precept.

64

Part II. *Rescuing an old house*

5 The first stages

Old houses are much in demand in most parts of Britain, and finding a suitable house may be the most difficult part of the exercise, particularly if you want one in an unspoiled condition. All too often, especially in popular residential or commuter areas, you will find that what is advertised as a 'delightful period cottage' has been drastically altered and over-restored, with genuine features replaced by pseudo-Tudor details.

If you are looking for an unspoiled country house, this is most likely to be found among the farmhouses and cottages belonging to an estate which has not carried out a recent programme of improvements (probably for financial reasons). Sometimes these houses have been occupied for many years by elderly tenants who did not want to be disturbed and, when they fall vacant, the estate may offer them for sale rather than spend money on improving them. Such houses are often in need of considerable repair, but they are unlikely to have been over-restored. Houses which have been through a recent series of owner-occupiers may well be in better structural condition, but as each owner will probably have carried out alterations to suit his own lifestyle fewer original features are likely to have survived.

The same principle generally applies to town houses; the fewer the changes of owner, the more likely it is that the house will retain its authentic character. It is generally best to avoid houses which have been deliberately 'done up' for sale.

In looking for a house, the first obvious step will be to approach local estate agents, but there are other sources which should be explored. Many local authorities publish registers of buildings at risk in their areas, and Save Britain's Heritage and English Heritage produce national registers. Some of these registers are available on the internet. The Society for the Protection of Ancient Buildings compiles a list of historic buildings for sale, circulated quarterly to its members.

As I have said, in popular residential areas, most old houses coming on to the market may well have been 'restored' to a greater or lesser degree, and if it proves impossible to find an unrestored house it may be necessary to consider one of these. Here it will be important to distinguish between houses where old features have simply been

A timber-framed house at Faversham, Kent. In spite of suffering from prolonged neglect, the frame was basically sound, and this house has since been repaired and extended over the adjacent vacant site. Grants were obtained from the Historic Buildings Council and from the Borough Council, under a town scheme.

65

In this terrace of traditional buildings in Newport, Essex, some intrusive uPVC windows damage the group value. This is permitted development, even in a conservation area.

covered up and those which have been treated more drastically — sometimes completely gutted. A knowledge of the local architecture of the period of the house is essential — you must know what to look for. If, for instance, the large chimneys remain, the old fireplaces may survive behind the modern tiled surrounds. If the partitions are in the right positions the old plank and muntin or other earlier construction may still be there under the plasterboard. Staircase balustrades may be covered in hardboard, and panelled doors may have been 'flushed up' by DIY enthusiasts. All these things are reversible, and 'unmodernising' a house which has been treated in this way can be quite a rewarding exercise.

The problem becomes more difficult when windows and doors have been replaced by modern or pseudo-'period' designs. Sometimes the window openings have been left untouched, with lintels or arches intact, but all too often the openings have been enlarged, obliterating all traces of the original fenestration. In many other cases you will find that the interior has been completely remodelled, destroying the original plan form, and most if not all early features. In these cases, while it may be possible to improve the appearance of the house its true historic significance has gone; it is in effect a new building, and really beyond the scope of this book.

Timber-frame construction and jetties are evident from the form of the houses on the left. Removal of the render to reveal the timber framing might remove some elements of the building's history.

Assuming, however, that you have found a house that attracts you, the next stage will be to commission a survey, and this should certainly be done before making any firm offer to purchase. The survey can be carried out by a qualified architect or surveyor, but it is most important that he or she should have a real understanding of historic buildings, particularly of local styles and construction. Not all architects or surveyors have this expertise: it does not form part of the normal professional courses and requires further training or postgraduate study. The Royal Institution of Chartered Surveyors runs a conservation accreditation scheme for members and there is an independent scheme for Architects Accredited in Conservation. Some architects and surveyors are members of the Institute of Historic Building Conservation, indicating a level of understanding and competence well above the average. Your conservation officer or the Society for the Protection of Ancient Buildings may be able to recommend suitable professionals in the area. Whoever you appoint, I

ABOVE *Removal of render and a modern doorframe revealed a sixteenth century wooden carved doorway and jetties, in what appeared to be a much later house.*

suggest that you go to the house with him, as his attitude to old buildings will soon become apparent. Of course, he will point out its defects and problems—he would be failing in his duty to you if he did not—but his concern should not be limited to these matters. If he has any real knowledge of and interest in old buildings he should be able to tell you something of the age of the house, its original form and subsequent development, and the likelihood of uncovering hidden features of interest. Because traditional construction is often quite different from that of modern buildings, someone with this knowledge will be better able to interpret signs of structural movement and decay, and to advise on their treatment. A lack of knowledge has often resulted in over-drastic repairs with consequent loss of original work. For instance, it is not always necessary or desirable to take down and rebuild a leaning wall; there may be other more appropriate remedies.

If care is needed in the choice of an architect or surveyor to make the initial survey, this is even more true when appointing one to plan and supervise works of repair and alteration. It is not essential to employ the same person for these two tasks, but as he will already be familiar with the house it is often an advantage to do so, particularly if he has shown a real understanding of the house and its problems.

Choosing the right builder is equally important. I do not think the size of the firm matters as much as is sometimes thought. We hear a lot about the advantage of employing a small firm but there is no point in this if they sub-let most of their work, and it is generally best to choose a builder who has his own carpentry and joinery shop. It is wise to see examples of his work, particularly on old houses but, as with the architect, I would always advise taking him round the house and noting his reaction to it before deciding whether to employ him. It will soon become apparent whether or not he has any feeling for old houses. If his reaction to any wall slightly out of plumb is that it should be taken down and rebuilt, that all timber showing any sign of beetle attack should be stripped out, that it is not worthwhile to repair old doors and windows when new standard ones are much cheaper, and that an old house is bound to give trouble, it will be best not to employ him. The result will be a continual battle if you are really trying to preserve, not reconstruct, the house.

There are good builders today; craftsmanship is not 'dead' as is so often stated, and in many trades, such as thatching, many intelligent young people are coming forward for training and achieving a high standard of work. They may not be as cheap as the average jobbing builder, but in this, as in so many things, you get what you pay for. For this reason, and because of the nature of the work, where discoveries made during progress may mean a change of plan, it is not always practicable to obtain competitive tenders. The specification is bound to include a number of provisional sums, and it is sometimes better to work on a 'cost plus fee' basis. It is of course essential to be able to trust the builder to stop work and inform you or your architect if any unusual features are uncovered during the work. If he is working to a fixed price he may be less inclined to do this if the resultant delay could mean loss of profit.

As we have seen, alterations to a listed building will require the consent of the local planning authority. In addition, planning permission may be needed if substantial alterations or additions are proposed, and consent may also be necessary under the Building Regulations. For this reason it is advisable to consult the appropriate officers of the council at an early stage, preferably before completing purchase of the house, and certainly before submitting any formal applications. For one thing, as we have seen, a strict interpretation of the Building Regulations and Housing Acts could result in damage to the historic and architectural qualities of the house, and the requirements of the highway authority about vehicular access and turning spaces could materially affect its setting. It is often possible to obtain relaxations of some or all of these requirements, provided that the authorities are satisfied with the alternative proposals, but as this takes time—the proposals have to be advertised—the sooner the process is started the better. Applications for relaxations should not be left until just before the work is ready to start.

The initial approach is generally best made to the Planning Officer. He may have a specialist conservation officer in his department, or he may consult the county council conservation section, or an independant consultant. The conservation officer will probably have a considerable knowledge of the local architecture, and may already be familiar with the house in question. Although final decisions on planning and listed building applications will sometimes be made by a lay committee who may reject the advice of their technical officers, this rarely happens in straightforward cases.

Unless the proposed works are of a minor nature, the planning officer will probably suggest a meeting at the house, and it is sometimes helpful if the building control officer can also be present. In this way, problems can be anticipated and remedies suggested before final plans are prepared. The council officers may be able to advise on possible sources of financial assistance for the work. If the house is in a historic town or large village where a Heritage Economic Regeneration Scheme is in operation, a grant might be available. Some Grade I and Grade II* buildings may be eligible for help from English Heritage of the equivalent body in Wales, Scotland or Northern Ireland. Local authorities may offer grant aid under the Housing Acts, subject to means testing. Some local authorities run Historic Building Grant Schemes but such grants are not automatic even for listed buildings, particularly not for recently purchased ones as most local authorities take the view that the cost of repairs should be reflected in the purchase price of the building. I am afraid that some purchasers of old houses, querying the price being asked, are glibly assured by the vendor or his agent, 'You can get a grant from the Council.' It is

In this nineteenth century urban terrace, the modern windows and door inserted in one house have destroyed the unity of the design. The installation of modern amenities need not be accompanied by assertive alterations of this kind. They are, however, reversible; unaltered houses on each side could provide the pattern for reinstatement of the original design. A house treated in this way, though, is likely to have been gutted internally.

important to check the position with the council officers before completing purchase.

The planning officer may also be able to provide some information about the history of the house, or to suggest possible sources, for instance, in the local record office. The Crafts Council and many local authorities keep a register of craftsmen concerned with building conservation, and this may be a useful source of information if specialist work is required.

The procedure for applying for listed building consent has been described in an earlier chapter. If planning, and/or Building Regulation approvals are also needed, these will involve separate applications, and work must not be started until all these consents have been issued. Sometimes, the Building Regulation decision will be issued before the planning and listed building decisions, as fewer consultations are involved, but it should not be assumed that, because the scheme has received Building Regulation approval, the others will follow automatically. Incidentally, many councils allow members of the public, including applicants, to attend planning committee meetings, but not to speak. It is sometimes helpful, particularly if consent is refused, or granted subject to conditions, to know the reasons for these, and the views of councillors.

Once the necessary consents have been received and the work started, it must be carried out in accordance with the approved plans. Problems can occur here, especially with an old building, as conditions may arise making a change of plan desirable. Quite apart from the owner having second thoughts, features of interest may be uncovered during the work, involving a change of plan if they are to be preserved. Also, defects are often discovered after work has started and changes to the approved scheme may be necessary to facilitate repair. Strictly speaking, if material changes are proposed, a fresh application should be submitted, and this can cause delay, inconvenience and possible extra expense. The best course in these cases is to inform the Planning Officer of the situation at once, and to ask whether he requires a fresh application, or whether the change can be dealt with as a minor amendment. Most councils will adopt a reasonable attitude in these cases, but it is not wise to proceed with the work, saying nothing and hoping that it will not be noticed. The changes may be reported to the council either by a local resident or amenity society, concerned that the character of the house is being affected, or by a neighbour complaining that his rights are being affected-for instance by the insertion of an additional window overlooking his property. A council failing to take action in such cases could be found guilty of maladministration, and while it may be annoying to have one's plans frustrated in this way by third parties it must be borne in mind that the roles may one day be reversed. Unauthorised work may also come to light when you try to sell the house. Most prospective purchasers will check that alterations have been carried out in accordance with the approved plans, held by the

local authority, and will be unwilling to buy a building where the necessary consents have not been granted. For one thing, they may become liable for rectifying unauthorised works and this is likely to put off a great many potential buyers, and could even make it impossible to sell the building.

Depending on the nature of the work it may be inspected periodically by the council's Building Control Officer, who may ask for additional work to be carried out; for instance, the rebuilding of a wall which he considers to be unsafe. This does not absolve the owner, or the builder, from the need to obtain listed building consent for this additional work, or at least to obtain the agreement of the Planning Officer. I am afraid that councils vary considerably in the co-ordination, or lack of it, between departments, but while the present system of separate controls survives it is the building owner's responsibility to see that he has the approval of all necessary parties for any changes to the original approved plans.

This may all sound rather discouraging, but in fact schemes which genuinely aim at saving an old house, and retaining its authentic character are generally welcomed and encouraged by planning officers who, all too often, are faced with insensitive and crude proposals for 'improving' old houses. It is the perpetrators of such schemes who are most likely to complain of 'bureaucratic obstruction'.

From all this, it will be clear that after you have bought the house there is bound to be some delay while drawings and specifications are prepared, the necessary consents obtained, and builders' estimates submitted and accepted. During this time it is most important to protect the building from further deterioration. A comparatively small sum spent on first-aid repairs, to keep out the weather and vandals, can result in far greater sums being saved when the main work is put in hand, and may prevent the loss of irreplaceable historic features.

An ideal subject for rehabilitation is a house which retains all its original features, even if decayed, as in the case of this late Regency villa in Bruton, Somerset.

6 Repairs: the basic principles

Preserving an old house does not simply mean keeping it standing; any work we carry out should aim to maintain its historical and architectural integrity. This applies to the whole building, not just the façade. We often hear proud owners of old houses say 'I haven't altered it outside,' or 'at the front'. All too often this means that the interior has been completely gutted, leaving at most only a shell. We must surely think of buildings, indeed of streets and towns, as having three dimensions. Often interiors are as important, or even more important, than the exteriors.

Assuming then that we are really trying to preserve the character of our house, we shall find that there are nearly always two aspects to be considered, and that these may sometimes conflict with each other. The first problem we have to face is that of the straightforward repair and maintenance of the building in such a way as to protect it from decay, without destroying its historic value. The second is that of adapting the building, where necessary, to give it a new lease of life today. The question of straightforward repair generally only arises on its own if we are carrying out what might be described as a 'museum piece' restoration: for example, that of an ancient monument in the guardianship of English Heritage. In these cases, all we have to worry about is the 'welfare' of the building itself, regardless of its suitability for any modern use. Occasionally too we may have a building which is in perfect structural condition, but which needs altering if it is to be used today. In most cases, though, we shall find both considerations arising in the same building, often at the same time.

The straightforward repair of an old building is generally the easier problem. Of course it is important for the work to be carried out in a knowledgeable and sensitive way if the building is not to be ruined in the process. This is largely a matter of acquiring and applying the necessary technical knowledge, and it does not involve the often difficult decisions which may have to be made when we are adapting an old building for use today.

Let us look first at the relatively simpler problems of repair, and some of the questions which can arise when we are dealing with an old building. There are of course no universal answers to these ques-

A timber-framed building under reconstruction at Norwich. At what stage does conservation really amount to rebuilding?

Repairs: the basic principles

Neglect of such simple matters as regular cleaning of gutters and downpipes can lead to serious problems of decay.

tions. Every old building is different, and needs individual treatment, but there are some basic principles which can guide us.

My first point may seem very obvious, but I think its truth will be apparent as we look round our old towns and villages, and that is the importance of regular maintenance of old buildings; as William Morris put it, 'to stave off decay by daily care'. I am referring to such matters as the regular cleaning of rainwater gutters and drains, repairing small roof leaks as they occur, regular painting of softwood joinery, and dealing with defective pointing before it causes serious damage. These are all matters which, if neglected, can cause deterioration in an old building more quickly than anything else, and all too often will lead to pressure for its demolition because of its bad state of repair. The worst cases of neglect arise when no one apparently has the particular responsibility for dealing with these matters, churches, for instance, have all too often suffered from this kind of neglect. Houses too may be affected, particularly some rented properties where neither the tenant nor the absentee landlord seem interested, and where the rents have, over a long period, been insufficient to provide for proper maintenance. In some cases, too, the landlord may be hoping eventually to redevelop the property, and be unwilling to spend anything on its repair.

Having made this point, we all know that there are many cases where substantial repairs will be needed to an old house, possibly because of past neglect. You may well have bought a house, fully aware of its condition, and accepting the fact that much work will be required. Faced with a house in this state, how do you proceed?

Referring to the previous chapter, you have, I hope, had a survey of the house carried out before purchase, and will therefore have some idea of the likely problems, and the first question to be decided is whether you should employ an architect or surveyor to specify and supervise the repairs, or whether you feel able to do the work yourself, either physically, or by directly employing a builder. The decision will probably depend on the complexity of the work as well as on the nature of the building. Let us take a parallel situation in the field of health. There are many simple, straightforward ailments for which it is quite satisfactory to go to a chemist and buy a suitable patent medicine. For anything really serious, though, or when we are not sure what our symptoms mean, it is better to go to a doctor, and a responsible chemist will probably advise us to do so in such cases. In the same way, a conscientious builder, faced with a difficult structural problem, will probably advise you, in his own interests as well as yours, to employ an architect or surveyor and, as previously mentioned, it is important to find one with a specialist knowledge of old buildings, their construction and their problems. I often hear people say that they do not want to employ an architect because they will have to pay a fee. This is a very short-sighted attitude. You may be dealing with a building worth many thousands of pounds, which may possess features of historic interest which can easily be lost through ignorance or carelessness; you are probably spending a considerable sum on the work itself, and surely should not begrudge the cost of professional fees if this will ensure that the house is repaired without loss of character. The employment of the right architect or surveyor may indeed save you money, since he will have the necessary knowledge to prevent unnecessary renewal and loss of genuine old work, and to specify long-lasting work rather than a quick fix. It should be remembered, too, that if you are obtaining a grant from English Heritage or the local authority, professional fees can generally be included.

Although no two old houses are likely to present precisely the same set of problems, and each one must be considered on its merits, I would recommend that independent professional advice from a conservation architect or surveyor be obtained if any of the following symptoms are apparent.

FRACTURES indicating possible settlement or foundation failure. There could be several reasons for this, and each case will need individual diagnosis and treatment. Rebuilding, or even underpinning, is not necessarily the answer; it may be possible to stabilise the building by other means.

LEANING OR BULGING WALLS, possibly combined with fractures. Again, this can be due to a variety of reasons — spreading of the roof, failure of main floor beams, differences in moisture content of the subsoil inside and outside the house (a condition possibly aggravated by faulty drainage), failure of bond between the facing and the core of the wall. Once again, rebuilding may not be necessary or desirable.

SERIOUS FAILURE IN THE ROOF STRUCTURE This may be due to faulty design in the first place, to later alterations (tie-beams have often been cut away to form doorways), to beetle or fungus attack, particularly at eaves level. Accurate diagnosis is necessary before a remedy can be prescribed.

ANY EVIDENCE OF FUNGUS ATTACK IN TIMBER unless this is very slight and local, its full extent clearly apparent and its cause obvious. Coupled with this, any signs of beetle attack sufficiently serious to affect the structural strength of the timbers.

ANY SIGNS OF DAMPNESS where the cause is not obvious, and simple to rectify.

ANY SERIOUS DECAY IN STONEWORK, BRICKWORK OR TIMBER FRAMING Wholesale refacing or renewal in an old building can result in its losing a patina which has been acquired over the centuries. It may sometimes be unavoidable, but often a more conservative treatment is possible.

SERIOUS DETERIORATION IN A LEAD ROOF OR GUTTER Lead flat roofs are more often found in churches and other public buildings, and in large houses, but they were sometimes used on smaller houses in the later

Although this timber-framed house at Lincoln appears to lean over in an alarming fashion, the movement is probably of long standing, and not indicative of an unstable condition.

Defective pointing and surface erosion of stonework needs careful repair, but does not normally indicate structural problems.

ABOVE *and* RIGHT *Structural fractures, particularly in old walls showing signs of earlier repairs, should be taken seriously and appropriate professional advice obtained.*

eighteenth and nineteenth centuries. Damage can be physical or chemical, and in both cases professional advice should be obtained.

Apart from these basic defects, which will probably be apparent from the start, it may well be that, during the progress of the work, unexpected problems will arise. These may be 'positive'. For instance, when wallpaper or hessian is stripped from an old wall, early paintings may be revealed, or when opening up an old fireplace you may find unusual features, such as a curing chamber. When this happens, you may want advice on the best way of preserving these finds. On the other hand, problems may be 'negative': apparently sound panelling may, when removed, reveal a wall infected with dry rot fungus. Even if you started work yourself, or by employing a builder directly, do not hesitate to obtain professional advice in these cases. As mentioned before, if you do not know a suitable architect or surveyor, an organisation such as the Society for the Protection of Ancient Buildings, or your local authority, will probably be able to recommend one.

Incidentally, don't expect to get impartial advice from someone who has a product to sell. Most timber treatment or damp proofing firms are unlikely to specify improved ventilation or re-pointing in lime mortar as solutions to insect attack or damp problems. Their recommendations often involve copious amounts of chemicals or cutting out of historic fabric and replacement with hard, inflexible, modern alternative. This is unlikely to help preserve the character of the building and may even cause more problems in the future. If you employ a conservation architect or surveyor you can be sure that they will put the needs of the building first.

Let us now look at some of the repair problems we are likely to meet in an old house, and the way to approach them. First, we must discover the original con-struction of the house. This may seem obvious, but traditional con-struction, particularly in its local variations, is often very different from that of a modern building, and before we can decide how to repair a house we must understand how it was built.

For example, when we are dealing with a timber-framed building, it is important to know whether it is of cruck, one of its variations such as jointed cruck, or box frame construction, as the functions of and the stresses in the timbers may be different in each case. Ignorance of these matters can result in unnecessary work, and even in damage to the building we are trying to save. You may have had a 'historical' survey carried out before buying the house, but if not, this should be the next step. As well as ascertaining the original con-struction of the house, it will be necessary to find out what alterations and repairs have been carried out in the past, and the effect these have had on the stability of the building. Of course, however thorough this survey has been, it is always possible that more information will be revealed as the work proceeds. What appears to be a brick house may turn out to be timber-framed, clad externally in brick, and plast-ered or panelled internally, and this could mean a complete change in your plans for its repair. All this of course illustrates the need for continuous and careful supervision of all work on an old house.

BELOW *This Tudor' Wealden' house in Kent is at right angles to the road. The end wall, abutting the road and forming the new 'front' elevation, has been refaced and gives no clue to the age or interest of the house.*

RIGHT *Another altered 'Wealden' house. One of the end bays has been rebuilt, destroying the jetty.*

7 Roofs

In any house, the roof is probably the most important element. A defective roof, allowing water to penetrate or perhaps causing the walls to spread, can soon result in structural deterioration. At the same time, in early houses the roof may be of considerable historic interest. and one of the greatest helps in dating the building. Clearly, from all points of view, roof repairs must be carried out with great care.

The roof structure

The condition of the roof structure can only be ascertained by an internal inspection, and whenever possible this should be carried out before purchase of the house. In some cases, however, there is no access into the roof space, and one can only guess at the condition of the timbers by looking at that of the roof finish. A certain amount of unevenness is quite common in old roofs, due to the use of unseasoned timber and its subsequent movement, but any bad dips in the roof surface, or the ridge line, will make its condition suspect. If the interior of the roof space cannot be examined before purchase

RIGHT *Badly sagging tiling may indicate decay in the rafters, not simply in the battens.*

LEFT *Repairs in progress to the roof of an eighteenth century house. Some of the common rafters have had to be repaired or renewed, but the main trusses are generally sound.*

Roofs

it should be done as soon as possible afterwards, and trap doors should be provided to give good access to all parts of the roof, to facilitate future maintenance.

As previously stated, any major defects in the roof structure will need professional advice. Areas needing particularly careful inspection will include the bearings of roof members on external walls, and the spaces below parapet and valley gutters. While this inspection is taking place it will be advisable to take the opportunity to clear all rubbish from the roof space. As well as harbouring fungus and beetle this can be a fire risk, and prevent ventilation of the roof timbers.

In an early house, up to, say, the later seventeenth century, the roof will probably be of oak, and may well be of an interesting design. Evidence of smoke-blackening may be found, indicating an original open hall, and even if the timbers are not blackened it may be obvious that they were designed to be seen, indicating perhaps a first-floor hall or solar open to the roof. If a roof of this type is in good condition you may want to consider exposing it, by removing the later ceiling, but the practicality of any such scheme will depend on the design of the house and the extent of any later alterations. What is important is that these early roofs should be preserved as far as possible, even though they may not be visible. They are of historic interest, and their exposure may be possible at a future date. We must always remember that our period of ownership is probably only a very short episode in the life of the house. If it is absolutely necessary to remove any early roof timbers they should be carefully recorded, by drawings and/or photographs.

Minor damage to roof timbers can often be repaired by plating or strapping with steel, or by carefully scarfing in new matching timber, to avoid unnecessary renewal of old work. Even when major repairs are necessary it is often possible to retain the main trusses, which in early roofs are likely to be of quite massive construction. Old roof timbers should never be removed simply to facilitate levelling up the roof, ready to take a new covering, or because it is more trouble to repair them than to replace them with a modern structure.

TIMBER DECAY Before leaving the subject of the roof structure I should like to look briefly at the two main causes of timber decay: fungus and beetle. These are of course found in other parts of the house, but trouble often starts in the roof.

The term 'wet rot' is often used, rather loosely, to describe either the simple breakdown of the timber fibres by the action of water, or some of the less virulent forms of fungus attack. These 'wet rot' fungi, of which the most common is probably *Coniophora cerebella*, the 'cellar fungus', will only attack wet wood, and will die out once the source of the dampness has been removed and the timber dried out. Repair in this case need consist only of replacing badly damaged wood. True 'dry rot', a fungus called *Serpula* (previously *Merulius*) *lacrymans*, is

Early roofs may show interesting details of construction and jointing. Wherever possible, such timbers should be preserved.

much more serious and can be difficult to eradicate. Although it needs moist timber to enable its spores to germinate it can, once established, travel to dry wood, taking its own moisture with it, and can penetrate plaster, and even brickwork. In the early stages of an attack it is not easy for anyone but an expert to say what type of fungus (possibly more than one) is present, and this is why it is important to obtain independent professional advice. Much fine old woodwork has been needlessly destroyed because it has been wrongly suspected of suffering from dry rot. On the other hand, if this fungus is really present, no short cuts should be taken in the process of eradicating it. However, there is now much evidence that even dry rot can be successfully treated simply by increasing ventilation or heating in problem areas, thus reducing the moisture content of affected timber.

The two species of wood-boring beetle most commonly found in old houses are the common furniture beetle and the death-watch beetle. The furniture beetle is, indeed, all too common, but, in oak, its damage is likely to be confined to the sapwood: the outer part of the log which was still growing when the tree was cut. The heartwood of oak is unlikely to be affected, unless it has become wet over a long period. Furniture beetle is a greater problem in softwoods, where it can penetrate the heartwood.

The death-watch beetle, distinguished from the furniture beetle by the larger flight holes (which may be up to $\frac{1}{8}$ inch or 3 mm in diameter), will attack both oak and softwoods, but again, in oak it is unlikely to do much damage to the heartwood unless the timber has become wet. This is why timber below parapet and valley gutters, and the ends of beams and joists bearing on, or buried in, external walls, are particularly vulnerable. Once the death-watch beetle has become established at these points it can sometimes penetrate the adjoining heartwood, and spread along much of the length of a beam before the extent of the damage is realised.

We must remember that both species of beetle have a long life cycle, spending five or more years as larvae before emerging as adult beetles to mate and die. It therefore takes many years for them to cause serious damage, but there is some evidence that the life cycle is speeded up in damp, unventilated conditions. The presence of flight holes in timber does not necessarily mean that there is active beetle attack—it may have died out, or been eradicated by earlier treatment. The adult beetles emerge during the early summer, and their presence will be announced by small piles of dust in or below the flight holes. In the case of the death-watch beetle, their characteristic ticking sound (the mating call) will also be heard at this time of year.

The treatment of the affected timber will depend on the extent of the damage, and whether this has affected its structural stability. In many early houses the beams and joists were of a far larger section than was structurally necessary, and even if the sapwood has been badly attacked there may still be enough timber left to carry its load.

Timber affected by true dry rot, Serpula lacrymans, showing fungus growth and disintegration of the material.

Roofs

Small local outbreaks can be treated with a reliable insecticide, but professional advice should be obtained if the trouble is widespread, and particularly if the ends of main beams appear badly affected. Wholesale removal of affected timber is not always necessary, and is certainly not desirable if we are trying to preserve the character of an old house.

The British Wood Preserving and Damp Proofing Association, should be able to provide a list of reputable firms to carry out treatment of affected timber.

Modern insecticides can be very effective, but as they are strong poisons care is needed in their use, particularly in enclosed spaces such as lofts, as they can give off harmful fumes. Some manufacturers of these materials can supply respirators for use in these situations, and their instructions should be carefully followed. Products based on boron do not contain harmful solvents and are currently thought to be the least harmful to humans.

The roof finish

Even if you are fortunate enough to find that the roof structure is substantially sound, the roof finish may well require attention. If, for instance, it is obvious that a tiled or slated roof has been repeatedly patched in recent years the trouble is probably due to failure of the nails or pegs, or of the battens, and it will be better to strip and re-lay the covering than to continue patching. This will also provide an opportunity to make a thorough inspection of the timbers, and to carry out repairs. Treatment with a fungicide/insecticide is also generally advisable. Let us look at the various traditional roof finishes.

THATCH is probably the oldest form of roof covering. Until the end of the middle ages nearly all smaller houses were thatched and it was common, especially in rural areas, until the mid-nineteenth century. Two factors contributing to the decline of thatch were the changes in farming methods, resulting in less durable straw, and the availability, by cheap transport, of Welsh slate in all parts of the country. Thatching as a craft, however, is not dying out, as is sometimes asserted; in recent years many young thatchers have been trained, and the standard of thatching today is probably higher than it has ever been. Although most thatchers are fully employed, the supply of materials is sometimes a problem. In the past a variety of materials has been used, including heather, but today three main materials are in use in Britain, *long straw, combed wheat reed* and *water reed.* The methods of laying the thatch differ in each case, and not all thatchers are trained to use all three. All these materials require a steep roof pitch, a minimum of 45°, while 50° is advisable.

Long straw This is straw which has passed through a threshing

Contrasting styles in thatch. ABOVE *Long straw thatch in East Anglian style, in Bedfordshire, and* RIGHT *wheat reed thatching in progress in Dorset.*

machine (not a combine harvester which leaves the straw useless for thatch). The straw is bruised to some extent, and this affects its life, which is from fifteen to twenty years. It is found in all parts of the country except the south-west, but its short life is undoubtedly a drawback, and its use may decline.

Combed Wheat Reed This is wheat straw which has passed through a reed-comber, an attachment to the threshing machine which 'combs' the grain from the ears without harming the stems. It cannot be cut by a combine harvester, and a farmer growing wheat for reed (which is now quite profitable) must either have it cut by hand, or by the old-

Sculptural thatch well maintained at Ringmore, South Devon. Cob walls are particularly vulnerable if thatch is neglected.

81

ABOVE *Water reed thatching in progress on a barn in Dorset, and* BELOW *preparation of the material. Note the length of the reed.*

Water reed thatch on a house in Suffolk. The sharp gables and up-swept ridges are typical of East Anglian thatch.

Projecting brick weathering on a chimney in a thatched roof. It would appear that the roof was originally of a steeper pitch than at present.

fashioned reaper and binder. Combed wheat reed is more durable than long straw, and should have a life of about twenty-five to thirty years. It is used mainly in Devon, Somerset, Dorset and Hampshire, and may supersede long straw in other areas.

Water reed was traditionally used in much of East Anglia as well as in Scotland and other localised areas. In the dry, cold eastern counties a life of fifty or even sixty years can be expected. In the warmer, wetter western counties, where it is increasingly being introduced, we are seeing lives of closer to thirty years. It is still grown in Norfolk and Scotland, but demand for its use in areas where wheat reed or long straw were the traditional materials has outstripped the domestic supply and water reed is now imported from various parts of Europe, particularly Hungary, Austria and Poland.

In recent years there have been experiments using imported African grass for thatching. This material does not appear to be long lived and it does not make sense to pay high costs for the labour of re-thatching in a material without a good track record.

With all these materials, re-ridging and other minor repairs will be necessary every ten years or so, particularly around chimney stacks, where the thatch tends to sink after a time.

Apart from the differences in the appearance of a thatched roof resulting from the use of the different materials, thatch shows distinct regional characteristics. East Anglian thatched roofs, with their ridges swept up to the verges of gables, and rather spiky gabled dormers, can never be mistaken for those of the West Country. Here, the roofs are often hipped and may be given a slightly convex profile. Dormers are usually of the 'eyebrow' form, and the roof has a rounded appearance.

Thatch is, of course, a very individual form of roofing, and every

Replacement of thatch by tiles on the roofs of these cottages has resulted in the tiles round the dormers being laid at too flat a pitch, causing deterioration of the tiling.

thatcher has his own style, often recognisable in a particular area. If you have bought a thatched house, and the roof needs repair, it is often advisable to find out who thatched it last time, or who has carried out recent repairs, and to ask him to look at the roof, as he will know it, and be aware of any trouble spots. Thatching is not cheap, and if the roof is in a really bad state of repair it may be tempting to consider replacing the thatch with another material. If the house is listed, any such change will require listed building consent, and most councils will be reluctant to grant this, particularly to a new owner who presumably knew what he was buying! Councils will be particularly opposed to losing a thatched roof in an area where there is a strong thatching tradition, or where the house forms part of a group of thatched buildings. In any case, it seems a pity to buy a thatched house and proceed to remove the thatch when there are generally far more tiled or slated houses available!

When a roof is re-thatched it is not always necessary to strip all the old thatch first, particularly in the case of combed wheat reed, where it is usual to fix a new coat on to the old base layers; the thatcher's advice should be taken on this. If, however, complete stripping is necessary, it is worth while considering laying a fire-resistant barrier between the rafters and the new thatch. Various suitable materials are now available, and the thatcher will probably be able to advise you on this. As well as reducing the fire risk, the use of such a barrier helps to keep the roof space clean.

Of course, the higher fire risk and the consequent high insurance costs, is one of the main reasons some people seek to remove thatch. Research into methods of reducing the fire risk is continuing, and in addition more favourable terms have been negotiated with certain insurance companies.

Because of the high cost of thatch and the fire risk, there have been various attempts to produce artificial thatch in a less vulnerable material. One such experiment consisted of fibreglass sheets, moulded and coloured to imitate thatch, but this met with little success. Attempts have also been made to produce actual 'reeds' in a synthetic material, rather like drinking straws, but it has not yet been possible to make these economically in a tapered form — essential if the roof is to be laid correctly. If this problem is ever overcome, artificial thatch may be a possibility, although it is never likely to be appropriate for listed buildings.

One decision which has to be taken when a roof is re-thatched is whether or not to wire it. Birds can do a considerable amount of damage, especially on long straw or wheat reed, although they will be less likely to attack a well-laid water reed roof. On the other hand, the wiring is rather unsightly, and it may restrict the flow of water off the surface of the roof, and prevent the easy removal of moss. It is also sometimes said that wiring prevents the removal of the thatch in case of fire, but in this connection two points should be remembered. First, if the wire is fixed correctly, it can if necessary

Replacement of thatch by corrugated iron. Often, corrugated sheeting is laid over old thatch.

be removed quickly and easily, and most thatchers are now trained to use this method. Second, if a thatched roof does catch fire, it is *not* always advisable to remove the thatch: this can increase the draught and make matters worse, and it should certainly not be done by amateurs before the fire brigade arrives. Generally, the advice of the thatcher should be taken on the question of wiring; he will probably know the roof and the likelihood of birds attacking it. Wiring may sometimes be advisable round the eaves and ridge, which are the most vulnerable areas.

Thatched roofs, having wide eaves, do not need gutters or downpipes, but care should be taken to see that the dripping eaves do not allow water to saturate the wall bases. Paving may be laid round the walls, sloping away from them, or a French drain may be laid, consisting of land drains laid on hardcore, draining to soakaways, and covered with pea shingle at ground level. Sometimes, where the dripping eaves would be a nuisance, as along a town street, V-shaped wooden gutters were used. If gutters are needed, this form is best.

Under the Building Regulations, a new thatched roof must not be constructed less than twelve metres from the site boundary. This does not affect the re-thatching of an existing roof, but it does apply in the case of an extension to a thatched house, or to the restoration of a thatched roof which has been replaced or covered with, say, corrugated iron. The local authorities have the power to grant a relaxation of the Building Regulations if they consider it reasonable, and subject to various additional fire precautions being taken. Most councils will probably do this unless there are special risks involved. An early discussion with the planning and building control officers is desirable.

There is no doubt that the 'social' position of thatch has changed completely in recent years. At one time it was the poor man's roof; now it is probably the most expensive form of roofing, its disadvantages accepted by those who appreciate craftsmanship. It is also an excellent insulator, a factor in these days of high energy costs.

85

Roofs

Stone slates laid in diminishing courses.

Stone slates pointed in cement. Although this practice is common it could cause decay in the timbers by trapping water, preventing it from draining away at the eaves.

SHINGLES Oak shingles, or 'shakes', were sometimes used in medieval times as an alternative to thatch, but their use diminished, possibly with the introduction of clay tiles. Shingled roofs have survived on churches, particularly on timber spires. The oak shingles were rent or split along the grain, and were quite tough. After a serious decline in use they are currently enjoying a modest revival. Sawn cedar shingles are a more modern alternative to oak. These have sometimes been used on old houses, but compared with the oak shingles they have a rather thin, mechanical appearance. Their use on an old house would not generally be appropriate.

As far as the Building Regulations are concerned, shingles are in the same category as thatch, and a relaxation of the regulations will be needed if a new shingled roof is to be constructed within twelve metres of the site boundary.

STONE SLATES Thin slabs of stone have been used for roofs, in areas where they were available, from medieval and, indeed, Roman times. At first, their use was probably confined to the more important buildings, but from the seventeenth century we find them used on smaller houses. They are a familiar feature of parts of Yorkshire, of the Cotswolds and other parts of the limestone belt, in some parts of Sussex, and of the Purbeck Hills in Dorset.

Because of the great weight of these 'slates' they require a heavy roof construction. The roof pitch varies, steeper pitches being used for the comparatively small Cotswold slates and flatter pitches for the large Yorkshire slates. Like plain tiles and true slates, they are laid with a double lap, i.e. there are two thicknesses of stone over the whole roof, all adding to the weight of the structure. The individual slates were fixed by being hung on battens, either with wood pegs or, in some areas, sheep's bones, and the underside of the slating was sometimes 'torched' or pointed with mortar to improve weather-resistance. The slates were graded in size, larger slates being used at the eaves, decreasing in size nearer the ridge, with the courses being correspondingly reduced, producing a very attractive effect. Ridges were generally of cut stone. Valleys were 'swept' formed with tapered slates, and hips were either cut and mitred, or covered with cut stone, similarly to the ridges.

Today, many of these roofs need repair, due to failure of the wood pegs and, often, of the battens. When we look at the underside of an old stone slate roof the battens often seem very thin to carry the weight of the stones. They were, however, rent, or split along the grain, and were stronger for their size than modern sawn battens.

Unfortunately, we often find that repairs to these roofs have been carried out by re-bedding the slates in a hard cement mortar, or even by applying a cement slurry over the surface. The reason for this is clear — while it is fairly easy to replace the odd slipped tile, or true slate, it is far more difficult to slide a heavy stone slate back into position, and almost impossible to re-peg it. When the stone slates have

Two traditional dormer designs in stone slate roofing. RIGHT *A gabled dormer with laced valleys, in the Cotswolds.* BELOW *A pent-roofed dormer in a Purbeck cottage. In this area the slates are generally larger than those of the Cotswolds.*

been bedded or slurried in cement, it is often difficult to remove them for re-laying without a considerable amount of breakage. However carefully the roof is stripped, a proportion of new slates will almost certainly be needed, and unfortunately they are now very difficult to obtain. Only certain beds of the various stones are suitable to be split into slates, and most of the old quarries are worked out, or have been closed down due to lack of regular demand and high costs. Some Forest Marble and Cotswold slates are still being quarried. New Purbeck stone slates were until recently unobtainable, but they are now being quarried again on a small scale. Second-hand slates may sometimes be obtained, but because of the limited supply these are expensive, and there is no doubt that a demand for these is itself actually encouraging demolition of old buildings, particularly barns, or at least their re-roofing with corrugated iron or asbestos, in order to cash in on this demand. This is a very real problem. The long-term solution is to encourage the re-opening of the old quarries which still contain suitable stone, but this will not help the owner of the stone-slated house faced with the problem of renewing his roof now.

Assuming, first, that you have been able to salvage all or most of the slates, and have been able to obtain enough second-hand slates

The underside of a stone slate roof, showing batten failure.

to make up the deficiency, they should be relaid in the traditional manner, in graduated courses. It will be advisable to felt the roof, thus avoiding the need for torching, and the slates should be hung with copper or stainless steel (not iron) pegs or nails. As will be explained in a later chapter, ventilation should be provided in the roof space, at the eaves level and the ridge. Ridges, hips, valleys and verges should follow the local traditional practice, with the addition of lead soakers at abutments, and at cut and mitred hips. Valleys should preferably be swept. Open lead valleys are rather unsightly, and secret valleys (where the slates overhang and conceal the lead) easily become choked with leaves and dirt. The slates, if properly laid, should not need to be pointed in mortar. This looks unsightly and can trap water in the roof if the pointing shrinks or cracks.

Old stone slate roofs, with wide overhanging eaves, did not normally have gutters, and if there is sufficient overhang dripping eaves may still be appropriate, with provision for drainage as suggested for thatch. Today it is more usual to fix gutters, although the roof looks better without them. If the roof has never had gutters it may be worth experimenting with dripping eaves before deciding to introduce them.

We now have to face the more difficult problem, where the stone slates are in such poor condition, or have been so badly damaged by earlier 'repairs' that there are insufficient left to recover the roof, and no suitable replacements can be found to make up the deficiency. The house owner in this situation will have to consider the following alternatives, always remembering that any change to the roof finish of a listed building will require consent.

1. To renew the roof covering completely, with another material. This may well be tempting, especially if you are offered a good price for the remaining old slates, which may almost pay for a new roof. It is a drastic solution, but there are occasions when it might be justified. For instance, if yours is the only stone-slated house in the street, or group, it may be acceptable to use tiles or slates matching those on the other houses. At this stage we should perhaps consider the artificial (concrete) stone slates that are now available. Some of these have quite a good colour and texture, but it remains to be seen how they will weather in the long term. They may be appropriate in some cases, but I would not recommend trying to mix them with natural stone slates on the same roof slope. The difference will be very apparent.

2. To use the old stone slates on the more important or visible roof slopes and another material on the less visible slopes. This can be successful, but a word of warning is needed. Any other material, including artificial stone slates, is lighter than a true stone slate, and if the two materials are used on the opposite slopes of a roof, they will cause eccentric loading, with a risk of structural problems. Professional advice should be taken before deciding on this course.

Repairs in progress on a stone slate roof.

3. To use the old stone slates on the lower slopes of the roof, with another material above them. This practice is traditional in some parts of the country, and there are various theories about its origin. In some cases it does appear to be a later repair, necessitated by a shortage of stone slates, and in these areas it would not be inappropriate to continue the practice.

In areas, however, where new stone slates are still available, they should really be used, rather than any of these alternatives, or second-hand slates. First, this will not encourage the demolition or mutilation of old buildings by creating a market for their materials, and, equally important, a steady demand for new stone slates will help to ensure the continuation of the industry.

PLAIN TILES Clay tiles appeared in south-east England from the Continent in the later middle ages and their use spread across the country, reaching most areas by the eighteenth century. Old handmade tiles are less regular in size and shape than modern tiles, and they generally have a double camber, or curve, in section, due to the method of manufacture. These factors, together with the use of rent or split laths for hanging the tiles, and the less regular lines of the old roof structures, gives old tiled roofs much of their character, contrasting with the more mechanical appearance of modern roofs.

The tiles were generally hung with oak pegs, necessitating larger holes than those in modern tiles, and they were not usually nibbed. To improve weather resistance, and reduce heat loss through the roof,

A tiled roof with lower courses of stone slates.

Sagging battens on a tiled roof.

the tiles were sometimes bedded or torched with lime mortar. Another method was to lay the tiles on a bed of straw.

In the nineteenth century, machine-made tiles were introduced. These were more regular in appearance than the old handmade tiles, and were generally flat in section, with no camber. Due to the method of manufacture, some of the earlier machine-made tiles tended to laminate, and this, together with the use of iron nails which were liable to rust, has meant that the life of a nineteenth century tiled roof was generally shorter than that of the older roofs. Later machine-made tiles were of improved quality and durability, but today they have been largely superseded by concrete tiles. Handmade tiles are, however, still being produced, and there is a demand for them in high quality work.

The fact that most of the old tiles were not nibbed means that it is more difficult to repair an old roof — replacement tiles cannot simply be pushed into place as on a more recent roof. Good handmade tiles will generally last indefinitely, apart from the risk of mechanical damage; the failure of an old tiled roof is generally due either to decay in the wood pegs (unfortunately sapwood liable to insect attack was often used for these), or the failure of the laths or the nails holding them. When this occurs it is advisable to strip and re-lay the roof. If the tiles are sound they can be re-used, and any machine-made or concrete tiles used in earlier repairs should be discarded. Occasionally we find old handmade tiles starting to laminate, due probably to faulty burning, and in this case it is better not to re-use them, as the process is likely to continue and increase.

If only a few tiles need to be replaced it will probably be possible to find suitable second-hand tiles. If, however, a large proportion of the tiles are defective, I would generally advise obtaining new handmade tiles, and using them on one section of the roof, rather than mixing them with the old tiles, or obtaining a large quantity of second-hand tiles. My reasons for this suggestion are twofold. First, as with stone slates, there is a considerable market for second-hand tiles, and this is encouraging the demolition of old buildings, or their re-roofing with inferior materials, and we should not support this trend. Second, we *should* encourage the continued production of handmade tiles. Many tile-makers have ceased production in recent years, and it would be tragic if they were all to disappear through lack of sufficient demand.

If you are going to use new tiles on all or part of your roof the question of colour choice will arise. In most parts of England the old tiles were a natural red colour, which has mellowed over the centuries. Today, the natural red tiles are still made, but artificially stained tiles, sometimes described as 'Tudor' or 'antique', are popular. These look quite attractive when first laid, but in time become almost black, and never attain the mellow variation in tone of the natural red tiles. I would therefore recommend using the natural red tiles, accepting the fact that they will look rather bright at first; they will soon start to tone down and resemble the rest of the roof..

Although red tiles were usual in most parts of England, there were some exceptions. For instance, in the Fenland areas of Cambridgeshire and Norfolk the clays produced a range of colours varying from dark brown to a light buff, thus producing rather a speckled appearance on the roof. If you have to re-roof a house in this area, these colours should be matched as closely as possible, rather than introducing a red tile. Local traditional practice should be taken as a guide in this as in other matters. I am of course speaking of hand-made clay tiles: machine-made or concrete tiles are rarely appropriate on an old house.

If we are to retain the character of an old roof when it is relaid it will be important to keep any levelling or firring up of the rafters to a minimum; there is no need to create a completely level roof line. Today it is usual to felt a roof, and this obviates the need for any bedding or torching in mortar. Felting, though, makes it difficult to hang the tiles as before, since the pegs would penetrate the felt, and this probably precludes the use of rent laths, although a perfectionist will prefer to use them! If the tiles are to be nailed to sawn battens, special large-headed nails will be needed to fit the large holes in the old tiles: these should be of copper or stainless steel to avoid rusting. The battens today are normally pre-treated with a preservative. As with stone slate roofs, if the roof is felted it is important to ventilate the roof space.

It is of course important for the details of a tiled roof to follow traditional practice. Let us look at these in turn:

Ridges Any old ridge tiles should be saved and re-used. They were generally of hog-back pattern at first; half-round tiles came later. Occasionally ornamental ridge tiles are found. Being handmade, these are fairly irregular in outline, unlike the Victorian ornamental ridge tiles which have rather a spiky and mechanical character. If these latter have been used on an older roof they are generally better removed, but they are of course entirely appropriate on a Victorian building.

Eaves These should be laid with a double course of tiles, and they were generally given a slight tilt or bell-cast, slightly flattening the roof pitch at the eaves. As we have seen, in some areas there was a tradition of using a few courses of stone slates at the eaves of a tiled roof. If a roof has this feature it should be preserved in the re-tiling.

Verges To maintain the tiling bond at the verges, half tiles were generally used on old roofs. Today, tile-and-half tiles are used, which gives a stronger finish. As old tiles were not made to this size, it will mean introducing new tiles, but these should soon tone down if they are of the right colour and texture. On plain tile roofs, before about the eighteenth century, bargeboards were generally used only on

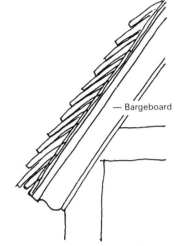

Bargeboard

Verge with bargeboard
in timber framed building

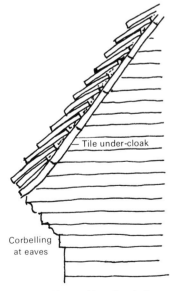

Tile under-cloak

Corbelling
at eaves

Verge with under-cloak

Traditional verge treatments.

Retiling in progress on an old roof. The felt is allowed to sag between the rafters, allowing any penetrating water to drain away at the eaves.

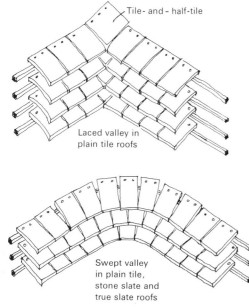

Tile- and – half-tile

Laced valley in plain tile roofs

Swept valley in plain tile, stone slate and true slate roofs

Traditional valley treatments.

timber-framed buildings, where they performed the function of covering the ends of the projecting purlins, and they were often moulded or carved. There is really no need for a bargeboard on a brick or stone building, and unless there is clear evidence that it was an original feature (as on some Victorian buildings) the roof will probably look better without one. The verge should overhang the wall a few inches, and be given an undercloak of one or two courses of tiles bedded on the wall top, so that the roof sweeps up to the verge, thus deflecting rainwater away from a vulnerable point.

Hips These were generally finished with special 'bonnet' tiles, pointed in mortar. Occasionally the tiles were cut and mitred together, but this is not a good finish. In the eighteenth century hips and indeed ridges were sometimes finished in lead, and where this appears to have been the original finish it would be appropriate to repeat it. The nineteenth-century practice of covering hips with half-round ridge tiles gives rather a clumsy appearance.

Valleys Today, purpose-made valley tiles are generally used: these are quite neat, and give a weather-resistant finish. The best old roofs, however, had 'laced' valleys. These look very attractive, and if properly laid are quite weather-proof. In the nineteenth century, open or secret lead valleys were often used. As already stated, secret valleys

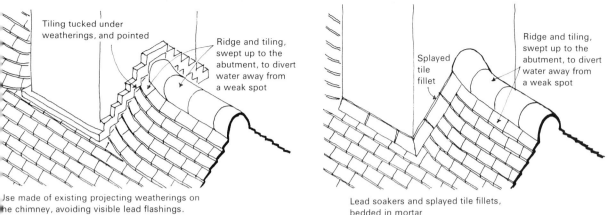

Tiling tucked under weatherings, and pointed

Ridge and tiling, swept up to the abutment, to divert water away from a weak spot

Splayed tile fillet

Ridge and tiling, swept up to the abutment, to divert water away from a weak spot

Use made of existing projecting weatherings on the chimney, avoiding visible lead flashings. Lead soakers should be used.

Lead soakers and splayed tile fillets, bedded in mortar

Vertical abutments to a tiled roof.

A laced valley in a tiled roof.

tend to get choked with leaves and dirt, and open valleys are rather unsightly. Both involve cutting the tiles.

Vertical abutments Today, lead or other metal soakers and stepped flashings are usual. These provide a good weathertight finish, but the flashings are rather unsightly and difficult to fix on, say, rubble stone walls. Some old brick chimney stacks had stepped oversailing courses following the line of the roof; the tiles were simply tucked under these and pointed in mortar. If the chimneys on your house have these oversailing courses the old method can be used, with the addition of lead soakers. A cheaper alternative was to form a mortar fillet along the joint between the tiles and the walling, but this tends to crack. A splayed tile fillet combined with lead soakers gives a better-looking and more durable finish. It is also advisable to fir up the battens so that the roof sweeps up to the abutment—as at the verge—to deflect water away from it. Plain tile roofs were generally steeply pitched, 50° being popular. Today they are sometimes laid to a flatter pitch, down to 40° or even less, but this is only satisfactory if the roof is felted, and is not to be recommended.

Tile hanging on external walls will be considered in a later chapter.

Rainwater drainage Until the eighteenth century, gutters and downpipes were rare on tiled roofs; they had wide dripping eaves. In the eighteenth century lead gutters and downpipes were introduced, and ornamental lead rainwater heads are a feature of many houses of this period. From the mid-eighteenth century it became more common for roofs to be finished behind parapets, with lead parapet gutters, and their repair will be considered later in this chapter. In the nineteenth century cast iron superseded lead for rainwater goods, while today they are often of plastic. As with a stone slated roof, if a tiled roof has never had gutters it may be worth while experimenting with dripping eaves before deciding to introduce gutters, unless there is evidence that the dripping eaves are causing dampness in the walls and this cannot be overcome by improved drainage. If gutters are to be used, the simple half-round shape looks best on most roofs, but if there is a moulded eaves cornice an ogee-shaped gutter may blend better with it. If cast-iron downpipes are used, they should be fixed clear of the walls on spacers or 'bobbins' to facilitate painting at the back; downpipes, especially those of square section, fixed flat against walls, have been responsible for much internal dampness — even for outbreaks of dry rot. The siting of the downpipes should be carefully considered; many old houses are spoilt by a rash of unsightly plumbing. Plastic rainwater goods have the advantage of not needing painting, but some of them are rather flimsy, and gutters tend to sag between the brackets. They have a much shorter life than cast iron as the plastic eventually becomes brittle and cracked. They are unlikely to be approved for use on a listed building.

PANTILES Large tiles with a flattened S-shaped section first appeared in East Anglia during the seventeenth century, probably introduced from the Low Countries, and became widely used over most of the eastern parts of England. They were less often used in the West Country except on some farm buildings. Unlike plain tiles, which are laid with a double lap, pantiles have a single lap only, but compensate for this by having a side lap, i.e. the adjacent tiles in each course overlap, instead of being butt-jointed like plain tiles or slates. Because of this difference, a pantiled roof is lighter than one of plain tiles, and needs a less substantial roof structure. Also, because of their larger size, pantiles can be laid at a flatter pitch than plain tiles. Most East Anglian pantiled roofs, though, are quite steep, probably because they were originally thatched, or continue the thatch tradition.

A pantiled roof on a Suffolk cottage. The gabled dormers and bargeboards are typical of East Anglia.

The older pantiles, like old plain tiles, were rather irregular in shape and section, and even with their side lap did not always fit perfectly on the roof. They were often bedded or torched in mortar to compensate for this, yet looking up at the underside of an old pantiled roof it is still often possible to see daylight in many places. In spite of this, the roof will generally be proof against normal rain, but may be vulnerable to driving rain or snow.

Like clay tiles, well-burned pantiles probably have an indefinite life, and failure of a roof is generally due to decay of the pegs or nails, or of the battens. When this occurs, stripping and re-laying is the only real solution. If the roof is then felted, torching should not be necessary, but, because of the irregularity of old pantiles, they must be skilfully laid if they are to fit properly. If second-hand tiles are to be used for repairs it is important to check that they are of the same size and section as those salvaged from the roof, as there is often considerable variation. As with plain tiles, if a large number of replacement tiles is needed it is probably best to use new tiles and to lay them together on one section of the roof. Clay pantiles are made today, but they are not often of exactly the same section as the old tiles. They are generally designed to overlap more efficiently, sometimes to interlock, to produce a more weathertight roof.

Most old pantiles are a natural red colour, but the clays used did produce variations in some areas. For instance, in Norfolk some very dark pantiles are found, with a hard, almost glossy finish. Modern

94

pantiles are made in various shades, and one should be selected matching the old local tiles as nearly as possible. Details in pantile roofs differ in some cases from those in plain tile roofs; let us look at each of them:

Ridges These were of half-round or hog-back form, and if needed suitable modern tiles can be obtained.

Eaves These generally had a course of plain tiles to form a base, and the hollows formed by the ends of the lowest course of pantiles were pointed in mortar, sometimes incorporating slips of plain tiles.

Verges in pantiled roofs present a problem, particularly at the right hand end of the roof slope where the last tile will finish with an upturn. Today, special verge tiles are made by most manufacturers with an extra roll, enabling the pantile to be bedded on to a plain tile undercloak, but, as we have seen, it is not easy to mix old and new pantiles on the same roof slope. Because of this problem, pantile verges are often finished with bargeboards. These, if used, should follow the local tradition in design; there is a tendency today to use very heavy bargeboards, splayed out at the bottom, giving a clumsy appearance to the roof. The difficulties in forming pantiled verges probably explain why gables in areas where pantiles are common, such as East Anglia and Lincolnshire, are often given parapets.

Another East Anglian pantiled roof, this time showing a cover fillet to the bargeboard, overlapping the tiling to provide a weathering.

Hips Pantiles are not very suitable for hipped roofs, as they do not adapt well to the necessary cutting. When they are found the hips are generally covered with half-round ridge tiles.

Valleys Here again, pantiles are not ideal. In old roofs they were sometimes cut and mitred together, but the only satisfactory detail is the open lead valley. Some makers of modern pantiles do make special trough valley tiles which can be used with them.

Vertical abutments As with plain tiles, these look best when formed with lead soakers and splayed plain tile fillets, unless there is an old oversailing course which can be used, again with soakers.

Apart from pantiles, various other forms of single-lap tiles have been used, particularly from the nineteenth century onwards. Of these, the double roman tile was probably the most popular; other patterns seem to have been peculiar to particular areas, or even to a particular manufacturer. Nearly all these have now ceased to be made, making the problem of repair very difficult. It may be possible to find second-hand tiles of the same pattern, and any spare ones should be saved for future repairs, but where these 'patent' tiles have been used, and a considerable amount of renewal is necessary, they may have to be used on certain slopes of the roof, with another form of tile, possibly a modern clay pantile, on the other slopes.

Gutters and downpipes on pantiled roofs are treated in a similar way to those on plain tiled roofs.

A slate roof in Yorkshire, laid in diminishing courses. The slates on the left-hand section have started to laminate, and they may have been too thin for this exposed position.

TRUE SLATES Unlike the stone slates, true slate is a metamorphic rock, relatively hard and impervious, and capable of being split into very thin layers. The main sources of slate in Britain are North Wales, the Lake District, and Cornwall, where it was both quarried and mined. Slate has been used for roofing in these areas since medieval times, but, except in some coastal areas where it could be brought by sea, its use only became widespread on smaller and medium sized houses since the introduction of cheap, efficient transport by canal or rail. In the nineteenth century Welsh slate was very widely used, especially in the growing towns. Thin Welsh slate became the usual roofing material for working class housing, and this is perhaps why it fell out of favour in the present century. Today, with many quarries and mines closed due to falling demand, slate has become an expensive roofing material — a similar 'social' change to the one we have seen with thatch.

The older slates were generally thicker and less regular than those produced in the nineteenth century when, to reduce costs, they were split as thinly as possible, giving a less attractive appearance. Although we tend to think of slates as being dark grey they can show considerable variation in colour. The slates of the Lake District are often a very attractive grey-green shade and, like stone slates, were generally laid in diminishing courses. Cornish slates are grey but sometimes have patches of a reddish brown colour, giving character to the roof. Even Welsh slates can vary from a blue-grey to a purple shade.

Slates are generally fixed by nailing them to battens, but in the nineteenth century they were sometimes nailed directly to boarding, providing a more wind-proof roof before felting became common. Good slates themselves probably have an indefinite life, and deterioration in slate roofs is generally due to rusting of the iron nails. This not only allows the slates to slip, but can actually split them, by expansion of the rusting iron. Isolated slates can be replaced by fixing them with lead or copper clips, but once a roof begins to suffer from 'nail-tiredness' it is better to strip and re-lay it. Indeed, the presence of a large number of refixed slates on a roof is a good indication that re-laying will soon be necessary.

If your house has an old slate roof which is clearly in need of stripping and re-laying, what are the alternatives? First, if the slate roof appears to be the original finish, which is most likely if it is in a slate-producing area, it should, ideally, be reinstated. It should be possible to re-use most of the old slates. Even if they have been split by rusting nails it may be possible to drill new holes: as with tiled roofs, copper or stainless steel nails should be used to prevent a recurrence of the trouble. It will be advisable to felt the roof, but, as previously mentioned, it is important to ventilate the roof timbers. In this connection, if the roof was boarded, and the boarding is to be retained, it will be better to felt, counter-batten and batten the roof, providing an air space below the slates, rather than to repeat the method of nailing the slates directly to the boarding.

In some cases, though, it will be clear that the slate roof is not original, that it is a nineteenth century replacement of another material — thatch, perhaps, or stone slates. If the slating is alien to the house, particularly if thin Welsh slates have been used, then a return to the original finish, or one more traditional to the locality, may be desirable. It will be necessary, though, to consider the roof pitch. Slates can be laid to a flatter pitch than most other materials — down to 30° depending on their size — and if the roof has been lowered it may no longer be suitable for the original material. Each case must be considered on its merits.

In the first half of the twentieth century 'slates' were made of asbestos and sometimes used, often in a diamond pattern, to re-roof old buildings. These are quite satisfactory if they are waterproof and left undisturbed. The problem arises when they have to be repaired or tampered with, as the regulations regarding toxicity require special handling by skilled operatives, and the expensive disposal of waste.

Today artificial slates are made from cement. These match Welsh slates reasonably well in colour, but they are thin and rather mechanical in appearance. If the roof is largely hidden behind a parapet their use may be acceptable, and they could be used on the hidden slopes of 'valley' roofs, but where the roof is an important feature of the design of an old house their appearance will be rather disappointing. In the twentieth century considerable quantities of imported slates were used. Some of these were less durable than locally produced slates, and have laminated badly. It is not worthwhile re-using these. When re-laying a slate roof, the traditional details at the eaves, ridge, hips and valleys should be followed, and if the slates were originally laid with diminishing courses this should be repeated. Let us look at the traditional details:

Ridges As on old stone slate roofs, these were originally often finished with specially cut slate ridges, which look very well. In the eighteenth century lead was used, and this blends quite well with the slate. In the nineteenth century tile ridges were common. If these are to be used they should match the slate colour — red ridge tiles rarely look appropriate on slate roofs.

Eaves These are finished with a double course of slates and, as with tiles, there may be a slight flattening of the roof pitch at the eaves.

Hips On old roofs, these were often formed by cutting and mitreing the slates. If this is done today, and it does look well, lead soakers should be used to give a more watertight joint. In the eighteenth century lead was used, as for ridges, while in the nineteenth century tiled hips were common.

Valleys These were sometimes 'swept' as with stone slates, particularly with Cornish and Westmorland slates. This looks very attractive: it is easier to do when fairly small slates are used. Later, either open or secret lead gutters became more common. Secret gutters are not ideal, for the same reasons as previously mentioned: they easily become choked with leaves and dirt. If swept valleys are not to be formed, open lead gutters are probably the best solution; the colour of the lead blends quite well with the slates.

Verges These are finished with two or three courses of slates, forming an undercloak. 'Slate and a half'-size slates may be used to form the bond. Bargeboards were sometimes used, particularly in the nineteenth century. Where these are clearly original features they should be reinstated, but, as with tiled roofs, the use of the clumsy bargeboards popular in new work should be avoided.

Vertical abutments In old slate roofs these were often formed similarly to those in tiled roofs, with the slating tucked under a projecting weathering on the wall or chimney stack, and simply pointed. Today lead flashings and soakers are normally used. The appearance of a lead flashing blends rather better with slates than it does with tiles, but if it is desired to avoid visible lead, a splayed slate fillet can be used, with soakers.

Rainwater drainage As with other traditional materials, old slate roofs generally had wide dripping eaves, without gutters or downpipes and, as we have seen, this can still be satisfactory provided that proper provision is made for drainage at the wall base. Otherwise, gutters and downpipes should be provided as described for tiled roofs.

Before leaving the subject of tiled and slated roofs, we must mention a practice which is becoming increasingly common: that of covering the whole of a defective tiled or slated roof with a fabric such as hessian or fibreglass mat, and sealing it with bitumen or some other liquid waterproofing compound. This has nothing to commend it, except short-term cheapness. It does, of course, alter the appearance of the roof, and effectively ruins any sound tiles or slates, making their re-use impossible. It can also, by sealing the roof, cut out all ventilation from the roof space, encouraging condensation and decay in the timbers. This treatment should only be used as an emergency repair on a roof where few if any of the tiles would be fit for re-use, and every care must be taken to see that the timbers are ventilated.

LEAD Lead flat roofs are more often found on public buildings and larger houses than on smaller and medium sized houses, but they were sometimes used in the late-eighteenth and nineteenth centuries. Lead was, however, often used in parapet and valley gutters and on porches, and in spite of the introduction of various modern substitutes it is still probably the most satisfactory material for these purposes.

Until the mid-nineteenth century lead sheet was cast, letting the molten lead flow over a bed of sand, and this cast lead, which is still produced by a few specialist firms, is generally considered tougher and more durable than modern milled lead, which is extruded between rollers. If your house has an old cast-lead roof which needs renewal, for reasons we shall consider later, it is certainly worth investigating the possibility of having it recast, rather than replacing it with milled lead. Sometimes, in an old lead roof, you will find the name or initials of the plumber who last cast and laid it, with the date. If the lead is to be recast, this panel should be cut out and incorporated in the new roof, together with a similar feature recording the current work, providing a good record for future owners of the house.

As I have said earlier, if a lead roof, and this includes lead gutters, is seriously defective, professional advice should be obtained, as the trouble could be due to a variety of causes. Lead has a comparatively high coefficient of expansion through changes in temperature, and if it is incorrectly fixed, restricting thermal movement, cracking can occur. Another potential cause of trouble is the practice of laying lead in over-large sheets, again increasing the risk of movement and cracking. Lead laid incorrectly on a pitched roof will tend to 'creep', reducing the overlap of adjoining sheets, and if laid on a flat roof or in a gutter with an inadequate fall, possibly combined with faulty detail at joints and drips, it will hold water and allow it to penetrate the roof through capillary attraction. All these faults were common in the nineteenth century and later, and we sometimes find them combined with the use of lead of inadequate thickness for its purpose — an example of false economy which can have very expensive consequences.

The worst way to deal with a leaking lead roof is to carry out 'jobbing' repairs, either with solder, or bitumen, or some of the products advertised for instant DIY repairs. Most of these materials have a dif-

Beaten lead on the roof of a new porch. The traditional concave profile neatly solves an aesthetic problem on a cramped site.

ferent coefficient of expansion from that of the lead, and are likely to fail again. More seriously, their use will make permanent repairs more difficult, as they will have to be removed before these can be carried out. The worst treatment of all is to cover the lead completely with a bituminous or similar compound. Not only does this make permanent repairs impossible without completely renewing the lead, but, by sealing the roof, cutting out ventilation, it can encourage condensation, and rot in the roof timbers. We must always remember that if a lead roof is leaking there is a possibility of decay in the timbers below, and these should be inspected before repairs are carried out.

Small isolated cracks in lead, particularly those which may have been caused by mechanical damage rather than by defective fixing, can be repaired by lead-burning, which must be carried out by a competent plumber. As no other material is introduced there is no risk of differential movement if the work is properly done. If, however, the lead continues to crack in the same or a similar position, more remedial work may be necessary.

A good lead roof, properly laid, should last for about a hundred years. After this time the lead tends to become crystalline, and recasting or replacement may be necessary. In recent years trouble has been experienced in lead roofs from chemical attack on the underside of the sheets. Research into the cause of this is continuing, but it may be connected with condensation, resulting from modern methods of heating and insulation, which tend to reduce ventilation in roof spaces. If the underside of the lead appears to be affected in this way professional advice should be sought.

When a lead roof or gutter has reached the end of its life, a decision will have to be taken on its replacement. As previously recommended, an old cast lead roof should if possible be recast. With a milled lead roof, it is probably just as good to replace this with the same, making sure that lead of adequate weight for its purpose is used, and obtaining the best available price for the old lead. Because of the cost of lead it will be tempting to consider using a cheaper alternative material, but none of these is likely to have the life of lead. Asphalt is sometimes used, but it is not ideal on timber roofs. Timber will expand and contract with changes in temperature and moisture content, and this tends to crack the asphalt. Asphalt is quite satisfactory laid on concrete, and can safely be used in parapet gutters which have been renewed in this material. Many forms of built-up felt roofing are commonly used on new buildings. These vary considerably in quality, but most of them carry a guarantee of twenty to thirty years only. Copper, zinc and more recently stainless steel have also been used. Copper can be very durable, but, as the sheets are thin, it is more subject than lead to mechanical damage, and care is needed to avoid corrosion if it comes into contact with iron, as in gutters and downpipes. Zinc suffers from the effects of atmospheric pollution, and has a comparatively short life in many areas. Stainless steel is a newer material; it is little if any cheaper than lead, and has been used mainly

Stainless steel roofing replacing lead on a church roof. The parapet gutter, BELOW, however, has been re-formed in lead, a more malleable material than the steel.

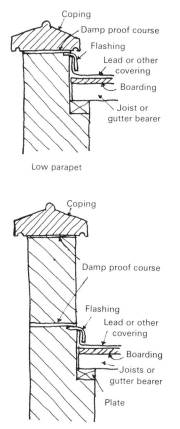

Low parapet

High Parapet

Parapet details.

Lead weathering to brick, stone or timber cornice.

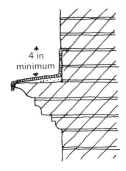

on churches which have suffered from lead thieves—less likely to be a problem in a continuously occupied building.

If a flat roof or gutter is likely to take much foot traffic, including access for maintenance, it may be advisable to fit timber duckboards, but these must be well maintained and kept clean. Defective duckboards do more harm than good.

Having accepted that the cost of a new lead roof is justified, it is of course important to see that it is laid correctly for the particular building, to ensure another hundred years of life, and to avoid the risk of physical and chemical deterioration. Professional advice should be taken, or the work should be entrusted to a specialist firm of lead roofers who are aware of the latest research on the subject.

Parapets, chimneys and dormers

Before leaving the subject of roofs, we should look at the structures associated with them.

PARAPETS These are often found to be defective, being exposed to the weather on both sides. In old houses, parapets rarely have damp-proof courses and when the brickwork or stonework becomes saturated it not only tends to decay in itself, but it allows water to penetrate below the roof finish, setting up rot in the adjoining timbers. Sometimes an attempt is made to remedy the trouble by rendering a parapet in a strong cement mix. This often does more harm than good, as the rendering may shrink and crack, allowing water to penetrate it but preventing it from drying out. If a parapet is badly decayed, and causing trouble inside the roof, it will probably be necessary to rebuild it, and the opportunity should be taken to insert a damp-proof course. In a low parapet a single damp-proof course, clear of the gutter and in line with the flashing, is normally adequate, but with a high parapet it is advisable to lay a second damp-proof course immediately below the coping to stop water penetrating the top of the wall through any open joints in the coping.

In some old houses, the parapets are an important feature of the design, perhaps incorporating moulded cornices and copings—or the wall itself may be treated in an ornamental fashion. If the parapet has to be rebuilt it is important to reproduce these features. When, in an attempt to reduce costs, the parapet and coping have not been rebuilt in the original form, the house can have rather an unfinished appearance. It may well be possible to re-use the old coping stones, if these are sound but weathered, and this will avoid creating a hard, obviously 'restored' skyline. If the bricks or stones are not too badly decayed every effort should be made to re-use them, otherwise matching materials should be obtained, also for the wall itself.

Very occasionally, we may find that an old roof originally had overhanging eaves, but was altered and given a parapet and back gutter at a later date, reflecting a change of fashion. If such a later parapet is found to be defective, it is worth considering whether the original form of the roof should be restored. This will probably reduce the long-term maintenance costs, but it will need careful thought. It may be that the fenestration of the façade was altered at the same time as the roof, as part of an overall face-lift. In this case, the reconstruction of the old roof line, with the new eaves much lower than the top of the old parapet, could spoil the general proportions of the façade. Each case must be considered on its merits, and it will be advisable to make a careful measured drawing, showing the existing and the proposed roof lines, so that the final effect can be judged before making a decision.

CHIMNEYS Like parapets, chimneys are exposed to the weather on all sides, and they may also be damaged internally by sulphate attack from the fire smoke, particularly if the old plaster lining has perished. In many old houses built of rubble stone we find that the chimneys have been rebuilt in brick, at a later date. The rubble stone has proved quite adequate for use in the thick walls, but not in the more severe conditions to which the chimneys were subjected. Also, as with parapets, old chimneys did not often have damp-proof courses. Internal dampness on or near old chimney breasts may be due to this, but it can also be caused by defective or missing flashings and fillets, or by rain coming down the flue. These troubles are exacerbated in chimneys that are not kept reasonably dry by regular use.

For all these reasons, and because open fires have become less common in recent years, there is a tendency today to take down old disused and possibly defective chimneys, rather than repair them. There are times when this is advisable, particularly when the chimneys are not original and do not contribute to the character of the house. In many cases, though, the removal of the chimneys is not to be recommended. They may be part of a formal design, symmetrically arranged, and an important part of the architectural composition. Sometimes, too, a later inserted chimney adds interest to the skyline, and tells part of the history of the house: for instance, the large chimneys inserted in early houses when the open halls were floored over in the Tudor and Stuart periods. Some old chimneys are themselves fine examples of brickwork or masonry.

Quite apart from the aesthetic considerations, there are other reasons why old chimneys should be retained unless there is a very good reason for removing them. Although open fires have been going out of fashion for some years, there are now signs of a reversal of this trend. Experience of power cuts and the rising costs of other fuels are encouraging many people to retain the option of an open fire, and it is now realised that the ventilation this provides in a room can help to reduce condensation and its associated problems. We shall be looking at the question of heating an old house in a later chapter, but at this stage let us assume that the chimneys are to be retained, but need repair.

Chimneys are often prominent features on old houses and display fine craftsmanship, as in this example from Dorset.

Although not of uniform design, and irregularly spaced, the chimneys form an important element in this terrace at Stratford on Avon, Warwickshire. Imagine how different the buildings would be without them.

Clearly, if the trouble is due to defective or missing linings, the chimney will have to be relined. The method used will depend on the fuel to be used, and professional advice should be obtained. Quite apart from the danger of sulphate attack from the products of combustion on the mortar or the masonry, a defective flue lining can be a serious fire hazard, and no chances should be taken.

When only the mortar in the outer face of the stack is defective, it can be raked out and repointed, taking care not to use too strong a mix—a subject we shall look at in more detail later. The method of pointing should match the original finish, if this has survived and can be seen. The hard trowelled finish beloved in the last century (and by many bricklayers today) should be avoided, as this draws attention to the joints, rather than to the bricks or stones.

If, however, the bricks or stones themselves are decayed, or badly fractured, rebuilding may be necessary, but this can sometimes be avoided by re-coring the flue with reinforced concrete, provided that, as is often the case with old chimneys, the flue is large enough to stand some reduction in its sectional area. This is specialist work, needing professional advice, but it sometimes enables a large chimney to be repaired *in situ*—particularly desirable if it incorporates ornamental brickwork or stonework. Rebuilding in such cases, however carefully carried out, always results in some loss of character and can easily produce an artificially 'restored' appearance.

If it is really necessary to rebuild an old chimney, it should be carefully recorded by drawings and photographs, and rebuilt in replica, re-using any sound old materials, at least for the external face. The opportunity should be taken to insert a damp-proof course.

103

Gabled dormer — plastered cheeks

Pent-roofed dormer in slate roof
— slate-hung cheeks

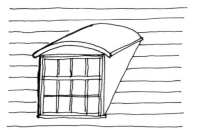

Segmental roofed dormer,
lead roofed, in slate roof.
Lead-covered cheeks.
Sash window.

Hipped dormer — tile-hung cheeks

Typical traditional dormers.

Roofs

When a chimney is not in use we often find that the top has been sealed off to prevent the entry of rain. If this is done it is most important to provide for ventilation, or condensation will occur, causing damp patches on the chimney breast below. One simple way of dealing with this is to cover the top opening with a half round ridge tile.

DORMERS AND SKYLIGHTS Dormer windows and skylights may be original features of a house, or be later insertions. They are frequently causes of trouble in a roof, all too often due to lack of maintenance, being found in little-used and sometimes rather inaccessible parts of the building. It may therefore be tempting to remove redundant dormers and skylights, especially when the roof is being relaid. Whether this is advisable will depend upon their importance in the design. If they are original or early features they should if possible be retained, taking care to provide adequate flashings and weatherings, and to maintain their original design and details. Sometimes, though, we find that rather unsightly later dormers have been inserted, particularly those of the 'chalet bungalow' variety, and these are better removed.

Since dormers often lit the servants' bedrooms and other less important rooms, they were sometimes of a more old-fashioned design than the windows in the rest of the house. We may find dormers with casements, or even lead lights, in a house where all the main rooms have sash windows. If the dormers need repair it may be tempting to renew them to match the other windows, but unless there are very good reasons for this it is better to retain them in their original form.

8 Walls

We will now look at some of the problems of repairs to external walls of an old house. I shall not be dealing with major structural defects; the treatment of these will depend on the particular circumstances of the building, and professional advice should be obtained. However, while a wall may be structurally sound, it may need surface repair, and it is important for this to be carried out in a sympathetic manner, in order to retain the character of the house. Apart from this, unsuitable surface repairs can actually increase the rate of deterioration.

The different materials used in the construction of old buildings are now described, with the principles to be followed in their repair.

Timber framing

A fine timber-framed house at Lavenham, Suffolk, showing sensitive treatment of the exposed timbers.

This is probably the oldest form of house construction. Until the end of the middle ages most small and medium sized houses were built

Walls

of timber. In some parts of Britain its use continued into the eighteenth century. In recent years, with growing interest in sustainable construction, there has been a revival of traditional timber framing.

In spite of losses by fire (especially in towns), fungus and beetle attack, and the general process of rebuilding, many early timber-framed houses survive in nearly all parts of Britain. A timber-framed house may need substantial structural repairs, arising not only from deterioration of the original structure, but from later alterations such as the removal of main beams and posts to create larger internal spaces. In such cases professional advice should be sought. It is not always necessary to renew all defective timbers: they can often be repaired by splicing in new oak, by the right use of steel ties and plates, or, a recent development, by a combination of steel or fibreglass rods and epoxy resin. This last method often enables nearly all the original work to be retained. Each case will need individual consideration, but it is often the case that a timber-framed building, being a more resilient structure, is easier to repair than one of brick or stone.

Turning to more minor repairs, when dealing with a timber-framed building we have to consider both the framing itself and the infilling between the timbers, either or both of which may need attention. We may also have to deal with a timber-framed house which has been clad externally with another material, and to decide whether the cladding should be retained or removed. Sometimes the cladding is a later addition to the building, where the timber framing was originally exposed, but in many later houses the walls were clad from the start, and the timbers never intended to be exposed to view, or to the weather.

If we take first a house with exposed framing, we must determine whether it was designed as such. In recent years many later timber-framed houses have been wrongly stripped. The timbers are comparatively thin and rough, and were not intended to be seen. In these cases it is better to reinstate the cladding; the house will probably look better, and will certainly be warmer and drier. Before carrying

ABOVE *Repairs to a timber-framed house in course of re-erection on a new site in Cheshire. A damp-proof course has been inserted under the cill, as indicated in the drawing,* RIGHT.

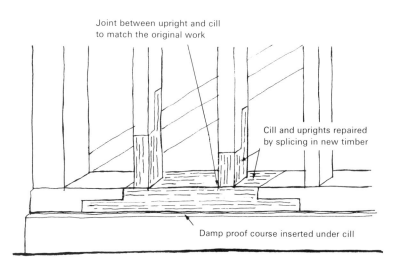

Joint between upright and cill to match the original work

Cill and uprights repaired by splicing in new timber

Damp proof course inserted under cill

Limewashing on the timber frame of a well-maintained house at Frampton on Severn, Gloucestershire.

'In situ' repairs to a timber-framed building in Norwich, Norfolk.

out this work, any necessary repairs should be carried out to the framing, and it is wise to treat it with a combined fungicide/insecticide. We shall be looking later at the various materials used for cladding timber-framed buildings, but it may be possible to ascertain the original finish from other 'unrestored' houses in the area, or even from old photographs.

If, however, the framing was originally exposed, and it is in generally good condition, you will probably want to retain it in this state. But if, though structurally sound, the surface of the timber is badly eroded it may be better to apply a cladding, rather than to carry out considerable surface renewal, which can result in an over-restored appearance. Provided that the framing is generally sound, repairs can be carried out by splicing in new or good second-hand oak. This needs to be done carefully, to avoid forming a water trap between the old and new work. It is no use simply nailing new oak boards on to the face of the framing members. The main areas likely to need repair are the sill plates, the feet of the main posts, and joints between main framing members. Generally the sill plate of a timber-framed house was set on a stone, flint or brick base, above ground level, but over the centuries the ground level may have been built up, level with or even above the sill, resulting in damp and decay in the timber. Where this has happened, the ground should be lowered round the house, to its old level. If the sill needs much renewal, it is often desirable to insert a damp-proof course below it during the work. Alternatively, the wall base, below the sill, can be damp-proofed by silicone injection. To ensure you employ a reputable firm for this work you can refer to the British Wood Preserving and Damp Proofing Association, which will supply a list of members.

The positions of missing framing members can sometimes be determined by the presence of mortice holes in the adjoining timbers, and if the structure has been weakened by the removal of a member it may be desirable to replace it. Conjectural 'restoration' should,

Alterations to timber-framed houses often resulted in old doors and windows being built up. LEFT *Removal of later plaster, leaving later window frames projecting, has revealed an earlier doorway.* BELOW *An old oak mullioned window can be seen next to the later casement.*

however, be avoided. Some of the existing timbers may have been re-used from another building, or another part of the same building, and in these cases mortice holes and slots can be misleading. I have already emphasised the importance of having a historical survey carried out before starting work on an old house, and this is particularly important with a timber-framed building. Far too many of them have been spoilt, and their history falsified by well-meant 'restoration' of this kind. If new timbers are to be inserted it is generally best to leave them with a sawn finish. It is true that early timbers were often adzed, but unless the craftsman is very skilled, modern attempts at adzing can look rather self-conscious and contrived. In repairing a timber-framed house we must be careful to avoid creating a 'Tudor Tea Shoppe' effect.

Many timber-framed houses will have been altered, even if the framing is still largely intact. Old doors and windows may have been removed, and the openings either blocked, or filled with later ones. Should we try to restore the original design? If the later features are themselves well-designed, and in scale with the building, it is probably best to leave them. Georgian doors and windows in a Tudor house can look attractive, and tell us part of the history of the building. Modern reproductions of earlier work, however well designed and made, tend to look what they are, and it is rarely that firm evidence will exist for the original design. There is certainly no justification for inserting modern pre-fabricated 'Tudor' or 'Jacobean' style doors and windows, which are generally a travesty of the real thing.

Sometimes though, the later features will be more recent, and quite unworthy of the house, such as modern metal or standard timber casements, and flimsy suburban-type doors. Here, there is a case for replacing them, though not necessarily with strictly 'reproduction' features, unless there is clear evidence for their original form. Where there is any doubt about this it may well be best to use simple battened

RIGHT *A standard modern 'Tudor' door inserted in a genuine Tudor house. Its rather fussy detail contrasts with the solid construction of the jetty above it.*

doors, avoiding mock strap hinges and other pseudo-antique iron-work, and simple cottage-type casements, with well-proportioned panes, designed to fit the original openings where these survive.

If the original doors and windows have survived, these should of course be kept and carefully repaired, with the minimum of renewal. If they have been mutilated, for example by inserting modern timber or metal casements into old mullioned windows, and where the original form is clear, careful restoration is justified. One problem we may find is that the original windows may have been unglazed, fitted only with shutters. Clearly, it would not be practicable to restore these to their original form in a habitable room. One common form of unglazed window had square section mullions set diagonally and housed into the head and sill. The best treatment for this type of window is probably to fix a plain sheet of glass internally, over the whole window area, which will maintain its general character. There is no point in, for instance, inserting lead lights into such a window.

When glass was first introduced into mullioned windows it was in the form of leaded lights, fixed direct to the mullions, sometimes stiffened with a central vertical timber or iron stancheon. Opening lights had flat section wrought iron frames, sometimes with ornamental fasteners, and were generally hung on iron hooks or 'rides', not on modern style hinges. Any surviving windows of this type should be carefully repaired. If the leading has perished the windows can be re-leaded, re-using any old glass, and the iron frames can be repaired and rust-proofed by a good blacksmith. Windows of this type are not of course particularly draught-proof. The best way to deal with this problem is probably to fix internal secondary glazing, which does not affect the original windows. Old windows should not be replaced by the pseudo-'Jacobean' double-glazed windows widely advertised today. When these are compared with genuine old work the difference is all too obvious.

At this point it is worth looking at the question of diamond versus rectangular panes in leaded windows. From the available evidence it would appear that the earliest glazed windows had diamond panes—possibly copied from the wooden lattices sometimes used in unglazed windows. In larger houses some quite elaborate patterns are found in the leading, but this was rare in smaller houses. By the mid-sixteenth century rectangular panes were coming into use, and by the end of the century they seem to have been the usual pattern. In the 'picturesque revival' of the early nineteenth century diamond panes again became popular, probably because of their medieval associations.

Since most smaller and medium sized houses did not have glazed windows before the sixteenth century, unless there is clear evidence of original diamond pattern glazing it would seem to be more appropriate to use rectangular panes. In a house where the old windows have survived we may find rectangular panes in the 'best' rooms and diamond panes in the attics and other less important

TOP *A seventeenth century oak mullioned window with lead lights. The feet of the mullions have been carefully repaired.* ABOVE *A modern 'Tudor' style lead light window, with its mechanical character and lack of depth, all too apparent when compared with what it is trying to copy.*

rooms, just as casements were still being used in these situations after double-hung sashes came into fashion. If old diamond-paned windows do survive, they will probably be rather irregular in pattern. Perhaps this is why the modern standard diamond-paned windows look rather self-conscious in an old house.

Sometimes you will find that old windows and doors have been blocked, new ones being inserted in other positions. This blocking was often done very crudely, and you may find the old mullions, or even the glazing, still in position, under the plaster. If it does not suit your plans for the house to open up these windows it is sometimes possible to cut back the blocking so that the form of the old window can be seen, either on the external or the internal face of the wall.

So far we have been considering the timber framing itself, but the infilling panels may also need repair. The original material was nearly always wattle and daub. Cleft oak or hazel staves were inserted in holes and grooves in the framing, and hazel or some other pliable timber woven round them, basket fashion. The wattle was then covered with daub, a mixture of clay, lime and straw, sometimes mixed with cow dung, and finished with a soft lime plaster. This material was less durable than the timber framing, and we therefore often find that it has been replaced with brick, especially in the more exposed walls. Some later timber-framed buildings were built initially with brick infilling, which was sometimes laid in herring-bone fashion. The problem with both forms of infilling is that timber tends to move, both in the initial seasoning process (green timber was normally used for framing), and later, due to changes in temperature and moisture content. This in time loosens the infilling, creating cracks round the panels through which water can penetrate, making the house damp and draughty. Indeed, this is one reason why many timber-framed houses were eventually clad externally.

If you are proposing to leave the timbers exposed, the panels will

Blocked windows in timber-framed houses often have their frames and mullions intact, and can be re-opened with little difficulty.

Infilling to timber-framed houses. LEFT *Wattle and daub and* RIGHT *brick filling. In most cases brick will be found to be a replacement of earlier wattle and daub, evidenced by holes and grooves in the framing.*

In this house in Lincoln, the plaster panels are recessed behind the timber framing, less usual than a flush finish. The nail holes indicate that the wall was at one time plastered.

probably need some attention. If wattle and daub panels are generally sound they can be repaired by patching in a similar daub mix, finished with a soft lime plaster. This last point is very important; a hard cement mix will shrink and pull away from the backing, allowing water to penetrate. When the panels are beyond repair, either because the daub has perished completely, or because the wattle is badly affected by beetle or rot, they will have to be replaced. I would not recommend using brick, although this was done in the past, as it is heavier than the daub, and will put additional strain on the framing. It is better to use a lighter material, such as wood-wool slabs, or one of the newer, ecological building materials such as reed mats or hemp mixed with lime, finished with soft lime plaster. Generally, the plaster was finished flush with the timber, but sometimes it was slightly set back from it, and the original design should be followed. Sometimes a lead tray is inserted at the bottom of the panel to improve weather resistance. If this is done, the underside of the lead must be well painted to protect it from attack by tannin in the oak. Old brick panels can be pointed or repaired as necessary, using a fairly weak mortar to minimise the effect of any subsequent movement in the timber.

Sometimes we find a house where some only of the infilling panels have been replaced in brick, with no regard for their appearance. A decision then has to be taken, whether to remove the brick panels and replace them with a more suitable infilling, with a plaster finish to match the remaining wattle and daub. There can be no hard and fast rule about this. If the brickwork is sound and not too unsightly it is probably better to leave it, but if it is in poor repair it may be right to replace it. Much will depend on the character of the house. If this is of a fairly sophisticated design, restoration of the original appearance may be justifiable, but in a humbler building the effect of mixture of materials may be more appropriate. It is all too easy

Bramall Hall, Cheshire. It is now becoming apparent that even in the north-west, timber-framed houses were not originally blackened. A start has been made on cleaning off the timbers of some houses, but it will probably be a long time before the 'black and white' image dies.

to destroy the unselfconscious charm of a simple farmhouse or cottage, and to turn it into something reminiscent of the 'stockbrokers' Tudor of the suburbs.

As we have seen, movement can occur around the edges of the infilling panels, and if the timbers are to be exposed externally it will often be advisable to cover them with an internal lining, except for the main framing members, to keep the house reasonably warm and draught-free. If the timbers are clad externally they can of course more easily be exposed internally.

Having dealt with the repair of the timbers, the panels and the doors and windows, a decision will have to be taken on the decorative finish to be applied. Many old timber-framed houses have suffered from the nineteenth-century fashion for blackening the timbers. Examination of houses which have escaped this treatment shows that it is not traditional, even in the so-called 'black and white' houses of the north-west. In some districts colour was applied to the timbers, but in most parts of Britain these were left in their natural state, or even limewashed over with the panels, the limewash sometimes being tinted with umber or ochre.

It may be possible to discover the original finish of the timber and the panels, particularly if an original external wall was covered by a later extension (thus becoming an internal wall) and has therefore escaped Victorian and more recent treatment. Other unrestored houses in the district may provide a clue. If there is no firm evidence for the original treatment it will probably be best to leave the oak framing uncoloured and to limewash the panels in a neutral shade. If the oak has been blackened it may be possible to clean it by using a chemical stripper, although this will not be easy if a bituminous compound has been used, or a stain which has penetrated the grain of the timber. If this is the case, or if the framing has had a considerable amount of repair, giving it rather a patchy appearance, it can be improved by limewashing the timber with the panels, and brushing the timbers down when nearly dry. This leaves a residue of limewash

Houses in Faversham, Kent, showing timbers left in their natural state, or limewashed and brushed off.

When this house in Lavenham, Suffolk, was reconditioned most of the plaster cladding was retained. Many other houses in the town have been stripped, in some cases producing rather an over-restored effect.

in the grain, and softens the appearance of the framing. It will also help to disguise nail holes left after the removal of later cladding. If there are signs of beetle activity the timbers can be treated with a clear, non-staining insecticide, allowing this to dry before any limewashing. Apart from this, sound oak should need no preservative treatment. Linseed oil, in particular, should be avoided as it tends to become sticky, attracting dirt, and possibly encouraging beetle attack.

Let us look now at the case of an early timber-framed house which has had a later cladding applied, such as plaster, tile-hanging or weatherboarding. As I have said before, if this cladding is sound, and there is no evidence of decay in the framing, it is generally better to leave the cladding in place. The cladding itself may, however, have perished; it may be of a material, such as a hard cement rendering, which could damage the structure by trapping water behind it, or it may be found necessary to remove it to repair the framing. Should it then be replaced? The answer to this question will depend on a number of factors.

First, is the framing sound, or will it need so much repair that it will have a patchy appearance? Second, were other alterations carried out when the cladding was applied, such as the insertion of new sash windows? If so, these will probably project, proud of the original wall face, and if the timbers are to be exposed it will be tempting to replace them with (probably conjectural) 'restorations' of the earlier windows. Third, why was the cladding applied in the first place? Was it simply because of a change of fashion, or because movement had taken place between the framing and the panels causing the problems we have already discussed? Generally, the presumption should be in favour of replacing the cladding, although there will always be exceptions; the timbers may be in excellent condition, and of a very attractive design.

As we have seen, many later timber-framed houses were designed to be clad, and these claddings should always be reinstated if they

Decorative plasterwork on a restored seventeenth-century timber-framed house in Saffron Walden, Essex.

have to be stripped to enable the timbers to be repaired. We will now look at the various materials used for cladding timber-framed buildings and the problems of their repair. Some of these were used on other structural materials, and the same principles will apply.

PLASTER This is probably the oldest form of cladding. In some areas, such as East Anglia, timber-framed buildings were being plastered in the late sixteenth and early seventeenth centuries, and it is in these areas that we find ornamental plasterwork, known as pargetting, incorporating floral, conventional and heraldic designs. The plaster was generally applied on split oak laths, and a lime and sand mix was used, often reinforced with ox or goat hair, giving a tough, durable finish, which was further protected with coats of limewash. This old lime plaster was sufficiently resilient to absorb any movement in the timber framing. Later repairs, from the nineteenth century onwards, were often carried out in a strong cement mix, which tends to crack and trap water behind it, leading to decay of the timber.

Deterioration of old external plaster may be due to a number of causes: the decay of the plaster itself, probably due to neglect and lack of regular limewashing, the decay of the laths or of the nails holding them, or the failure of the key between the plaster and the laths. If the laths are sound, the plaster can be repaired, using a similar mix to that of the old plaster. It should be finished with a wood float, not a steel trowel, and allowed to follow the contour of the wall face without trying to achieve a completely flat finish. On the other hand,

A timber-framed wall was covered in later plaster. Decay has been caused by failure of the plaster key, possibly aggravated by water penetration.

114

an exaggerated 'antique' finish should be avoided; some finishes of this type in common use today can give rather an artificial effect.

If the laths themselves are decayed, or are coming away from the framing because of failure of the nails, they will have to be replaced. Today, metal lathing is often used in place of wood, but this should be of stainless steel to avoid rusting. If the house has ornamental plasterwork every effort should be made to preserve it. Small areas of decay or damage can be repaired by a skilled craftsman, but our aim should be to preserve rather than to renew. If the trouble is due to failure of the key, or decay of the laths, it may be possible to remove the ornamental section, and to refix it to new laths with screws and washers. This, however, is specialist work and should not be attempted by an amateur, or a run-of-the-mill plasterer.

When carrying out repairs to old plastering, it is important to follow the original traditional details around door and window openings. These will vary according to the style of the building: for example, whether the window frames are recessed or flush with the outer face of the wall. Sometimes, today, lead weatherings are inserted around these openings to make the junction of the plaster and the timber more weathertight. If this is done, the lead should be painted to avoid any direct contact with the oak. If a damp-proof course has been inserted under the sill of a timber-framed building, care should be taken to see that this is not bridged by the external plaster.

Old plaster, as we have seen, was generally finished with limewash and tallow, and this is generally the best material to use. Some of the modern cement-based and other patent paints recommended for external walls are too hard for use in this situation, and may crack and come away from the plaster. If, however, the wall has already been treated with a modern paint which cannot be removed, it may be better to continue its use, as limewash may not adhere to it. Colour is, of course, a matter of personal choice, but it may be possible to discover the original finish by carefully flaking off the later layers of paint in a small area. The limewash was often tinted with umber or ochre, and these 'earth' pigments will resist the bleaching effect of the lime better than other types.

WEATHERBOARDING This was a popular finish for timber-framed buildings in the later seventeenth, eighteenth and early nineteenth centuries. Sometimes the boards were of uniform thickness, but more often they were tapered, and in later work the lower edge of the board was often moulded. The original design should be matched in repairs, as should the details round door and window openings.

If a large area of the boarding has to be renewed, it may be worth fixing building paper to the timbers before re-boarding. Some later timber-framed houses which were weatherboarded from the start did not have any infilling between the timbers. With houses of this type, if substantial re-boarding is needed, it may be advisable to take the opportunity of improving the insulation by fixing fibreglass quilt or

A Kentish house under repair. The framing in this case was probably always covered, and the weatherboarding is correctly being retained.

some other suitable material between the timbers. It is important, though, in all these cases, not to create conditions which could encourage condensation, and professional advice should be taken if you plan to modify the original construction in these ways. Weatherboarding is best finished just below the sill of the timber framing—well above ground level—to avoid risk of decay through rising damp.

Weatherboarding was generally painted, but sometimes, especially in coastal areas, it was tarred. Where this has been done it will be very difficult either to remove the tar or to paint over it, and it will generally be best to continue the same treatment. Natural, unpainted weatherboarding, of oak or elm, is popular today. In the past waney-edged elm boarding, split along the grain to give an irregular profile, was used only on farm and other outbuildings. Although it is going through a fashionable phase now, it is not really appropriate on old houses. In some areas elm is plentiful, as a result of the felling of elm trees affected by Dutch elm disease (the timber is perfectly safe for use once the bark has been removed), but it should be sawn to give straight edged boards. Today, too, artificial weatherboarding is made, in plastic and aluminium sheeting. These can be acceptable on new houses, and may save on maintenance, although their long-term durability is unknown. However, their very regular appearance makes them inappropriate for use on old houses.

A Sussex timber-framed cottage, with its upper walls tile-hung. The lower walls have been rebuilt in brick.

TILE-HANGING Many timber-framed buildings in the south-east were tile-hung in the eighteenth century. Sometimes this finish was applied to the upper walls only, the lower storey being rebuilt or refaced in brick. The warm, mellow colouring of the old tiles, combined with white paintwork, enhances many town and village streets from Kent to Hampshire. Tile-hanging is in fact a very efficient form of weatherproofing, and it was often applied to porous brick walls, especially

116

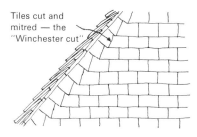

Tiles cut and mitred — the "Winchester cut"

Tile-hanging: traditional finish against the verge.

those facing the prevailing wind. As with tiled roofs, the tiles themselves, if well burned, should last indefinitely and any trouble is generally due to failure of the pegs or nails, or the laths. The principles to be followed in repairs are similar to those we have seen in respect of tiled roofs, but two details needing particular care are the external angles, formed by adjoining walls, and the finish under the verge of a gabled roof.

In old houses, the external angles were formed by simply cutting and fitting the tiles together, but often this vulnerable joint was covered by a timber fillet. Today, purpose-made angle tiles are manufactured, which give a more watertight joint; however, as with the tile-and-half tiles made for roof verges, they are unlikely to be an exact match for the old tiles. If it is desired to retain the old appearance, using a timber cover fillet, it is advisable to fit lead soakers to the tiling, as on a tiled roof.

Where the courses of tile-hanging met the verge of a gabled roof the last two tiles at each end of each course were cut on the splay to give an upward tilt to the courses, known as a 'Winchester cut'. This was probably partly for aesthetic reasons, but it also avoids cutting the end tiles at a very acute angle, leaving a point which could easily break off. If the old tiling was finished in this way, it should be repeated in any re-tiling.

The finish of the tile-hanging round doors and windows will need care, both to match the original appearance and to ensure a weathertight joint.

Sometimes we find a special form of tile-hanging, known as mathematical tiling. These tiles were made to imitate brickwork, and, like a brick wall, were pointed on completion. At first sight, we might think that the building was indeed of brick, but on close inspection it is generally possible to see the difference. The finish at external angles, and the fact that these tiles were sometimes hung on jettied first floor walls, are two of the more obvious clues. If we have to repair a building faced with mathematical tiles, replacements may be a problem. It may be possible to obtain second-hand tiles, but as there was no uniformity of size they may not match the existing ones exactly. It is, however, possible to obtain purpose-made mathematical tiles from certain manufacturers, and if this is done it is advisable to order enough for future repairs. Some firms are now producing mathematical tiles in coloured concrete, but these are unlikely to blend with old work.

Mathematical tiling on the upper walls of a timber-framed house, probably originally jettied.

SLATE-HANGING is another very efficient form of weatherproofing, both on timber framing and porous brick and stone walls, and was particularly popular on the coast, and other exposed areas. Sometimes, especially in the West Country, the slates were cut to form ornamental patterns, and these should be maintained or repeated in any repairs. The general principles of repair will be similar to those for tile-hanging.

Contrasting styles in Devon slate-hanging. ABOVE *Plain, utilitarian work on houses at Kingsbridge, and* LEFT *ornamental cut slate on the front of an Exeter house.*

Both tile-hung and slate-hung walls were sometimes painted over at a later date. This presents a problem when repairs have to be carried out. Generally it will not be possible to remove the paint without damage to the tiles or slates, and it is best to accept the situation and to repaint on completion of the repairs.

INSERTED DOORS AND WINDOWS As we have seen, when timber-framed houses were given a later cladding they often had new windows and doors inserted as part of a general face-lift. By the eighteenth century the most popular form of window was the double-hung sash, but side-hung casements, and horizontally sliding windows, sometimes known as Yorkshire sashes, were also used. For a time, around 1800, cast iron windows were popular. All these should, if necessary, be carefully repaired, following the old design. Particular care should be taken to copy the old sections of the frames, sashes, and glazing bars, including any mouldings. When sash windows first appeared the glazing bars were quite thick, and heavily moulded. Later, they were made more slender, especially when, as often happened, hardwood was used. If it is necessary to renew an old window completely, it should be purpose-made to match the old one. The modern standard casements and sashes are very unlikely to be suitable as replacements, as the timber sections used, as well as the proportions, will probably be different from the existing windows. Any old glass, particularly crown glass, with its slightly uneven surface, should be saved and re-used. Modern pseudo-'bull's eyes' are best avoided. Originally the 'bull's eye' was the waste piece of glass, in the centre of the spun sheet, where the glass stem was attached, and it would only have been used in some unimportant place, such as a kitchen, or servant's

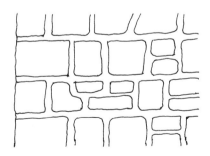

Stone walling: fine ashlar. The joints are very fine and need careful pointing.

Coursed rubble with rough ashlar quoins. A coarse, sharp sand should be used for pointing, kept back slightly from the stone face.

118

room. It is strange that it should now have become some sort of status symbol. Old cast iron windows may be badly rusted, but they can generally be cleaned off, treated with a rust-proofer, and repainted. If they are beyond repair, their replacement is less easy than that of timber windows, but there are firms who will make replicas of any design.

With its new windows the house would probably have been given a new panelled door, perhaps set into a classical surround. These features, too, should be carefully repaired, telling us as they do part of the story of the house. If really necessary, they should be replaced in replica. There are many modern standard 'Georgian' style doors available today, but most of them are unsuitable for use in old houses. Apart from the triviality of much of their detail the proportions are often wrong, since most old doors are wider in relation to their height than the standard modern door. The same thing applies to most 'Georgian' style door surrounds and porticoes produced today, which can be far too pretentious in style for the small houses on which they are so often used.

In an earlier chapter I emphasised the importance of employing a builder with his own joinery shop, and I hope the reason for this is now clear. If he has to sub-let all his joinery work he may not be particularly interested in trying to retain and repair old doors and windows, or to replace them in replica if necessary, when it is so much easier to order standard items from a catalogue.

Stone

We find houses built of stone in most parts of Britain. Owing to the varied geology of the country there are many kinds of stone used in buildings and, until the coming of cheap transport, it was, particularly for smaller and humbler buildings, obtained from the nearest possible source. Today, many of the old quarries are worked out, or have been closed for economic reasons, with the result that it is often difficult, or impossible, to find matching material for repairs.

Stone as used in buildings is generally found in one of two forms: ashlar and rubble. Ashlar is the term used to describe stone accurately cut to form smooth rectangular blocks, laid in regular courses, with fine joints, and we generally find it in the larger and more expensive buildings. Rubble describes stone roughly cut to shape, and laid either in courses or 'random', with thicker joints to compensate for the less regular sizes and shapes of the stones. It is found more often in the smaller houses and cottages, but, especially in its coursed form, was sometimes used in rather grander houses. Sometimes, indeed, the main façade of a house will be built of ashlar, while the side and rear walls are of rubble.

As I have already stressed, if a stone-built house shows signs of major structural movement professional advice should be obtained. There is another symptom of trouble peculiar to stone construction

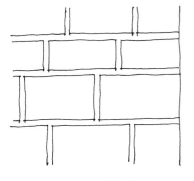

Stone walling: rough ashlar. The joints are wider, and a coarser sand can be used for pointing.

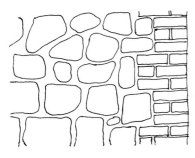

Random rubble with brick quoins. Pointing should be similar to that for coursed rubble.

which also needs professional diagnosis and treatment. Stone walls, whether of ashlar or rubble, were not always solidly built and bonded together, as in a good brick wall. The inner and outer skins were built of faced stone, and the space between them — the core — filled with very rough rubble with little or no mortar. In these walls the core may settle, or the facing may pull away from it, causing bulging and bowing, perhaps accompanied by cracking. If, in an old stone wall, the outer face is bowing, while the inner face appears reasonably plumb, this is probably the cause of the trouble. The remedial treatment will depend on the extent and seriousness of the failure. Rebuilding or refacing is not always necessary; it may be possible to tie back the facing and to consolidate the core by grouting, but this decision needs an expert opinion.

POINTING Leaving aside, then, these major problems, we may have an old house where the walls are structurally sound, but need some surface repair. The most common problem will be defective pointing. Until the nineteenth century, most stone walls were built in lime mortar, the joints being finished as the wall was built, rather than being subsequently raked and pointed. The outer face of the mortar may have deteriorated, particularly in areas of high atmospheric pollution or subject to salt impregnation, as in coastal areas, or where the wall has at some time been covered in ivy or other creepers. In the nineteenth century, and later, cement mortar was used, both for new work and to repoint older walls. This can be harmful in two ways. A strong mortar tends to shrink and crack, trapping water behind it, causing internal dampness and increasing the risk of frost damage. It also means that when the wall becomes wet, it can only dry out through the stones (these being more porous than the joints), and any harmful salts in the wall will tend to be deposited on or just behind the face of the stone, causing at best unsightly efflorescence on the surface, and at worst spalling or flaking of the stone face.

This explains why, in any repointing, it is essential to choose a mortar mix slightly *weaker* than the stone. Lime was the traditional binder for mortars, plasters and renders. Nowadays, there is a variety of different types of lime available, suitable for different purposes. Non-hydraulic limes are suitable for re-pointing very soft stone or for very sheltered locations. Natural hydraulic limes come in three grades called, in order of increasing strength, NHL2, NHL3.5 and NHL5. They are suitable for pointing harder stones and for more exposed locations. The choice of sand is also important: it should be clean and free from salt, and should contain a good proportion of coarse, sharp material. The joints should be well raked out and wetted before pointing. Shallow pointing in a strong mortar is not only unsightly but will accelerate decay in the stone.

The finish of the joints should match that of the original work if this survives. In ashlar work the joints were generally flush, or very slightly recessed. In rubble walls they were also generally flush, but

Bad pointing of brick and stone. BELOW *Raised or 'ribbon' pointing, which draws attention to the joints rather than to the bricks or stones.* RIGHT *On worn brickwork or stonework, flush pointing smeared over the edges of the bricks forms a 'feather edge'. This tends to pull away from the brick, allowing water to penetrate. It also looks unsightly, covering much of the brickwork.*

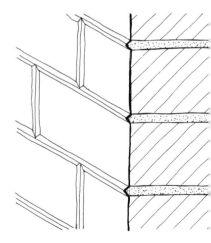

in repointing an old wall, where the stones have probably weathered and lost any sharp edges they may have had, it is generally best to keep the mortar back slightly, to avoid forming a 'feather edge' over the stone, since this would tend to shrink and form a water trap. The hard 'struck' pointing loved by some bricklayers, and the double-struck pointing sometimes known as 'snail creep' should always be avoided, as should the practice of smearing the mortar over the edges of the stones. It is not always possible to remove unsightly pointing without damaging the stones, but if, as is likely, a strong mortar mix was used, it will probably come away in due course, and can then be replaced with a more sympathetic treatment. The pointing is best placed into the joints with a narrow pointing iron, not a trowel, and when nearly set can be finished with a stiff bristle brush to expose the aggregate.

STONE REPAIRS Pointing is a relatively simple exercise. The problem becomes more difficult when the stones themselves are suffering from erosion. How far, in these cases. should we attempt to 'restore' the original appearance of the wall? The answer to this question will depend upon a number of factors, including the nature of the building and the extent of the decay. If this is widespread, and in particular if the whole of the wall surface appears to be soft and crumbling, professional advice should be obtained. It may be, for instance, that the stonework was never intended to be exposed to the weather, and would be best covered again, a decision which will of course change the present — though not necessarily the original — character of the house.

If the walling is generally sound, and the decay confined to certain individual stones, the degree of justifiable restoration will probably depend on the nature of the house. For instance, in a fairly formal ashlar building, such as a Georgian house with good classical details, it may well be right to aim at a restoration of the original appearance as far as possible, by cutting out and replacing damaged stones. The main problem here may be to find the right stone to use, if the original quarry is no longer being worked. As well as trying to match the colour of the original work, the new stone should also be of similar chemical composition. In some cases the use of limestone to repair a sandstone building, and vice versa, has resulted in decay of the sandstone from chemical action.

Sometimes, in an ashlar-faced building, we find that iron cramps were used to secure the stone, and that these have rusted, causing the stones to split. Where this has happened the only real remedy is to cut out the iron completely, replacing it with new non-ferrous metal cramps. Simply facing up the stone and leaving the iron will not cure the trouble, which is likely to recur.

Today, of course, pre-cast reconstructed stone is widely used, but I would not normally recommend it for repairing an ashlar stone building. However carefully the original colour may be matched

LEFT *Good and* BELOW *bad pointing of a rubble stone wall. In the lower example the joints compete for attention with the stone itself.*

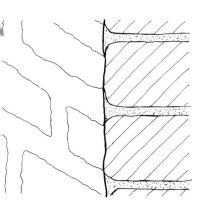

121

initially, the reconstructed stone may weather very differently from the natural stone, resulting in an increasingly patchy appearance. The other method of stone repair, not using natural stone, is what is often known as 'plastic repair'. This is rather a misleading term, since it does not involve the use of 'plastics' in the usual modern sense. It is perhaps better described as the 'dentistry' method. On the whole it is better suited to the repair of rubble walls, and to small details such as mouldings, window mullions and tracery, than to plain ashlar walling. Its main virtue is that it can enable a stone to be repaired, not renewed completely, and can be modelled to blend with adjoining sound but weathered stones, thus making the repairs less obtrusive and preserving more original work. It may also be less expensive, but if well and carefully done may not be much cheaper than new stone. It should certainly not be thought of simply as a cheap alternative, and badly done it can ruin a building.

Before going into the details of plastic repair, let us consider the general treatment of rubble stone walls. As we have seen, these are generally found in less sophisticated buildings: the simple farmhouses and cottages. Here it is important not to over-restore; by so doing it is easy to destroy the simple charm of the house. Generally, it is only necessary to renew or repair a stone if it is so badly decayed that it is structurally unsound (i.e. incapable of carrying its load), or is creating a water trap. Otherwise, all that may be necessary is to scale or brush down the wall to remove any loose or crumbling surface. This action alone, by removing possible water traps, will at least slow down the rate of decay. The loss of one, or even two inches off the face of a two-foot thick wall is not going to affect its structural stability.

If a stone is very badly decayed, or shattered, it may be necessary to replace it and, as with ashlar work, a matching stone should be obtained, and care taken to see that it is laid on its correct bed, i.e. with the bedding planes, or layers of sedimentation laid horizontally. If, however, most of the stone is sound, plastic or 'dentistry' repair may be the best solution. It is not, though, simply a case of 'facing up' the stone in a mixture of crushed stone and cement. This will not only look unsightly, but will in time pull away from the old stone. First, the decayed section must be cut away to sound stone, and be cut back square with the wall face or, better still, slightly undercut, to avoid any 'feather edge'. The key for the repair may be formed either with copper dowels and wire, or with slips of clay roofing tile let into the old stone, in layers about the thickness of a tile apart. The mix for the repair should be slightly weaker than the stone, and made of lime and sand as for pointing, but perhaps with the addition of some crushed stone. It should be built up in fairly thin layers, to avoid risk of shrinkage, each layer being allowed to set before the next is applied. In hot weather the work should be kept damp to avoid too rapid drying. If two adjoining stones are being repaired they should be treated separately, and the joint between them afterwards pointed in a

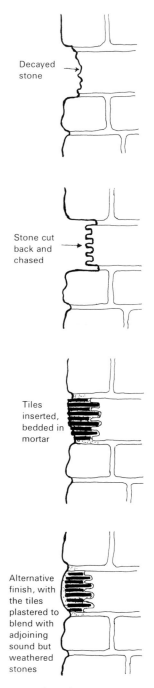

Decayed stone

Stone cut back and chased

Tiles inserted, bedded in mortar

Alternative finish, with the tiles plastered to blend with adjoining sound but weathered stones

Tile stitching repairs to stonework.

slightly weaker mix. The final surface can be moulded to match the adjoining stones, and should be brushed off when nearly dry to expose the aggregate. It will be obvious that this is work needing a skilled and sensitive craftsman, but it can be useful in dealing with rubble walls, and, as previously stated, with small sections of mouldings and similar details.

TREATMENT OF DAMP Deterioration in a stone building is often caused by damp and we should of course try to remove the source of the problem. Much damage is done by leaking rainwater gutters and downpipes, and by loose or missing pointing. Hard cement pointing can also lead to dampness inside; cracks in the cement allow rainwater to penetrate into the wall, but, because the pointing does not breath, it cannot escape. These matters are fairly straightforward to put right, but rising damp may be more complicated to deal with. Very few houses built before the mid-nineteenth century had a damp-proof course so moisture was able to rise up from the ground on which the wall was built. Sometimes the problem may have been aggravated by allowing the ground level round the house to rise above the ground floor level, perhaps as a result of garden works or the formation of a terrace. At other times defective rainwater drainage has made matters worse, but there is often another reason: originally the ground floor may, in a very early house, have been of beaten earth, or later of brick or stone paving laid on sand, or even of timber — all permeable materials which allowed moisture to evaporate through them. If a modern, solid concrete floor, incorporating a damp-proof membrane, has been laid this creates a barrier to upward moisture movement, which can divert the water and drive it up the walls.

Today there are several methods of dealing with rising damp. If possible, ground levels and drainage should be improved to reduce the source of moisture reaching the base of the wall, and in many cases this will be sufficient to solve the problem. In a solid ashlar wall it may be possible to insert a conventional damp proof course in a suitable horizontal joint by cutting through it with a special circular saw, and this is probably the most reliable method. It is, though, impossible to do this in a random rubble wall. Most damp proof firms advocate the use of injected silicone damp proof courses for rubble walls, but these are often of limited effectiveness on their own, and seem to rely more on the associated internal re-plastering, using hard, cement-based materials, which the contractor normally insists on, to keep the damp at bay. In a building severely affected by damp it may be necessary to strip internal plaster to remove hygroscopic salts, as these will attract moisture from the atmosphere and cause damp patches to appear even after the wall has dried out. However, provided the wall has dried out, re-plastering can be in lime plaster.

WINDOWS AND DOORS In older stone houses, up to the mid- to late seventeenth century, the windows will probably be of the mullioned type, of stone or timber, and would have had leaded glazing, as we

Dampness at the wall base of this Purbeck cottage may be due to rising damp in the wall itself, or to water dripping from the gutterless eaves and splashing up from the paving. The cause must be found before a decision is taken on treatment.

Traditional mullioned windows. ABOVE *A Yorkshire example, with no hoodmould and plain chamfered mullions. Decay in the stone may have been aggravated by the hard pointing.* LEFT *A Somerset window with hoodmould and hollow chamfered mullions.* BELOW *The use of timber instead of stone enables lighter mullion sections to be used.*

have seen in timber-framed houses. In the oldest examples the windows would have been unglazed, but as stone was not often used for small houses before the later sixteenth century we are not so likely to find these unglazed openings as we are in a timber-framed house. If old mullioned windows survive it is important to retain and repair these in their original form. Today it is possible to obtain 'Tudor style' mullioned windows made up in reconstructed stone, but these are generally unsuitable as replacements for old stone windows for several reasons. First, the standard mullion sections used are thinner than those of the old windows and, second, they are designed to take modern standard metal windows, and are therefore spaced wider

Small Yorkshire houses of stone have a distinctive, rather austere character, with their simple design and solid mullioned windows. An attempt has been made to give the house on the left of the picture a 'period' character with standard 'Georgian' type doors and windows, involving the loss of the centre mullion in the ground floor window. Both houses have been rather disfigured by the external plumbing – not necessary under modern Building Regulations.

apart. Their scale is therefore wrong, quite apart from the fact that their regular, rather mechanical appearance can never match that of the original work.

By the eighteenth century, double-hung sash windows were usual in superior houses, and we have considered their preservation, and that of early doors, elsewhere. In ashlar stone houses these later openings generally had either stone lintels or flat stone arches, with tapering voussoirs, externally, and timber lintels internally. The earlier mullioned windows also had internal wood lintels, and in the simpler rubble stone houses the windows, often of casement or horizontally sliding type, generally had external wood lintels also. We may find that the inner wood lintel has decayed, and this is a common cause of fractures above door and window openings. It is usual today to replace the decayed timber with pre-cast reinforced concrete lintels. It is important to retain or replace in replica the original external lintels or arches, including the external wood lintels in the simpler houses. Sometimes these are replaced in concrete, which looks wrong even, or perhaps especially, if this is 'faced up' in cement in an attempt to imitate stone. If the outer lintel has to be replaced it is important to use seasoned timber to avoid risk of subsequent movement.

EXTERNAL FINISHES Having completed the repairs to the external stonework, you may want to consider some preservative treatment. Over the past few decades many patent chemical treatments have been produced, but on the whole their long-term value is unproved. Indeed, some of them have done more harm than good, by sealing the surface of the stone so that it could not breathe, or trapping water behind it, sometimes encouraging the surface to peel away even more than before. Even products which claim to be microporous or breathable can significantly hamper moisture movement and cause problems. Experiments are still continuing, but I would not recommend the use of any chemical treatment without very specialised advice from an independent conservation professional, not from a salesman.

There is a great deal of controversy today about the merits and demerits of colouring external stonework. Most people probably prefer to see it unpainted, but there is clear evidence that, on rubble stone buildings at least, sometimes even on ashlar, limewashing was general, probably until the nineteenth century. Apart from its decorative value, limewash helps to preserve the stone, particularly limestone, by acting as a binder and also as a protection from the weather. Unlike some modern finishes, it is not completely impervious, and allows the stone to breathe. Even when the limewash has been scraped off you may still find traces of it on old rubble walls. As on timber-framed buildings, it was often tinted with umber or ochre.

Whether or not to re-limewash an old house must be a matter of individual choice, but, in the case of a soft rubble wall it could help to prolong its life. Much will depend on the style of the house, and its setting: it might be rather anti-social to limewash one house in a street or terrace where all the others are uncoloured. As we have seen with old plastered timber-framed walls, it is best to avoid the modern impervious finishes.

As I have suggested earlier, there is evidence that some very rough rubble walls, particularly where the only available stone was of a soft, porous nature, were not merely limewashed, but were given a thin coat of plaster. This has often been stripped in Victorian and later times, just like certain timber-framed houses which were never meant to be exposed. Replastering may be the best treatment in these cases, but this should not be done without professional advice, as it will be important to select a suitable plaster mix for the particular stone. Again, as we have seen with timber-framed houses, some old stone houses were plastered at a later date, when rough stone had become unfashionable, and they may have been given new doors and windows at the same time. Removal of this later plaster sometimes

At Bradley Manor, Devon, the external rubble stone has been limewashed in the traditional manner, showing up the details of the mouldings and carved work. On limestone, limewash properly applied can act as a safe preservative.

This house at Melksham, Wiltshire, has been well pointed, but the projecting window surrounds indicate that it was originally plastered.

reveals evidence of these changes — old windows blocked and new ones made with brickwork — resulting in rather a patchy appearance. Although each case must be considered on its merits, it is often best to retain or restore the plaster in these cases.

If an old rubble stone wall is to be plastered, a suitable lime plaster should be used, and the plaster should be allowed to follow the contour of the wall face, without trying to obtain a perfectly flat finish. A wood float should be used, rather than a steel trowel. If the wall was originally plastered it may be found that the stone quoins, and the jamb stones at the door and window openings are slightly proud of the general wall surface. If so, the plaster should be finished flush with these, avoiding any hard edge or 'cut back' effect, which can look rather contrived. The old plaster was probably limewashed, but you may prefer to leave it exposed, particularly if the sand is carefully chosen to produce an attractive coloured finish.

Although, as we have seen, the old stone walls were often limewashed from the start, there may be occasions when you will want to remove limewash, or other paint, from external walls. Old limewash, particularly if it has already started to flake off, can often be removed by hard scrubbing with water and a stiff bristle brush. Incidentally, a wire brush should only be used on old walls if the stone is very hard and dense, or it may damage the surface. With other paints, it may be difficult to remove them without damaging the stone face, and independent professional advice should be obtained if it is desired to do this. Both chemical and abrasive methods may be used, and are widely advertised, but their success will depend on the nature and condition of the stone as well as of the paint.

Cleaning of unpainted stone also needs to be done with care. For most stones, water cleaning is the safest method: a water spray will eventually remove most soot and other deposits from limestone, but it is a long process, and not always convenient, particularly on buildings adjoining a street. There are many firms carrying out stone cleaning by a variety of methods, chemical, abrasive, or a combination of these with water. Again, professional advice should be sought, as an unsuitable method can result in permanent damage to the stone.

If it is desired to remove lichens from stonework various proprietory materials are available, but most lichens do no harm to the stone. Certain creepers and climbing plants can be harmful. by preventing the stone from drying out. Ivy, in particular, should never be allowed to grow on old stone walls, as its aerial roots can penetrate the mortar joints, resulting in dampness, and even, in extreme cases, in structural damage. Where ivy growth has become established, the best way to remove it is to cut the roots, treating them with weedkiller, and to allow the plant to die down. It should not be pulled off the wall while still growing, as this can damage the pointing, or even the stone if it is of a soft, porous nature. If you want to have climbing plants on the walls of an old house it is best to grow these on a trellis or other framing which allows air to circulate behind it, and which can allow the plant to be taken down when repointing or other maintenance becomes necessary. These remarks apply equally to most other old walling materials.

Brick

Bricks were used in Britain in Roman times, and seem to have been reintroduced in the thirteenth century. The earliest post-Roman brick buildings are in East Anglia, and the use of brick spread gradually across the country, replacing first timber framing and cob, and, later, stone, for smaller houses. By the mid-nineteenth century brick had probably become the most common building material.

Before the advent of cheap transport, bricks were mainly used in areas where clay suitable for brick-making was available, and there were many small brickworks scattered over the country, producing bricks of various colours, according to the type of clay and the method of firing. In recent times many of these small brickworks have closed and modern machine-made bricks are transported to all areas. There is still, however, a great variety of brick available in different colours and textures, so that it is generally possible to find a reasonable match for old brickwork in need of repair. The main problem may well be to match the size rather than the colour of the old bricks since, until the eighteenth century — later in some areas — their size had not been standardised. Some brickworks will, however, make bricks specially to non-standard sizes, and will match specially shaped or moulded bricks if required.

True bricks are made from burnt clay. Today, many so-called 'bricks' are made of a mixture of sand and lime or flint and lime, not burnt, but moulded under steam pressure. These are really more akin to concrete than to true brick, and they will rarely be suitable for use in exposed walls in old buildings.

As with other materials, if a brick building needs major structural

Seventeenth century brickwork, in garden wall bond, with stone quoins.

repairs, professional advice should be obtained. Wherever possible an old brick wall should be repaired in situ, rather than taken down and rebuilt. With brickwork, even more perhaps than with other materials, it is tempting to say that it is easier and cheaper to rebuild than to repair, but against this must be set the inevitable loss of authenticity. However carefully the rebuilding may be carried out, it is almost impossible to re-create the texture and patina of the old work. This is particularly true with medieval, Tudor and early Stuart buildings. In these periods, the bricks were not always laid to any recognised bond, and there might be considerable variation in the thickness of the mortar joints. This, with the irregular size and shape of the bricks themselves, and the fact that early walls were not always completely plumb, gives old brickwork much of its character, very easily lost in rebuilding. This is perhaps less vital in later houses where the bricks and the walling are of a more regular nature.

If a brick wall has to be rebuilt it will probably have to be as a cavity wall — indeed, the local Building Inspector may require this. The outer leaf of the cavity wall is generally only 4½ inches thick, which means that it will probably be built in 'stretcher' bond, to avoid having to cut bricks. This at once gives the game away: the wall

Brick bonds found in old buildings. TOP LEFT *English bond, common until the end of the seventeenth century. The bricks were narrower than those in use today.* TOP RIGHT *English garden wall bond, also found in early buildings, popular in nine-inch-thick walls.* CENTRE LEFT *Flemish bond, common from the eighteenth century onwards.* CENTRE RIGHT *Header bond, popular in the eighteenth century, often had contrasting coloured brick for quoins and other details.* LOWER *Flemish garden wall bond. A version of Flemish bond often found in nine-inch-thick walls.*

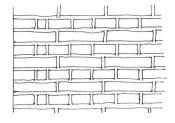

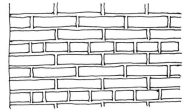

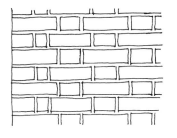

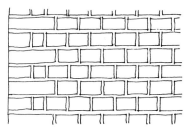

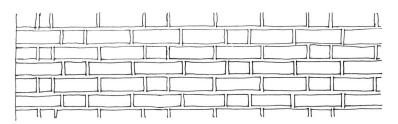

is clearly modern and will not harmonise with the old walling. If rebuilding is unavoidable the original bond should be repeated, either by cutting bricks or by building the outer leaf 9 inches thick.

Another point which must be borne in mind is that the brickwork may only be a facing, on a timber-framed, cob or even stone house, added when brick was the more fashionable material. This should always be checked before work is started, as it could affect the repair methods adopted. On the other hand, what appears to be a brick wall may be clad in mathematical tiles (described earlier in the chapter), and this again should be checked before any work is started.

POINTING The more superficial problems of repairing brick houses are similar to those applying to stonework, the most common one probably being defective pointing. As with stone, it is important to choose a mortar mix slightly weaker than the bricks. The decision about which type of lime to use will depend on the hardness and porosity of the bricks, and the degree of exposure of the wall. Again, as with stone, the mortar should not be 'struck' with a trowel, or finished proud of the face of the bricks. It is best finished with a brush when nearly set to remove any lime skin and expose the sand. Before starting any repointing it is important to rake the joints out well, and to wet them to prevent water being drawn out of the new mortar by porous bricks.

The thickness of the mortar joints in old walls often varies. In early work, where the bricks are of irregular size and shape, the joints may be quite thick, while by the late seventeenth century they were often much finer. Where the original pointing survives it should be used as a model for any repointing. Bad later pointing, often in too strong a mix and either raised, or smeared over the edges of the bricks, should not be repeated, and neither should the use of black ash mortar, popular in some districts in the nineteenth century.

For a time in the nineteenth century there was a fashion for 'tuck pointing'. In this, the mortar was coloured to match the bricks: a fine groove was cut along the centre of each joint and filled with white mortar, giving the effect of a much finer joint than actually existed. If there is clear evidence that this was the original finish there is a case for repeating it, but if so it must be done very carefully, by a skilled craftsman.

BRICK REPAIRS Apart from defective pointing, we may find that the bricks themselves have decayed. This is generally due to their having been under-burnt, since well-burnt bricks are very durable, but even these may decay if they have been subjected to prolonged saturation with water, perhaps because of defective roofs or drainage. The only real remedy in these cases will be to cut out the defective bricks, replacing them with matching bricks, carefully bedding and pointing them to blend with the old walling. Second-hand bricks may be available, perhaps from another part of the house which is being altered, but if large numbers of bricks are required, it is generally better to

Ornamental sixteenth century brickwork on a house at Methwold, Norfolk.

find suitable new bricks than to encourage the demolition of old buildings by creating a market for second-hand materials. The old method of firing bricks often resulted in the ends of the bricks being much darker than the sides, and these 'burnt headers' were often used to make decorative patterns in the walling. If this feature exists it should be retained in any repairs.

Brick walls may, of course, be affected by rising damp. This can be remedied in the ways described for stone walls. In the case of brickwork, however, it is easier to insert a conventional damp-proof course, by cutting through a mortar joint with a specially designed circular saw. A number of firms specialise in this work.

In some early brick houses we may find specially moulded bricks used to create architectural features, including classical details, often showing Flemish influence. Houses of the sixteenth and seventeenth centuries generally had the mullioned windows typical of the period. Sometimes these were of stone, or timber, but they were often built up in specially moulded bricks. If these features need repair it will be necessary to have bricks specially made, and fortunately there are firms who will do this. As the process is comparatively expensive, since separate moulds have to be made for each feature, it is worth having some extra bricks made, for future repairs.

WINDOWS AND DOORS In later brick houses you will find windows similar to those in stone houses: casements, horizontally sliding and double-hung sashes, and cast iron casements in wood frames. All these generally had timber lintels internally and brick arches externally. These arches might, in simpler houses, be formed with ordinary bricks, with tapering joints, but in the better eighteenth- and nineteenth-century houses the bricks themselves were made, or

Early nineteenth century cast iron windows of various patterns, often enhancing the character of simple houses and cottages.

rubbed, to a tapered profile, enabling the joints between them to be very fine. Sometimes these arches had stone, or raised brick keystones. Another popular eighteenth-century feature was the raised 'apron' under the sill, and the window jambs were sometimes formed in a contrasting coloured brick. All these features should be carefully retained in repairs. Many old houses have been spoilt by replacing the original arches with the modern 'soldier' arch, which is not only structurally meaningless (it has to be carried on a steel bar or angle), but is quite out of character with the old walling and windows.

While on the subject of windows in eighteenth-century houses, let us consider that of the bow window. Generally, these seem to have been more common in shops than in houses, although they were popular in the late eighteenth- and early nineteenth-century seaside developments. Their construction demanded a very high standard of joinery, as each pane was curved on plan, necessitating specially made glass. The shop windows were generally fixed, without opening lights, but in private houses bow windows were normally fitted with double-hung sashes. Where these windows survive, and are authentic, they should be carefully repaired. Recently, though, we have seen a fashion for introducing pseudo-bow windows, loosely described as 'Georgian', into many houses which never had them, and this is tending to turn some of our old towns into replicas of the 'Quality Street' advertisement. Worst of all are the standard 'bow' windows produced by some of the modern window manufacturers. These are of the wrong proportion, generally too wide in relation to their height, they are made up of a series of straight sections, i.e. they are *not* curved on plan, their glazing bars are generally of a very clumsy section, and their opening lights are in the form of side-hung casements often combined with top-hung lights—all completely out of character with genuine Georgian design. To make matters worse, they are often given a fibreglass capping in a style quite unknown in the eighteenth

A nineteenth century brick terrace with an assortment of 'ad hoc' alterations, destroying the unity of the design. In unlisted buildings all this work would be permitted development.

A modern bow window inserted in a Georgian house – an attempt to be 'traditional' – but the scale of the new window is completely different from that of the original ones above it.

132

In this nineteenth century house at Stratford on Avon, Warwickshire, the ornamental cast iron verandahs add interest and liveliness to the façade. All too often, when such features need repair they are simply removed.

A good eighteenth century timber door and surround on a brick house in Suffolk.

century, and fitted with one or more mock 'bull's eyes'! As we have already seen, the standard 'Georgian' type windows are rarely suitable as replacements for genuine work, and these mock bows are probably the worst of their type.

It is perhaps with Georgian brick houses that we associate the attractive classical timber door hoods, pediments and surrounds that give so much character to old town and village streets. Although these features are found on stone houses, they are, in these cases, more often formed in stone themselves. Painted woodwork can be a perfect foil to mellow brick, and these features should be carefully repaired, retaining and if necessary renewing any lead weatherings. Today, as with windows, standard so-called 'Georgian' door surrounds are obtainable, sometimes made up in fibreglass, but while these may have their uses in new buildings, they should not be used to replace genuine Georgian work. There *are* good joiners today, quite capable of repairing these features, and they should be sought out.

The doors themselves in old brick houses will be similar in character to those in contemporary stone houses, and, like them, should be retained and repaired, or, if necessary, replaced in replica.

EXTERNAL FINISHES Brick is often found in conjunction with other materials. As we have seen, stone was often used for early mullioned windows, as it was for door surrounds, quoins, string courses, and cornices and copings. Brick was also used in some areas in conjunc-

133

tion with flint, generally in alternate horizontal bands, and, as we have seen, for quoins and door and window surrounds. All these features should be retained and repaired.

Although in many early houses the ornamental value of brick was exploited, it was sometimes plastered from the start, possibly because the builders were not sure of its weathering properties. In these cases, the quoins and door and window surrounds were generally of ashlar stone, finished proud of the brickwork to allow the plaster to be finished flush with the stone, a feature we have already seen in connection with rubble stonework. Again, as we have seen with other materials, this early plaster was often stripped in more recent times. Whether or not to replace it in these cases will probably depend on the character and condition of the bricks and on whether the wall is weatherproof without its protective plaster. If you do decide to replaster, the choice of plaster mix is important, as the wall must be allowed to breathe. As with pointing, the mortar should be weaker than the brickwork, so a weak or moderately hydraulic lime will be the likely choice, depending on the softness of the brick and the degree of exposure of the wall.

A more difficult problem can arise when an old brick building has been plastered at a later date, perhaps in conjunction with other alterations. Here, as we have seen with timber framing and with stone, removal of the plaster may create more difficulties than it solves, and it is often better to retain and repair it.

Another subject which we have already considered in connection with stone is the controversial one of colouring brickwork. Just as some early brick buildings were designed to be plastered it is probable that some were always limewashed. Many more have been limewashed, or painted, at a later date. It is not always easy to remove this paint without damaging the face of the brickwork. Various methods are now in use, but it is advisable to test any proposed method on a small area and to leave it for a time to see how it weathers, before proceeding with the whole building. Indeed, sometimes if a brick house has been patched, or if the bricks are not particularly attractive, it is worth considering colouring it. As we have seen there is good traditional precedent for this, but on an early house the decision should not be taken without professional advice. The house should not, of course, be considered in isolation: if it is part of a terrace or group it might be rather anti-social to colour it.

Other traditional materials

CHALK BLOCKS The building stones of Britain vary from the hard granites of parts of Scotland and Cornwall, through the many types of sandstone and limestone to the soft chalk-like clunch of the Chilterns. In some downland areas we even find chalk itself used for building, in spite of its comparatively low strength and weather-resistance. Usually it is found in internal walls, and on the inner faces

RIGHT *Polychrome brickwork used to decorative effect on a nineteenth century lodge at Swallowfield, Berkshire.* BELOW *Brickwork window surrounds emphasised by a flush render, which should be made of lime.*

of external walls, and when it was used for the outer faces of external walls it was usually plastered. Occasionally though, in sheltered areas, we may find external, exposed chalk block walling, more often in barns and other farm buildings than in houses.

When repairing chalk walls, it is important to use a weak mortar for pointing, as a strong mix will encourage decay in the soft chalk. Chalk block walls are generally built off a footing or base of harder material, and this should be maintained in any repairs or alterations. It is also important to see that the wall has a good protection at the top, for instance, by a good overhang to the eaves. If chalk walling is allowed to become saturated it will soon disintegrate, a process hastened by frost. If the surface of the chalk is badly eroded it may

RIGHT *Chalk blocks banded with harder flint, in Dorset.*

well be best to plaster it, using a soft lime mix as described for rubble stone.

Window and door openings in chalk block buildings generally had timber lintels. As we have seen, these may decay, resulting in movement in the walling over the opening. When this has happened, the lintel should be carefully removed, the walling supported, and a new lintel inserted. Although concrete lintels are normal practice in modern work it is probably best not to use them in chalk block walls, as the concrete is a denser, harder material, and could cause further movement. Untreated hardwood or painted softwood lintels are likely to be more satisfactory, and will retain the original appearance of the wall if this is not plastered.

FLINT Flint is often found in the chalk downland areas, and may be used in conjunction with chalk blocks for walling. The flint itself is a very hard material, unlikely to decay, and the main problems are likely to be defective pointing and, in extreme cases, the actual falling away of the surface flints.

Flint walling can vary considerably in character, but basically it is of two main types. In its less sophisticated form the flints are used whole, just as they are found, and either laid random or roughly coursed. It is probable that many of these rough flint walls were originally plastered, and traces of the original finish may be found on buildings which have not been 'restored'. As we have seen with other materials, since the nineteenth century there has been a fashion for stripping rough flint walls and pointing them up, sometimes in a very unsympathetic manner, with a hard trowelled joint which emphasises the mortar, rather than the flints which were so laboriously stripped.

In the rather grander buildings the flints were generally split or 'knapped' to expose the dark, shiny interior, and to produce a reasonably flat face. In these walls the flints are more likely to be laid in courses, and were probably always exposed. In some areas, flint walling reached a very high standard; the flints were not only knapped to produce a flat face, but were cut into regular square or rectangular shapes, and laid with fine joints. This work sometimes incorporated stonework in a panelled or traceried pattern, known as 'flushwork', and is seen at its best in some East Anglian churches. In the nineteenth century we find flint houses and cottages built with brick or stone dressings of a very ornamental character — perhaps, to our eyes, rather fussy and assertive looking. These are now, however, starting to mellow, and their richness is being appreciated.

Although flint is a strong material, it cannot be used easily for quoins, or for door and window jambs. These were therefore generally built up in stone or brick, and these materials were also used to form horizontal bonding courses in flint buildings, and had a structural value, as well as being ornamental.

Pointing of flint can be carried out in a slightly stronger mix than

Banded brick and flint in nineteenth century Dorset estate cottages.

that for most stones, using a moderately hydraulic lime (NHL3.5) and sand. In knapped work it should be kept back, off the face of the flint. Pointing of the rougher walls is more difficult, as these were generally intended to be covered. If you wish to leave the flint exposed the mortar should still be kept back slightly, to avoid forming a 'feather edge' over the flints.

Where the facing flints are actually falling away, owing perhaps to the building having been covered in ivy, they should be carefully reset, after cleaning out and wetting the backing to assist adhesion. As flint was generally used very near its place of origin, it should not be too difficult to find any necessary replacements, as they often occur on or near the ground surface, and do not have to be quarried. Any bonding or other patterning with brick or stone should be retained. The repair of finely jointed knapped flintwork will need more care, and a specialist craftsman should be employed. It is still possible to obtain knapped flints from a few places, mainly in East Anglia.

In flint-walled buildings, the door and window openings will have either lintels or arches of stone, or brick arches, with timber lintels internally. Some very simple cottages may also have external timber lintels. As with other walling materials, movement may be caused by failure of timber lintels. These may be replaced by concrete lintels internally, taking great care to support the flintwork above, as this could easily start to run. The original external lintels or arches should be retained, or, if necessary, replaced in replica.

COBBLES AND PEBBLES Rather similar in character to flint walling is that made up of cobbles and pebbles from the seashore and river valleys. These may be laid random, or roughly coursed, and as with flint the quoins and jambs to window and door openings are generally built up in brick or stone. Stone and brick banding courses are also found in cobble walls, helping to give them stability, since it is difficult to obtain any real bond with these materials. In many buildings they were probably originally plastered, but as with other materials they are often now found stripped and pointed.

Methods of repair and the general treatment of buildings with cobble and pebble walls are similar to those of flint, but, since some of the cobbles are less hard than flint, a rather weaker mortar should be used.

COB, AND SIMILAR 'EARTH' WALLING Cob, pisé de terre, and similar forms of earth or mud walling, have been used since early times, particularly in areas with no readily available supplies of timber or stone. Its composition varies according to the place of origin, and the nature of the subsoil, but it may contain a mixture of clay, loam, chalk and small stones, bound with straw or heather, mixed with water, and well trodden down to form a stiff, dense mix. This is then built up in a series of 'lifts', about eighteen inches high, each lift being allowed to harden before the next one is laid. Sometimes the walls were built up between parallel boards, the equivalent of shuttering for mass con-

Banded stone and flint at Cerne Abbas, Dorset.

Devon cob and thatch at Hope Cove.

ABOVE *Cob walling on a rubble stone base. A solid foundation is essential for cob.*

crete, but often they were constructed without this, the face of the wall being trimmed off when partly set, to give either a vertical, or slightly battered (i.e. inwardly sloping) finish.

Good cob eventually becomes very hard, and may be thought of as an early form of concrete, or of unbaked brick. It needs, however, to be protected from damp, and it was therefore built off a base of stone, brick or flint, and was protected at the top by a good overhang at the eaves. It is no coincidence that many cob buildings are, or were originally, thatched. The finished cob was generally plastered and limewashed, although this finish was sometimes omitted, particularly on farm buildings. The walls were often built with a batter, tapering towards the top, and the external corners might be slightly rounded. These features give cob buildings a pleasant, soft, rather irregular profile, and it is important to retain this when carrying out repairs.

Apart from structural movement caused by faulty or missing foundations and changes in subsoil conditions, or thrust from a defective roof (troubles which can occur with most materials), the main defects to be found in cob buildings are due to water penetration. If a roof is allowed to leak, allowing water to soak into the top of a cob wall, it will soon start to deteriorate. In an exposed position, decay of the external plaster may result in erosion of the wall face. If the ground level is allowed to build up above the level of the stone or brick wall base, decay will soon begin to affect the cob. As we have seen, structural movement is a matter requiring professional advice, but, in the case of a cob building more than with others, it is important to employ an architect or surveyor who understands cob building and is used to repairing it. Someone used only to modern

Cob on a rubble stone base in a new building at Northleigh, Devon.

construction is likely to be put off by the idea of a house built of 'mud' and may recommend more drastic measures than are necessary or desirable. It is also, for the same reason, important to choose a builder who is used to working with cob.

If the top of a cob wall has been allowed to deteriorate through water penetration it can be taken down to a sound base and built up, either in reconstituted cob, or new cob mixed in the traditional manner, or in pre-fabricated cob blocks, and subsequently plastered. Where the surface of the cob has eroded, it is best to clean it down, wet it, and make it good in a fairly soft plaster, say 1:3 lime putty and sand, finished with a wood float, and following the contour of the wall face, as I have described for plaster on rubble stone. Large holes are best filled with cob blocks, or cob tiles bedded in lime mortar, after cleaning out, and well wetting the old cob. The problem of trying to use reconstituted, or newly made cob for this purpose is that the cob will shrink on drying, perhaps as much as $\frac{1}{4}$ inch in a foot in height, and will not therefore form a proper key to the old work. This difficulty does not of course arise in the same way when building *up* in cob on top of an old wall.

Small cracks in cob walls can be well wetted, and pointed up in a fairly weak mortar. Larger cracks are better repaired by 'stitching', possibly with courses of clay tiles bedded in mortar.

Door and window openings in cob houses generally had wood lintels. If these have decayed, causing movement in the walling above, it is better to replace them in wood, either hardwood or treated, painted softwood, rather than to introduce concrete. If the lintels are exposed externally they should certainly be replaced in timber. If new door or window openings are to be formed in a cob wall it is important to avoid causing unnecessary vibration or disturbance. Rather than knocking holes with a pick, it is better to cut out the cob with a saw, after drilling holes at the corners with an auger.

I have mentioned the importance of providing a good overhang at the eaves of a cob building. Cases have been known of serious failure after a thatched roof on a cob house has been replaced by tiles, with a much smaller overhang; this should always be borne in mind if a change of roof finish is contemplated. On the other hand, the insertion of a damp-proof course in a cob building should not be undertaken lightly. There is some evidence that the structure of cob can be weakened if it is allowed to become too dry. The wall base should be repaired and pointed as necessary, and the surface water drainage maintained in good order. If trouble is still experienced from rising damp, specialist advice should be obtained.

CLAY LUMP A variation on cob building found mainly in some parts of East Anglia is clay lump. Here, the clay was moulded into rectangular blocks, like large bricks, and left to dry. These blocks were then built up in courses, like masonry, and plastered externally. Like cob, this material is durable as long as it is kept dry, but will soon

Walls

deteriorate if allowed to become wet. New clay lump blocks can be made for repairs or, since these walls are always plastered, soft brick or stone could be used.

WINDOWS AND DOORS Houses built of chalk blocks, flint, cobbles and pebbles, and cob are likely to have simple timber windows— casements, horizontally sliding sashes, or double-hung sashes. Occasionally, in early examples, timber- and even stone-mullioned windows with lead lights may be found, and, as we have seen, cast iron casements were popular in some areas for a short period around 1800. Doors are likely to be of the simple boarded type, though some later houses may have panelled doors. The repair of these features has been described in a previous section.

Stucco

We have looked at the use of plaster to cover timber-framed, rubble stone and old brick walls, and have seen that this was sometimes done to improve the weather-resistant qualities of the wall, and sometimes to cover what had become unfashionable materials. This early plaster was generally plain in character, although it was sometimes ornamented with raised designs of a floral, heraldic or conventional pattern: the practice known as 'pargetting', which was such a feature of East Anglian buildings in the sixteenth and seventeenth centuries, and described earlier in this chapter.

In the later eighteenth and early nineteenth centuries, however, plaster was used, on brick and rubble stone, in a more formal manner, reproducing classical details in imitation of contemporary work in ashlar stone. By this time, harder mixes than that of the old lime plaster had become more common, using the stronger hydraulic limes of which the best known was probably the so-called 'Roman' cement. This stucco work was typical of the Regency period, the Nash terraces around Regent's Park in London being perhaps the most famous examples. The plaster was generally painted, although at first an oil-based stain was sometimes used.

If stucco is well maintained and painted regularly it should give little trouble, but if water is allowed to penetrate it — perhaps due to faulty gutters and weatherings — problems can arise. The brick or stone walling becomes wet, and cannot dry out through the hard plaster. This can result in internal dampness, possibly leading to dry rot attack, and salts carried through the brickwork may force the plaster off the wall, destroying the bond between the two materials. When this has happened it is necessary to remove the loose stucco, and to allow the brickwork to dry out thoroughly before replastering.

REPAIRS True 'Roman' cement is not easily available today, but hydraulic lime may be obtained, and it is generally better to use this than to introduce Portland cement. The strength of the hydraulic lime used and the proportion of lime to sand will vary depending on the

Renovated stucco detailing, Islington, London.

Ornate plasterwork on an eighteenth century house in Warwick.

strength of the original stucco and of the backing material. As with all repairs, the new work should match the original as closely as possible, including the texture of the sand; colour is less important if the wall is subsequently to be painted. It is of course important to see that the walling itself is sound before starting to repair the plaster; it should not be used to cover up trouble. If there is evidence of salts in the walling — these can usually be seen as a white crystalline deposit — professional advice should be obtained. If the salts cannot be removed it may be necessary to use a special sulphate-resistant plaster for the repairs to prevent a recurrence of the trouble. It is of course important to put right any defects in the building which could allow water to penetrate behind the plaster. Open joints in copings, and defective or missing lead weatherings to cornices and other projections are a frequent source of trouble.

In repairing stucco, all loose and defective sections should be removed, and the walling cleaned down and wetted. The new plaster should be applied in the same number of coats as the old work, allowing each coat to dry and set before applying the next coat, and finishing the final coat with a wood float.

DETAILS In repairing these Regency and early Victorian stuccoed houses one shoud retain and repair such features as cornices, moulded surrounds to doors and windows and projecting string courses. Many houses of this type have been spoilt by having had these features shorn off in the interests of economy or fashion — trying to make them look 'modern'. Apart from the main ornamental details we often find the surface of the stucco marked out to imitate the joints of ashlar stonework. This also should be retained in repairs as it helps to give scale to the elevation. If a considerable amount of repair is necessary to a stucco-faced house it may be tempting to consider stripping the remaining stucco to expose the brick or stone walls. This is almost always a mistake. The walling in these cases was not intended to be seen, or to be exposed to the weather. On practical as well as aesthetic grounds the stucco should be *renewed* if necessary.

Sometimes, when considerable sections of, say, a moulded cornice have had to be renewed, it has proved more economical to have them made up in fibreglass, rather than forming them in plaster. However, the long term weathering qualities of this material have still to be proved, and, although it does seem to be satisfactory, particularly if it is painted, it is unlikely to be acceptable for use on a listed building. Attempts to replace stone features in fibreglass have been less satisfactory, as it tends to change colour in time.

While the use of fibreglass or other modern materials to reproduce in *replica* missing or damaged features may be acceptable, the use of *standard* mouldings and features, unrelated to the building, is another matter, and is best avoided in old houses.

WINDOWS AND DOORS Typical of houses of this period are the ornamen-tal iron balconies, verandahs and porches which stand out so attractively against the plain plaster walls. They should be retained and carefully repaired. It is generally possible to find a good local blacksmith who can undertake this work, and there are a number of larger firms who will match existing details. Windows in these houses are generally double-hung sashes, although casements are sometimes found, and French windows were becoming popular when stucco houses were built. The glazing bars — by now very slender — did not always divide the windows into equal-sized panes, as in earlier Georgian work. Sometimes we find a large central pane surrounded by narrow borders. In other cases the glazing may be designed in imitation of medieval tracery, showing the influence of the Gothic Revival. Occasionally the windows themselves have pointed arched heads.

Windows of this period often had external louvred shutters, sometimes in addition to solid internal shutters. Where these features are original they should be kept and repaired. Today there is a fashion for fixing external shutters to windows in houses of all periods, but this seems rather pointless *if,* as often happens, they are not hinged, but fixed flat on the wall so that they cannot be shut. Genuine shutters were generally made so that the louvres or slats sloped down towards the front when they were closed, to throw rain away from the window. Modern pseudo-shutters are generally made the reverse

ABOVE *and* RIGHT *Regency-style, early nineteenth century stucco-faced terraces in Southampton, Hampshire, where a repair programme is in hand. The left-hand photograph shows decay, caused mainly by water penetration through the roof and parapet gutter. This must be remedied before starting to repair the plaster.*

way, so that, supposing they could be closed, the rainwater would be directed on to the face of the window!

Ornamental fanlights to doorways were still popular, but now glazing was more common in the door itself, of similar design to that in the windows. The door hoods and surrounds might be of timber, or formed in the stucco, generally of classical design, but sometimes like the window glazing, showing Gothic influence. All these features are worthy of retention and repair.

FINISHES As we have seen, this stucco work was normally painted, and this is the usual treatment today. Regular painting is particularly important in seaside areas, where stuccoed buildings are common, to protect them from attack by salt in the atmosphere. Gloss paints are generally more durable, and easier to keep clean, but limewash or silicate paint will allow the stucco to breathe. Colour is a matter of individual choice, but where the house forms part of a terrace or group it is best if the owners can all agree on a unified scheme, possibly introducing some variation in the colours of doors and minor features if desired.

BELOW and RIGHT *Careful renovation of a small house at Kidsgrove, Staffordshire, has included the reinstatement of the attractive verandah.*

9　Floors and ceilings

Ground floors

In early houses, the ground floor was often of beaten earth, or of lime ash, a composition which could be quite hard, and even given a polish. Some larger and finer houses had tiled floors, the tiles being either plain — generally red or buff in colour, or incorporating heraldic or other designs. These encaustic tiles were often copied in the nineteenth century, when they were particularly popular in churches. Later, stone flags, unglazed clay tiles and bricks were introduced, generally laid directly on the earth, or on a bed of sand. Timber floors were rare, unless there was a cellar, but by the nineteenth century the 'best' rooms were usually provided with timber floors, the joists often being laid directly on the earth, but occasionally they are found laid over older stone or brick floors.

All these types of floor are likely to be affected by rising damp, and in the case of timber floors laid directly on the earth, the joists are often found to be affected by fungus and beetle attack. Old stone and brick floors have sometimes been covered by a cement and sand screed in an attempt to provide a drier and more level surface, but in many cases these screeded floors have cracked, having no adequate key to the old floor below.

The treatment of defective ground floors depends on several factors:

An early seventeenth century ornamental plaster ceiling in a former merchant's house in The Rows, Great Yarmouth, Norfolk.

the character of the house and of the floor itself (for instance, surviving early tiled floors, or bricks laid in an interesting pattern) and the eventual purpose of the room. There is no doubt that some early houses have lost much of their character when an old flagstone floor has been replaced by, say, vinyl tiling, although it is probably easier to clean.

REPAIRS If you wish to retain an old stone or brick floor it is usually possible to take up the paving, dig out the earth below, and re-lay the flags or bricks on a bed of lightweight, insulating 'concrete' laid over a thick layer of coarse gravel or expanded clay granules. This will prevent liquid water from being drawn up but will still allow the floor to breathe. The joints should be pointed in hydraulic lime mortar. It is important not to cover the floor with vinyl flooring or foam backed carpet as this will trap moisture evaporating from the surface of the floor. If the floor is re-laid on a damp-proof membrane it could increase the effect of rising damp in the walls, necessitating further damp-proofing treatment.

If you have old timber ground floors which have decayed, and you wish to retain a timber finish, it is important to avoid creating conditions which will encourage decay. A timber suspended floor should be carried on brick sleeper walls, built honeycomb fashion, on top of site concrete, and an adequate number of air vents must be inserted in the external walls to ensure cross-ventilation. Solid timber floors can be constructed, the boards being nailed to wood fillets embedded in a screed laid on concrete, with a damp-proof membrane between the concrete and the screed, but the fillets and the boarding should be pressure-treated with preservative, and the boards not laid until the screed is thoroughly dry.

NEW GROUND FLOORS In many old houses you will find that the original floors have gone: there may be softwood floors of no interest, and in poor condition, or cement screed on concrete, nineteenth-century quarry tiles, or plastic tiles laid in a recent attempt at modernisation. In these cases the choice of a new floor will depend on personal taste, and the extent to which you want to restore the original character of the house. Clearly, it would not be practicable to return to beaten earth. If you want to lay a stone floor it is sometimes possible to obtain second-hand flagstones, and new flagstones are available from some quarries. Unglazed paving tiles are available new, as are a variety of stone and slate tiles. If you want a brick floor, it will be important to choose bricks with a hard-wearing surface. Timber floors can, of course, be laid in accordance with good modern practice, but if wood blocks are chosen, they generally look more appropriate in an old house if they are laid in straight lines, with broken joints, i.e. 'brick' pattern, rather than in the herring-bone pattern.

Some forms of modern vinyl tiles and sheet flooring are made to imitate old tiles, or even slate slabs. Whether these are appropriate

Floors and ceilings

in an old house is a matter for personal choice, but it would be unfortunate if their use resulted in the destruction of genuine early work.

ARCHAEOLOGICAL CONSIDERATIONS Any work involving the taking up or re-laying of old ground floors will need care to avoid destroying archaeological evidence. As we have seen, nineteenth century wood floors were often laid over older brick or stone pavings. These pavings themselves may cover an earlier tiled, lime ash or beaten earth floor, possibly incorporating a hearth serving an original open hall. Fragments of pottery, coins or other artefacts may also be found under old floors. It is fair to say that work involving the disturbance of the ground floor of an old house should not be carried out without proper supervision. If any traces of an earlier floor, or of old foundations to former walls, come to light, the work should be stopped until these finds have been examined and recorded by an archaeologist. The local museum will probably be able to help in this, by sending someone to inspect and advise. To avoid unnecessary delays, it is generally best to let the museum curator know in advance when work is to be carried out on the floor so that he can arrange to have someone at hand. The museum should also be able to advise on dating any artefacts that may be found. If these have to be taken up, their original sites should be marked on a plan, and, preferably, photographed before removal.

CELLARS If an old house has a cellar under part or all of the ground floor the floor above it will probably be of timber construction, although occasionally we may find brick vaulting. If the cellar has been kept well ventilated the floor may be in reasonable condition, but we often find the ends of beams and joists decayed where they are built into the external walls. In dealing with this problem it is best to remove the cause of the trouble, i.e. the embedding of timber in a damp wall. The ends of the beams can be supported on a stone, brick or concrete corbel, preferably incorporating a damp-proof course, or be given a steel shoe built into the wall. Where a series of joists were built into the walls, the ends can be cut off, clear of the wall, and carried on a new timber or steel beam laid parallel to, and just clear of, the wall face. All the timber should be well treated with preservative, and the ventilation in the cellar maintained, or if necessary improved. You may find that the old cellar windows have been blocked, and it is advisable to re-open them, and to provide some permanent ventilation.

Upper floors and ceilings

Upper floors in old houses are nearly always of timber joist and board construction, although very occasionally we may find floors finished with plaster on laths, or even of tiles, laid on plaster. Let us look at some of the common problems in these floors.

RIGHT *The repair of a suspended timber floor. The top drawing shows a decayed joist end in the wall. Below, the joist is cut back, clear of the wall, and supported on a new wall beam. The old opening in the wall is filled. Alternatively (in the third drawing) the joist is cut back, clear of the wall, and supported on a steel angle, built into the wall, and the old opening in the wall is filled. In the bottom drawing, the joist is cut back, and repaired by scarfing on a new end. Again the joist is supported on a steel angle shoe, built into the wall, and the old opening in the wall is filled.*

A timber upper floor at Stranger's Hall Museum, Norwich, with moulded beams and joists. The boards are laid parallel to the joists, and not across them as is usual in later work.

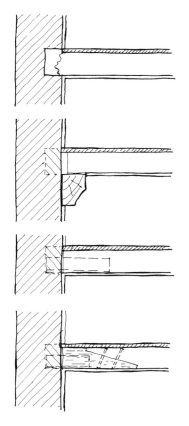

First, the floor may be uneven, owing partly to settlement of the structure, and partly to the use of unseasoned timber in many early houses. Clearly, if the settlement is serious this must be remedied, and as I have said earlier this is a matter needing professional advice. If, though, the movement has been checked and the building is stable it may be possible to take up the boards, saving them for re-use if they are sound, and to level or 'fir' up the joists. This may, though, create more problems at door openings, and it is not always possible to obtain a perfectly level floor in an early house without substantial reconstruction.

Next, you will often find that an old floor, where the boarding has been affected by beetle, has simply been covered with a new layer of boards, leaving the old boards in place, and probably doing nothing to eradicate the beetle attack! In these cases it is really best to take up all the boarding, and to re-lay the sound boards, firring up the joists as necessary and treating all the timbers with insecticide.

The next problem is one we have already considered in connection with cellars: decay in the ends of beams and joists built into external walls, and the same principles of repair can be followed. With an upper floor, though, the underside may be visible. In a house of informal design, where there may already be exposed ceiling beams, a new wall beam can be quite acceptable. If it is desired to avoid this, the joist ends may be carried on a steel angle, secured to the wall, and covered by the wall and ceiling plaster. A related problem occurs when, owing to settlement or movement of the walls, the beams and joists have lost most of their bearings, and where the joists have pulled away from their fixings to the main beams. In these cases the joints between the beams and joists can be strengthened with iron straps, preferably on the upper surface where they can be covered by the boarding.

The joints between intersecting beams are particularly vulnerable, not only to this kind of movement, but to beetle attack, and they should be carefully examined and repaired as necessary. The system of repair using steel or fibreglass rods and an epoxy resin filler, mentioned in an earlier chapter, can be very effective in these situations, but should only be carried out by a reputable and competent firm, under professional supervision.

In most old houses we find the floor boards laid on top of the joists, at right angles to them, but in some medieval buildings with wide, closely spaced joists, wide floor boards were laid parallel to them, the joists being rebated to take the boards (i.e. the top of the joist itself served as a board). This construction should be retained in any repairs, as it is usually an indication of early date.

BEAMED CEILINGS In medieval and Tudor houses, the main beams and the intermediate joists were generally exposed on the underside. In these cases it is often obvious that the joists were intended to be seen. They will be of uniform size, evenly spaced, and except in the very

humblest houses will have their arrises chamfered, or even moulded. By the mid-seventeenth century it was becoming more usual for the joists at least to be concealed behind a plaster ceiling, and by the eighteenth century even the main beams were generally plastered over, or concealed completely in a double floor structure. At this time, too, the exposed beams and joists in older houses were sometimes covered, to comply with the current fashion. Just as we have seen with timber-framed walls, there has been a recent fashion for stripping the plaster and exposing, not only old beams and joists which were originally exposed, but those later ones which were covered from the start, and which are often rather rough and irregular in character. Generally, I would recommend leaving these later timbers covered, and even re-covering them when they have been exposed, but the problem is less straightforward in the case of earlier beams and joists which have been covered by a later plaster ceiling, particularly if the plaster has decayed, or has to be stripped to enable the timbers to be repaired. If the timbers are generally in good condition, and particularly if they are moulded, there is a good case for exposing them, but sometimes they have been hacked for plaster, or badly pitted with nail holes for laths, or may even have had their mouldings pared down to accommodate a ceiling. Sometimes, too, the ceiling was part of a general 'Georgianising' and incorporates a moulded cornice, designed in conjunction with new panelling and other joinery. In these cases it may be better to retain or renew the plaster, after making sure that the timbers are sound. If we are going to leave an old timbered ceiling exposed, any necessary repairs should be carried out with great care, to retain as much original work as possible.

In some medieval houses, where the ceiling timbers are exposed, there was no plaster between the joists; the ceiling was formed by the underside of the floor boards. Today, you will probably want a better standard of sound insulation than that provided by this form of construction. A plaster ceiling can be provided between the joists in two ways. Timber battens can be fixed to the sides of the joists, close to the boarding, and plasterboard or a similar material nailed

Intersecting deeply chamfered ceiling beams, c. 1600, in a house at Okeford Fitzpaine, Dorset.

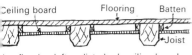

ing flooring left undisturbed. ceiling board
  to battens.

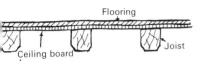

ing flooring lifted and relaid over continuous
ng board laid over the joists.

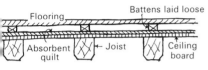

ting" floor, to improve sound insulation. (Careful
ing necessary, especially at junctions with walls)

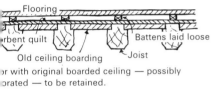

r with original boarded ceiling — possibly
rated — to be retained.

*Different treatments for open-beamed
ceilings.*

to these, finished with a coat of plaster. Alternatively, if the floor boards have to be lifted, the plasterboard can be laid over the joists, and the boards fixed to this, over any necessary firring. A better standard of sound insulation may be obtained by forming a 'floating' floor: laying an absorbent quilt such as fibreglass over the plasterboard, with the floorboards fixed to battens laid loose on this. Care must be taken at the junction of the floating floor with the surrounding walls, not to form a 'sound bridge'. It must be accepted, however, that there is almost bound to be more sound transmitted through a floor where the joists are exposed than through one with a continuous ceiling.

Another point to be remembered is that in medieval and Tudor houses the floor beams and joists were often coloured, and that this coloured decoration may continue over the boards, where these formed the ceiling. In these cases the colour should be preserved, and it will probably be best to lay a new floor above the existing one, preferably a floating floor to achieve some sound insulation.

Very often, on the other hand, you will find that exposed ceiling beams and joists have been given one or more coats of dark paint or stain, probably in the nineteenth century or later. The oak will nearly always look better if this can be removed. Blowlamps should *never* be used in an old house; the risk of fire is too great; there may be hidden timbers which can be set alight and smoulder for some time before the fire is discovered. It may be necessary to experiment with various types of chemical stripper. A paint which has simply been applied to the surface of the beam, possibly over old limewash, will be easier to remove than a stain which has penetrated the grain of the timber. Sometimes abrasive strippers are used, but care is necessary in their use, as the surface of the timber may be damaged. Because of the possibility that early coloured decoration may exist under later paint, the stripping should be carried out very carefully. If any signs of early colour are found the work should be stopped and specialist advice sought. The local museum may be able to help in this, as many of them employ a conservator who will have experience in dealing with these problems.

Old ceiling beams and joists may suffer from beetle attack, but this is often confined to the sapwood and, due to the fact that, in early houses, the timbers were generally far larger than was strictly necessary, the decayed sapwood or 'frass' can often be cleaned off, back to sound wood, still leaving enough timber to carry its load. Here again though, care is needed if the timber retains any early colour. In this case it should not be cleaned off, but specialist advice sought, as it may be possible to consolidate the crumbling wood and preserve the painting.

If it is found impossible to remove a dark stain, the appearance of the beams can sometimes be improved by applying a coat of limewash, and brushing it off when nearly dry. This leaves a residue of lime in the grain, producing a softer appearance.

Floors and ceilings

PLASTER CEILINGS When continuous plaster ceilings became usual in the seventeenth century they were, in the houses of the more wealthy, often formed with elaborate moulded decoration. By the eighteenth century, decoration was more often confined to the cornice, and perhaps a central feature, although later in the century we find ceilings with overall decoration of a more delicate character. Such old ceilings should be carefully preserved, but their repair can present problems. As we have seen with old wall plaster, three main causes of trouble can arise: decay of the plaster itself (less common in internal work unless it has become wet), decay in the wood laths or rusting of the nails securing them, and failure of the key between the plaster and the laths. In the case of ornamental ceilings there may also be mechanical damage, resulting from later alterations such as the insertion of partitions.

Fortunately, the old plaster generally contained a good proportion of hair, and its composition renders it both tough and resilient. If the laths are badly affected by beetle, they can be treated from above with an insecticide and the ceiling strengthened by a new backing, generally of plaster with a fabric reinforcement, and screwed back to the joists, using screws with wide washers, these being sunk into the plaster and the holes carefully made good. This can also be done where the trouble is due to failure of the key. Recently, systems of repair have been developed using fibreglass and epoxy resins, or polystyrene foam, which are lighter than plaster, but it must be stressed that the repair of an old plaster ceiling is specialist work, needing very careful supervision. Occasionally it may be necessary to take the ceiling down in sections and to refix it to new timbers — again a highly specialised operation. Only in the very last resort, if repair is really impossible, should the ceiling be reproduced by taking moulds from it and casting a new replica.

Substantial repairs to a farmhouse in Dorset have revealed an early timber and plaster firehood. Note also the jointed cruck trusses.

Of course, old plain plaster ceilings may also suffer from the same defects: decay of the plaster, decay of the laths, nail failure and failure of the key. Here again it is better, if possible, to repair the ceiling in situ, rather than to take it down and replace it. This applies particularly to early houses, and those of an informal design and character. Replacements today are generally in plasterboard or a similar material, producing a perfectly flat finish, which can look rather mechanical. This is perhaps less important in later, more formally designed buildings, but it is worth remembering that plasterboard ceilings are less effective at sound-deadening than old lath and plaster ceilings — particularly old ceilings where the plaster may be up to an inch thick. Riven laths and haired lime plaster are still available and are usually the most appropriate choice for repair or replacement. The rather self-conscious textured finishes sometimes applied on new ceilings will rarely if ever be appropriate in an early house.

10 Interior features

Fireplaces

We have already looked at some of the problems of repairing chimneys, above the roof level, and I have stressed the importance of retaining these where possible to enable fireplaces to be kept in, or restored to, use. I suppose that one aspect of repairing an old house which most people enjoy is that of opening up an old fireplace which has been blocked by a succession of later ones. This messy but satisfying operation is not, though, without its problems. These may be structural—for instance the main supporting lintel may have been cut away to take a later range or fireplace, so that the latter cannot be removed without the risk of a collapse. If anything like this is discovered, the work should stop until further advice can be obtained.

The other problem is the old one of how far to take 'restoration'; is it always right to remove all the later fireplaces to expose the original opening? I suppose that if we were to take this course to its logical conclusion we should, in an open-hall house, remove the fireplace and chimney stack completely and reinstate the open hearth. Few of us would have much compunction over removing a modern tiled or brickette fireplace surround, but the Victorian cast iron fireplaces incorporating ornamental tiles which, not so long ago, were being generally discarded, are now coming back into favour while Regency hob grates fetch high prices as antiques. If an old open fireplace has been altered to take a good eighteenth-century surround and interior

151

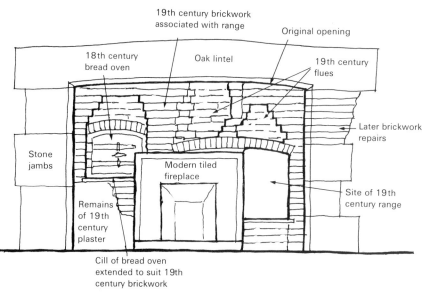

19th century brickwork associated with range

Original opening

18th century bread oven

Oak lintel

19th century flues

Stone jambs

Later brickwork repairs

Modern tiled fireplace

Site of 19th century range

Remains of 19th century plaster

Cill of bread oven extended to suit 19th century brickwork

it may well be best to leave it, especially if the rest of the room is now of similar character. Each case must be considered on its merits. If good later fireplaces are taken out they should not be destroyed; it may be possible to use them elsewhere in the house.

When opening up old fireplaces you may find such features as a bread oven, a curing chamber, or one or more recesses, possibly for keeping salt or other materials dry. Bread ovens are usually of eighteenth or early nineteenth century date, and when they are found in earlier fireplaces they are probably later insertions, often on the site of an older newel staircase. The repair of all these features is generally straightforward, consisting of repointing, and perhaps replacing some defective bricks.

If the restored fireplace is to be used for an open fire it is of course essential to see that the flue is sound, and it should be given a smoke test. This is advisable for all flues in an old house. If the lining has failed, allowing smoke to penetrate the brickwork, the flue should be relined. There are several methods of doing this today, depending on the size and shape of the flue, and the type of fuel to be used, and professional advice should be obtained. The risk of fire is too great to allow for any half measures here.

Many people, having worked hard to open up and repair an old open fireplace are disappointed when they start to use it and find that it smokes badly. What can we do about this? First, we must remember that these early fireplaces were the immediate successors of the open hearth, the smoke bay and the fire hood, and even if they did sometimes smoke, were a great improvement on these earlier forms of heating. Our ancestors were used to smoke and probably did not expect perfection. Then, these large fireplaces required a large volume of air to keep them drawing, and this was supplied by doors and windows far less well fitting than we expect today. Again we must remember that these fireplaces first appeared at about the same time that the first glazed windows replaced the old shuttered openings—our ancestors were used to draughts as well as smoke.

A large open fireplace in course of excavation in a house at Witchampton, Dorset, has revealed alterations of various dates, as indicated in the drawing ABOVE LEFT, the most recent being the insertion of a c. 1950 tiled surround and grate.

An early nineteenth century hob grate inserted in a larger, probably seventeenth century fireplace opening, and itself covered over at a later date.

152

It should therefore be clear that if a large open fire is to draw properly it must be provided with an adequate flow of air. If we insist on draught-proofing all openings the air must come from another source, preferably introduced as close to the fire as possible. In a room with a suspended timber floor a grille can be inserted in this, in front of the hearth—this will also help to ventilate and preserve the floor joists. With a solid floor this is not practicable, unless the floor is being relaid, when a duct can be incorporated in it. A fireplace on an external wall can have an air brick inserted in the back, with a 'hit-and-miss' closer so that it can be shut off when the fire is not in use.

An improvement can sometimes be made by lowering the effective height of the fireplace opening, either by forming a hood over the fire, or by, say, a plate glass sheet fixed across the opening below the lintel. It may also help to remove any later chimney pot, which was probably fixed when a smaller coal-fired grate was inserted; this will allow an uninterrupted upward flow of hot air and smoke. To a large extent it is a matter of trial and error, and every old fireplace is different, and can be affected by such things as the siting of the house and the direction of the prevailing wind. It may not be much consolation to realise that the fireplace has probably always smoked to some extent and on some occasions, but it may help one to look at the problem in a more philosophical way.

Let us now look at the opposite situation. You may sometimes want to do away with an earlier fireplace, perhaps in a bedroom where it is not wanted, and where the wall surface can be used more effectively without it. What are the points to watch here?

First, any work of this kind should be reversible, a future owner may want to open up this fireplace, and this should always be possible. The simplest treatment is to leave the surround and possibly the interior, and to cover the opening with plasterboard or a similar material. If the surround is removed, and it is of interest or value it should not be destroyed, but if possible kept in the property for the benefit of a future owner. Whatever treatment is adopted it is important to ventilate the flue, by a grille or louvre vent into the old fireplace opening and, if the top of the flue is sealed to prevent the entry of rain, by another vent into the flue at as high a level as possible, to maintain a flow of air in it. Failure to do this can result in condensation and damp patches, possibly stained with soot if the old flue lining has perished, appearing on the wall of the chimney breast.

Staircases

The oldest form of staircase is the simple ladder, but we are unlikely to find one of these surviving, except perhaps into a loft in some very humble houses. The earliest surviving stairs are generally of the spiral or part-spiral type, with the steps tapering into a central newel post. These may be of stone (sometimes covered with timber at a later date), of solid baulks of timber, or, in later examples, with timber treads

Interior features

and risers as are in general use today. In some medieval and Tudor houses the stair consisted of a straight flight, with the steps formed from solid baulks of timber, and these are still occasionally found.

The main problem with most of these early stairs is that they are often very steep, and some of the early spiral stairs have very narrow treads. They are unlikely to comply with modern Building Regulations, and a local council may require them to be altered and made safer if they are offering an improvement grant, or if the house is subject to a closing order. These standard requirements may, as we have seen, be modified in a listed building, and if the staircase is original or early, it should, if possible, be left unaltered. Sometimes the best solution may be to construct a second staircase elsewhere in the house to comply with the council's requirements, and this may often be an advantage in the typical narrow plan of the old farmhouse.

An old stone spiral stair may have become very worn, and even dangerous. It can be repaired by cutting out and piecing in new stone, but this can be costly. Simply facing up the treads in cement mortar, or some of the patent fillers on the market, is unsightly and may not stand up to wear. Often the best solution will be to fix new timber treads, preferably of oak, over the stone, as was often done in the past.

Later stairs are likely to be of the straight flight, dog-leg, or open well form, with turned balusters. If these are of seventeenth, eighteenth or early nineteenth century date they will probably be of good design and should be kept. Sometimes, especially in less sophisticated houses, the balusters, instead of being turned, were cut out of flat timber to a shape approximating to the profile of contemporary turned balusters. The repair of these later staircases is generally straightforward, simply requiring a competent joiner. It is sometimes possible to strengthen an old stair by inserting additional bearers below it, to avoid unnecessary renewal.

When old farmhouses were converted to cottages in the nineteenth century, as often happened, new stairs were inserted and these are often of rather poor, cramped design. They can generally be removed if the house is to be reinstated as a single unit.

Internal wall finishes

From medieval times, the internal walls of all but the very humblest houses were finished with plaster, panelling or textile hangings. Today there is a fashion for stripping off the plaster, especially from stone walls, and pointing up the rough rubble. This may be thought aesthetically attractive — it was often done in medieval churches in the nineteenth century — but there is no historical justification for it. If the internal walls were of ashlar stone, they might have been left unplastered, but they would almost certainly have been limewashed, and were often embellished with painted decoration. Even in smaller houses, mural paintings were not uncommon. This is one reason why we should be extremely careful in removing old wall plaster; early

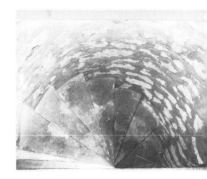

Seventeenth century staircases from Dorset. ABOVE *A stone spiral staircase in a house at Broadwindsor.* BELOW *A timber staircase, with square newels, closed string and turned baluster, in a house near Wimborne.*

154

paintings may well have survived under later decorations.

Let us look at some of the wall finishes we are likely to find in an old house, and the problems of their repair.

PLASTER In timber-framed houses, the main framing members were generally left exposed, but the intermediate studs may have been plastered. If you are not sure whether the plaster covering timber framing is original, a small section can be carefully removed, a layer at a time. If, under an outer layer covering both timber and the infil panels, there is another finished surface covering the panels only, finishing flush with the timbers, it will be clear that the outer coat is a later addition. It may not always be wise to remove it, especially if the timbers are exposed on the exterior of the house, a subject we have looked at in an earlier chapter. If, though, you decide to remove the outer layer of plaster, exposing the timbers and the earlier plaster, this work must be done with great care to avoid disturbing the earlier work. And if, in the course of this work, or when cleaning down old plaster at any time, signs of painted decoration appear, the work should be stopped at once, and specialist advice obtained. Paintings can be of various kinds: geometrical designs, floral patterns, pictorial and figure subjects, sometimes of a religious nature, imitations of text-iles and hangings, or, in the seventeenth century, scriptural or other texts. Such paintings, carefully repaired, can add much to the interest of a house.

A handrail, newel and moulded balusters painted on the stair wall of a house at Colchester, Essex, echoing the genuine work on the outer side of the stair. An insight into the seventeenth century sense of humour?

On stone and brick walls also, there may be several layers of plaster, and before any layer is removed it should be carefully cleaned down and examined for signs of paintings. Repairs to an old plastered wall should be carried out in a mix matching that of the old work as closely as possible: it will generally be of lime and sand, and, from the seven-teenth century onwards hair was often added. When the lower two or three feet of old, salt-laden plaster has to be stripped in connection with the insertion of a damp-proof course, the firm carrying out the work will probably insist on a waterproof plaster for the backing coat, but it may be possible to use lime plaster for the top coat. This will help to make the junction between the old and new plaster less noticeable, especially when decorating with limewash or distemper. It is, incidentally, rarely of any use to try to deal with rising damp in a wall by rendering the lower part with a waterproofed cement mix. This will simply drive the water, and any salts, higher up the wall.

In some medieval and Tudor houses where the internal walls are of rubble stone, the quoin stones at external angles and at door and window openings are built up in ashlar. This ashlar was generally kept slightly proud of the adjoining rubble, so that the plaster could be finished flush with it. Any limewashing or painted decoration was, however, almost always continued over the ashlar. Since the nineteenth century there has been a fashion for cleaning off the ashlar and leaving it exposed, in contrast with the adjoining colourwashed plaster, an effect never intended by the original builders, who were concerned with the lines of the architecture, not the constructional joint between the two materials. Churches in particular have suffered from this treatment, but we do find it in old houses, an example of the idea that it is somehow immoral to cover stone in any way. This produces rather a restless, jagged appearance, quite apart from the danger of destroying early painted decoration in the process. Indeed, the limewash was generally carried right over the stone window mullions, as can be seen in unrestored houses and churches. Sometimes, of course, there has been such a build up of coats of limewash that the profile of the mullions has been almost lost, and in these cases it can be carefully stripped, but it is generally best to re-apply a coat of limewash, particularly if there has been any patching or repair of the stone. The whole appearance of the window is softened, and light reflection into the room improved when this is done.

In the late eighteenth and nineteenth centuries, the inner faces of brick and stone walls were sometimes battened out to take plaster on wood laths, rather than plastering directly on to the solid walling. This was presumably an attempt to prevent internal dampness, but as the laths were in contact with damp brick or stone and the air space behind the plaster was generally unventilated, they were susceptible to decay. When fungus attack occurs in this situation it can spread rapidly, causing widespread damage before it is discovered. If a wall has been battened out in this way (it will sound hollow when tapped), it is advisable to open up sample areas for inspection, particularly if there are any signs of damp, for instance, from leaking gutters and downpipes or defective pointing.

Lime plaster, whether original or new, should always be painted with a breathable paint. This will allow dampness in the wall to evaporate and will reduce condensation. Vinyl, acrylic or oil-based paints can trap moisture and encourage condensation and mould growth. Limewash, tinted with earth pigment, was traditionally used for many cottages and farmhouses. If properly applied and cured it forms a durable finish which does not rub off onto clothing and it is the most breathable paint. Soft distemper, made from ground chalk mixed with size, is suitable for ceilings. For walls distemper should be bound with linseed oil or casein (a milk protein) to prevent dusting off. It is slightly less breathable than limewash but requires fewer coats to give good coverage.

PANELLING Wood panelling was an alternative finish to plaster. Originally intended simply to provide a warmer, drier surface, it soon became a vehicle for decorative treatment. In medieval, Tudor and early Stuart buildings the panelling was generally of oak, in fairly small panels. Later, imported pine was used, the panels became larger, with details and mouldings showing classical influence.

Old panelling may need repair for a number of reasons; the panelling itself may be affected by beetle or rot, it may have become cracked and warped by undue changes of temperature and humidity — for

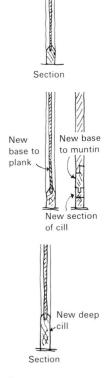

Section

New base to plank

New base to muntin

New section of cill

New deep cill

Section

Repair of plank and muntin partitions.

instance, from the installation of modern heating — or it may have suffered some mechanical damage as a result of alterations to the room, or even to accommodate a piece of furniture. More seriously, the timber grounds and battens by which the panelling is fixed to the wall may have decayed, generally owing to dampness, and where there are signs of beetle or rot in the panelling the timbers behind it should always be checked, by carefully taking down a section of panelling in the affected area.

Where only the panelling is affected, repair is generally straightforward, a matter of good joinery practice. Every effort should be made to preserve as much original work as possible, accepting some irregularity and wear — we are not trying to renew but to *preserve.* This is particularly important in early panelling, or where it incorporates linenfold or other ornamental work. Where the backing timbers are affected it will be necessary to take the panelling down, with great care, to renew the fixings, treating the wall with a fungicide if there are any signs of fungus attack, and treating the new fixings and the back of the panelling with a preservative. If the trouble is extensive, or if there are signs of active fungus attack, professional advice should be obtained.

Panelling fixed to an external wall is always liable to decay, and it is advisable to provide some ventilation behind it, preferably near the top and the bottom. This can often be incorporated in the repairs. In cases where the wall is obviously damp, remedial measures should be taken, such as improving ground drainage, lowering external ground levels, re-pointing or overhauling defective rainwater goods, as previously described.

Panelling was often moved from one part of a house, or even a building, to another. Sometimes it is obvious that it is not in its original position, from the way it has been cut to fit the room.

PARTITIONS Sometimes we find not only wall panelling, but partitions of panelled or similar all-timber construction, such as the plank and muntin partitions common in later medieval and sixteenth and seventeenth century houses. These may suffer from similar defects to those found in wall panelling; decay of the sill plate is common, due to rising damp. The principles of repair will be similar to those for wall panelling. It is often wise to insert a damp-proof course under the sill. If these partitions are in their original positions they should if possible be kept there. If, like wall panelling, they have already been moved from elsewhere, there may not be the same objection to moving them again if desired.

TIMBER FINISHES I have already mentioned the damage that can be caused to panelling, and indeed to other joinery following the installation of modern heating systems. Generally it is the later, pine panelling, made up in large units, which suffers most. The earlier oak panelling, in smaller sizes, is better able to accept a certain amount of shrinkage. We shall be looking later at the question of heating,

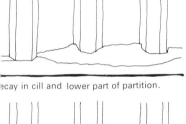

ecay in cill and lower part of partition.

muntins and planks repaired by splicing in
w timber. Damp proof course inserted under cill.

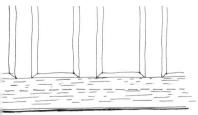

tensive decay to cill and base of partition
paired by a new, deeper cill.
amp proof course inserted under cill.

Plank and muntin partition, late sixteenth to early seventeenth century. The timbers have been hacked for a later plaster covering.

Interior features

but any repairs should be left until you are reasonably sure that all shrinkage has taken place. As I have said, it is the later panelling which will generally need most repair, and fortunately this can be hidden by painting. This later panelling was nearly always painted from the start; the fashion for stripped pine is comparatively modern, and the strong graining often found in pine rather obliterates the fine detail of the mouldings and carving. These can also, of course, be obliterated by repeated coats of paint, and this may have been responsible for the idea that it was not originally painted. The removal of a thick succession of coats of paint will need to be carried out with great care and, as I have already stressed, blowlamps should *never* be used in an old house. Chemical strippers are slower, but safer. If the stripping is done carefully it may be possible to discover the original colour used.

The older oak panelling was often left in its natural state, but coloured decoration was sometimes applied, just as it was on ceiling timbers. Where this survives it should be kept, and specialist advice sought on its preservation. If there is no sign of early colour, the oak should be cleaned and left unstained, indeed, it will generally look better if later dark stain can be removed. If any finish is required I would advise the use of beeswax and turpentine. Linseed oil should not be used, as it becomes sticky, attracting dirt, and it may also encourage furniture beetle attack.

The two pictures LEFT *show a late sixteenth to early seventeenth century door in a frame with a flattened ogee-shaped head, in what is now a party wall between two cottages – formerly one house. The wall itself is of plank and muntin construction.*

158

Before starting any work on an old house, a careful interior inspection is necessary. Early features may have been covered by later work. This West Country house is partly of open-hall form.

This seventeenth century house at Frome, Somerset, has had one of its mullioned and transomed windows replaced by a later sash. Should one attempt to 'restore' the original design in a case like this?

Repairs: conclusion

Before leaving the subject of repairs to an old house, we should consider the problem of 'restoration': the replacement of missing features, especially if there is no definite evidence of what they were like, so that any restoration must be conjectural. Here, as we have seen, the Victorians in their enthusiasm often went too far, thus depriving a building of much of its authenticity, and this practice is still quite common, especially where finance is no problem. Another related question is whether later alterations and additions to a building should be removed in order to recover its original design. For instance, as we have seen, a medieval or Tudor house may have had a face-lift in the eighteenth century, with its walls plastered to hide the unfashionable rubble stone or timber framing, and the old mullioned windows replaced by Georgian sashes. Generally, any attempt to restore the original design is likely to look rather artificial, although there may be exceptions.

What are we to do, though, when an old house has had some unsightly *recent* additions? I think most of us would want to recover something of its lost character, but the problem is not an easy one. Additions we may consider unsightly may be regarded very differently by the next generation. Perhaps the best rule is 'when in doubt, leave it alone'. If we do too little in the way of restoration of this kind it is always open to another generation, perhaps wiser than we are, to continue the work. If we do too much, it may be impossible to put it right.

11 Alterations: general principles

Having considered the basic repairs which may need to be carried out to an old house, we should now look at what may be a more difficult problem, that of adapting and converting it for use today. Of course, one way to do this is to be completely ruthless and utilitarian in our approach, as was often the case in the past. I think, though, that the situation now is rather different. In the past, particularly before the industrial revolution, building techniques and traditions were to a large extent continuous, even surviving the great change of taste which took place at the Renaissance. Today, completely new techniques in building have produced, and are still producing, new standards of design. Coupled with this is the fact that we now have a far greater ability to obliterate the past in our buildings even when we claim to be preserving them: for instance, by inserting steel girders and pulling out whole walls and chimney stacks to replan house interiors. In the past, alterations were often limited by structural considerations; this is no longer the case. Because of this, and the fact that unspoiled buildings are becoming more scarce, I think we should be more careful in our approach. In altering an old building of any interest or character we should, I believe, try as far as possible to retain its authenticity. This applies to the interior as well as to the façade. In many old houses, indeed, the actual plan form may be its most important historic feature.

If we accept this, the first step must be a thorough historical survey of the house, as we have already seen when considering repairs. We must know how the building we are proposing to alter originated, and how it has developed. How old is it? What was its original form? What alterations have been carried out, and why? What is its essential character? Once we have established these facts to the best of our ability we can then make our own decisions as to how the building should be altered today. For example, we may find that an old house originated as a medieval or early Tudor open hall, heated by an open hearth or as a long-house, with the living area and the byre for the animals under one roof, perhaps with no solid divisions between the two sections. Clearly we could not, even if we wished, bring a house back to this form if it is to be used for normal living accommodation. What we can and should do is to make sure that no alterations we

161

carry out during our period of ownership will destroy the evidence for the original form of the house or harm its character. It may well be possible to reveal some of the early features without affecting the efficiency of the house. It is of course, as we have already seen, essential to employ a builder who can be trusted to stop work and report any early features exposed as the work proceeds. Much of interest has been lost by a failure to do this.

A late medieval roof, with chamfered beams and wind bracing clearly designed to be seen, hidden in the attic of a farmhouse.

Official requirements and regulations

Some of the most common difficulties occur because of the need, when altering an old house, to comply with the modern Building Regulations and Housing Acts, and the requirements of the highway

This early seventeenth century stone mullioned window had been completely blocked, and was only discovered during alterations to the house.

ABOVE *A Wealden type house, probably early sixteenth century, divided into three cottages and refaced in a mixture of brick, plaster and tile-hanging. In spite of this the original form is apparent.*

Replacement of the old casements by larger, standard modern windows, as shown LEFT, *has destroyed the scale of this simple cottage. In an unlisted building such work is generally permitted development.*

163

Alterations: general principles

authority. It is important, as we shall see later, to distinguish between the Building Regulations, which apply only to *new* or *altered* work, and the Housing Acts, which can sometimes require *existing* features to be modified, especially if a grant is being offered.

Among the most frequent items affected by these regulations and acts are window areas and window head heights in habitable rooms, and the design of staircases. Ceiling heights are no longer controlled by the Building Regulations, but if the ceilings are unduly low, the building owner may want to increase them for his own convenience. If this is to be done it is important to see, first, that early and interesting ceilings are not destroyed by any change, and that the basic proportions of the room are not spoilt. In the ground storey it may be possible to lower the ground floor level to avoid disturbing the ceiling, but care must be taken not to undermine the walls or to create conditions which would encourage dampness. With windows, real difficulties can arise when these are original, perhaps with stone or timber mullions and early glazing, or where the proportions of the building would be spoilt if the windows were to be enlarged. I am afraid that this treatment has occurred all too often. If the windows are not too far below the minimum standards laid down in the Regulations it may be possible for these latter to be relaxed. Sometimes it is better to leave the original windows alone, and to look for somewhere else where an additional one may be inserted where it will be less obtrusive, perhaps in an end gable wall.

As we have seen in an earlier chapter, early staircases may not

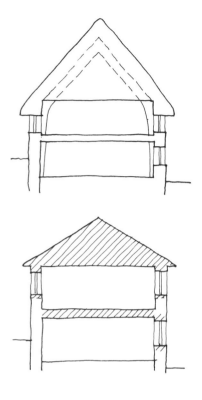

In this cottage additional daylight has been obtained by inserting a new window in the end wall, to avoid altering the earlier windows in the front wall. The choice of a standard window was perhaps rather unfortunate.

164

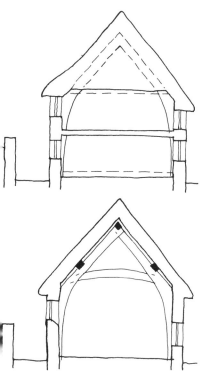

Standard windows and clumsy dormers destroy the scale of an end-of-terrace cottage. Alterations of this kind are sometimes a condition of an improvement grant.

Improving a sub-standard cottage: the drawing at the top of the left-hand column shows an old, cruck-framed cottage, originally of open-hall form. The insertion of an intermediate floor has produced rooms with very low ceiling heights and small, low windows. The old 'rule-of-thumb' Public Health Act solution is shown in the lower drawing, LEFT. *The walls have been raised to take a new roof. The first floor has been raised and the windows enlarged. The cottage has lost all its character and interest. A more sympathetic solution is shown in the top drawing above. The roof, first floor and front windows have been retained. The ground floor has been lowered, and the first-floor ceiling raised within the existing roof structure. The high ground at the rear has been excavated to allow the insertion of an additional ground floor window, and a dormer has been inserted at the rear. A better solution, if space allows, is shown above. The inserted floor has been removed, restoring the original open hall and exposing the cruck trusses.*

conform to the rather rigid standards of the Building Regulations, especially the old spiral staircases found in so many old houses. If the stair is original or an early insertion it should not be destroyed, and, as suggested earlier, it may be an advantage in a house of long, narrow plan form, to insert an additional stair which can comply with the Regulations.

Another problem concerns the use of thatch, which, as we have seen, cannot, according to the Building Regulations, be used on a new building which is less than twelve metres from the site boundary. This may make it difficult to use thatch on a new extension to an existing thatched house, or to reinstate an old thatched roof which has been covered with corrugated iron, both of which courses of action may be highly desirable on architectural and aesthetic grounds. Many authorities will, however, be prepared to relax the Regulations in these cases provided that additional fire precautions are taken, unless they have reason to fear that the use of thatch will create an *additional* fire risk in the area.

In all these cases it is up to the building owner to apply for the appropriate relaxations of the Regulations. The local authority officers will not necessarily draw his attention to his right to do so.

As I have said, the Building Regulations apply only to new work, or to existing features which are being altered, and they do not normally require existing unaltered features to be brought up to their standards. More difficult problems arise when the Housing Acts are involved, either because a Housing Act grant is being sought, or because the house has been made the subject of a closing order. In these cases the Authority can require *existing* features to be altered to comply with the requirements of these Acts, even if no alterations are being proposed to them. For example, if you apply for a grant to install a damp-proof course, you may be required to raise ceiling heights, enlarge windows and reconstruct the staircase.

Alterations: general principles

If the house has been the subject of a closing order, made by the local authority, the authority has to prepare a schedule of defects to be remedied before the house can be re-occupied. These schedules are generally prepared by the environmental health officer, who may or may not be aware that the house is of any historic interest, and may include such items as 'increase ceiling heights' or 'increase window areas', without specifying how this is to be achieved. Of course, if the house is listed the planning department of the same authority will have to approve the work, and may be able to suggest alternative and less damaging treatments. Local authorities vary considerably in the degree of co-operation between their different departments. Many unlisted houses also merit careful treatment, but if the alterations required under the Regulations or Housing Acts are within the limits of permitted development under the General Development Order, the planning department will not be involved. If an old house is not to lose much of its character and historic value by a 'rule of thumb' interpretation of the Regulations and Acts it is most important for all the authorities concerned to be consulted at an early stage, to see whether an acceptable scheme, from all points of view, can be worked out. I make no apology for repeatedly stressing this point, in view of the damage so often done. This is another reason why it is so important to employ the right architect or surveyor for work on an old house. It takes time and trouble to apply for relaxation of the Regulations; it is so much easier simply to say 'the council want it done this way'.

If the local authority is not prepared to relax the Regulations, the house owner has the right to appeal directly to the Department of the Environment. Such an appeal should be accompanied by all the relevant information.

There will, however, be some instances where it would be impossible to bring, say, an early medieval house up to modern standards without destroying its character, and in these cases it may be better to look for a different use, or a different approach. For example, a large number of 'difficult' buildings have been acquired by the Landmark Trust, who have repaired and adapted them for holiday accommodation. The Trust has found that for this use, the degree of modernisation or 'improvement' need not be so great as it would for normal habitation. At Purton Green Farm, Stansfield, Suffolk, for instance, the medieval open hall and service rooms have been restored practically to their original form, with beaten earth floors and shuttered windows, forming an annexe to the holiday cottage fitted into the rather later solar block. Even with a house intended for permanent as distinct from holiday occupation it may be possible to adopt this approach: to accept the limitations of the building and the fact that parts of it should be left as 'non-habitable' space, rather than to insist that the whole of it must be brought up to modern standards at the expense of its historic interest and authenticity.

Destructive 'improvements' to a simple three-roomed farmhouse. TOP *The un-altered house, with original timber casements—possibly with lead lights—and plain ledged door.* CENTRE *Modern standard windows, complete with night vents, dormers to achieve Building Regulation window head heights, and modern glazed door, all destroy the scale of the elevation.* BELOW *When so-called 'Georgian' components are used the effect is no better if the scale is wrong.*

For someone who wants a house like these, it is better to buy a new one—there are plenty being built.

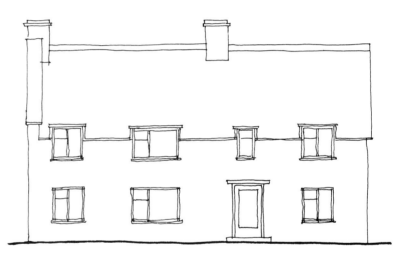

167

The problems of designing extensions to old buildings: ABOVE at Hall Place, Bexley, Kent, an eighteenth century addition to a sixteenth century house makes no attempt to copy the style of the original, but because of the quality of the new work and, perhaps, the mellowing effect of 200 years, we can now accept it. RIGHT A modern garage extension to a small eighteenth century town house has been designed to blend with the original building, but the difference in scale of the openings makes this difficult to achieve.

12 Improving the accommodation

Extensions

In adapting an old house for modern use it may be necessary to provide additional accommodation. This is not of course a new problem—many old houses have been enlarged, sometimes more than once. How should we approach this if the character of the house is not to be spoilt?

The first consideration should be the size of the proposed addition in relation to that of the existing building. It is fair to say that there is a limit to the size of an extension, however well designed, if the old house is not to be dominated by the new work. Many people buy a very small cottage and then immediately set about trying to turn it into a fair-sized house, destroying in the process the very characteristics which probably attracted them to the cottage in the first place! If the house really needs this degree of enlargement in order to suit your life-style it would have been better to buy a larger house in the first place. Although there can be no hard and fast rule in these matters, I think, as a general guide, that an addition should not be more than half the size of the original house if this is to retain its integrity. Indeed, the smaller the house, the smaller the addition should be in proportion to it.

As we have seen, most early houses were only one room deep, with rather a long, narrow plan. They can either be extended in this form, or the addition can take the form of a wing at right angles to the original house, producing an L- or T-shaped plan. In this case it is generally best to keep the span and the roof pitch of the extension the same as that of the existing house. A single-storey addition can sometimes be roofed by carrying the main roof slope down over it, as a lean-to or 'catslide'. What should be avoided at all costs is the flat-roofed addition, unrelated to the size and shape of the original house, and reminiscent in appearance of the surface air raid shelters of World War II. Unfortunately, additions of this style are all too common, disfiguring many old houses. Matching the original span and roof pitch will, of course, limit the size and shape of the addition, but if we are really trying to maintain the character of the house, this restriction must be accepted.

A rather unhappy flat-roofed extension to a stone and thatched cottage, in an alien material and with standard modern windows.

Death of a cottage.

'We found this lovely little thatched cottage—just what we were looking for.'

Improving the accommodation

MATERIALS Apart from the basic size and shape of the extension we have to consider its materials and detailed design. Should these attempt to match the existing house exactly, or should they be recognisably the work of our own age? Here I think that the size and character of the existing house should be taken into account. Generally, the smaller and simpler the house, the more important it is for the extension to be as unobtrusive as possible. This will generally mean matching the original materials and design. One problem which may immediately arise is that the original materials are no longer available. Many old stone quarries have been worked out, or closed down, and many old local brickworks have also disappeared. As we have seen, there is still a wide range of bricks available, and it should be possible to find a reasonable match, but this may well mean taking trouble to find the right bricks and not simply accepting the first ones offered by the local builders' merchant. The Building Centre, Store Street, London, has a very good collection of currently available brick samples, and is well worth a visit in this connection. With stone the problem may be more difficult. Stone of similar character may be available, but if not, it may be necessary to consider an alternative material. Generally, I would not recommend using 'artificial' or 'reconstructed' stone. These materials may be acceptable in a completely new house, but if used next to natural stone the difference will probably be all too obvious. Depending on the character of the house, it is sometimes better to use a suitably coloured brick, or plaster, or even weatherboard as a finish. If it is necessary to use a different material for an extension it will generally be more satisfactory to build this at right angles to the existing house, rather than as a continuation of it, or at least for some distinct break to be made between the two sections.

As with the walls, the roof finish should if possible match that of the existing house. Handmade clay tiles and natural slates are still

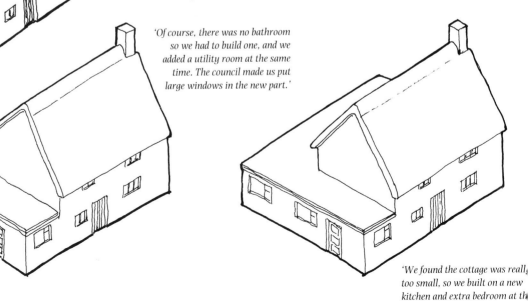

'Of course, there was no bathroom so we had to build one, and we added a utility room at the same time. The council made us put large windows in the new part.'

'We found the cottage was really too small, so we built on a new kitchen and extra bedroom at the back.'

'With the children growing up we needed more bedrooms, so we put another storey on the back addition. Then, when the children married and left home, the house was too big for us and we sold it.'

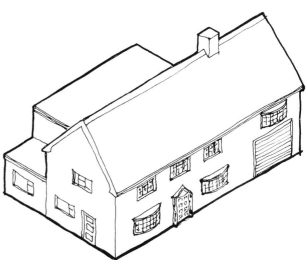

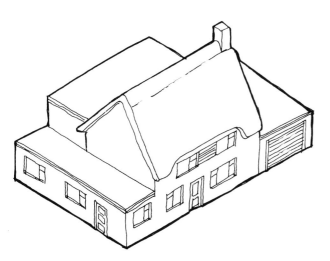

'When we bought this house the thatch was in a very bad state, so we decided to have it tiled. We needed more rooms, so we built up the front at both ends. We put a new Georgian-style door and windows in the front, to be more in keeping with an old house.'

'When we bought this house the old part was very dark, so we put in bigger windows and a glass door. We also added a garage. Just as we had got the house as we wanted it, we had to move to Scotland, and sold it.'

available, and should be used in preference to concrete or asbestos cement. Stone slates are more difficult to find, although as we have seen, they are quarried in some areas. Artificial stone slates may be acceptable if the roof is not actually continuous with that of the original house.

WINDOWS AND DOORS Next, we have to consider the design of windows and doors in an extension. Should these be exact copies of those in the existing house? I think that this again will depend to some extent on the age and character of the house. With a medieval or Tudor house, with stone or oak mullioned windows and lead lights I would not necessarily recommend repeating these in the extension—indeed, this could be considered an attempt to mislead future historians. What is important is that the *scale* of the windows in the extension should be compatible with that of those in the original house, and this will generally rule out the use of standard windows, including

In this extension to a terraced cottage an attempt has been made to match the walling and roofing materials. The stonework, however, has been laid in a non-traditional manner for the area, and the scale of the windows is quite different from those in the original building.

the so-called 'cottage', 'Jacobean', or 'Georgian' types. The main problem with all these is that individual lights are too wide, generally based on a 2-foot module, while the lights in old windows are nearly always narrower: 1 foot 6 inches to 1 foot 9 inches. This difference may seem small, but it can have a considerable impact on the appearance of the building. In addition, the top-hung ventilators found in most modern standard windows at once give the house a suburban character.

In an addition to an early house, simple casement windows of the right proportions, will generally look quite appropriate. If we are dealing with a later house, perhaps with double-hung sash windows, it is perhaps more justifiable to repeat these in the extension; after all, these are still in use today; we are not copying an archaic form. Once again though, standard sashes will rarely be of the right proportions, and their glazing bars are often of rather a clumsy section.

The choice of doors for an extension should not be too difficult. In simple cottages and farmhouses the plain ledged and battened door will generally look right—avoiding pseudo-antique ironwork and mock strap hinges—while in later, more formal houses a four or six panelled door will be appropriate. Some standard doors are of quite reasonable design, but I am afraid there are many 'horrors', including one found all too often, with glazing in the form of a mock fanlight,

In this Yorkshire terrace the various owners have tried to assert their individuality in the treatment of the doors: 1920s–30s 'rising sun' design on the left, ornamental Victorian cast ironwork in the centre, and a recent glazed timber porch on the right.

The problem of extending a simple cottage.

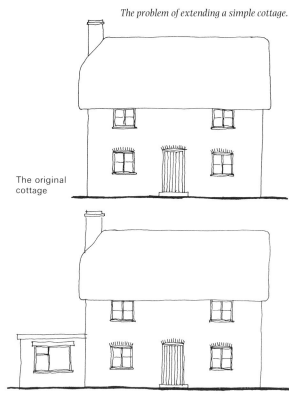

The original cottage

Simply continuing the line of the house may destroy the scale particularly if windows in the extension have to be raised to comply with Building Regulations.

Flat-roofed extension, with modern window out of scale with the building — an obvious "appendage".

Setting the extension back slightly may help to make the change of scale less obvious.

Extension with parallel pitched roof. A change of roof finish may be acceptable. Extension set back slightly.

Extension set forward, with cross-gabled roof.

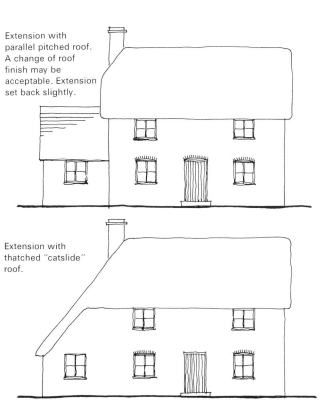

Extension with thatched "catslide" roof.

Extension set forward, with "catslide" roof; first floor windows set in end wall to avoid dormers breaking roof line.

New rear extensions need not be unsightly, as exemplified by these in Frome, Somerset.

which should be avoided in an old house. Door surrounds, porches and hoods are generally best kept simple, following the local traditional form. This also applies to any porch added to the original house.

DESIGN PROBLEMS We have already considered some of the problems posed by the Building Regulations. These may well affect the design of additions to old houses, by requiring larger and higher windows than those in the original house. This can often make it difficult to keep the new work in scale with the old. It may be possible, particularly with a listed building, to obtain a relaxation of the Regulations, but if not it will need a very skilful designer to overcome these problems—another reason for care in the choice of an architect.

I suppose that the extensions which are easiest to handle are those made to simple, informal, detached houses and cottages, where a resultant asymmetrical appearance is not necessarily harmful, and may even add interest to the building. Two other types of house will need even more careful thought. The first is the formal, symmetrical building, such as the typical Georgian or early Victorian house of classical design. Here an addition may produce an unfortunate lopsided appearance, destroying the harmony of the original design. Greater care will also be needed if the house forms part of a terrace or group. What we do in this case will affect not only our own house but those of our neighbours. Another point we must remember when considering an extension at the rear of a terraced house is that this could affect, not only the architectural character of the terrace, but the amenities of the adjoining houses by reducing the natural lighting and privacy. For this reason, planning controls over such extensions may well be more stringent than those applied when dealing with detached houses. Indeed, in the case of small terraced or semi-detached houses it is often best to convert two into one, avoiding the need for rear extensions, which may encroach on an already small rear garden.

It is a fallacy to think that the design of an extension does not matter so long as it is 'at the back'. In rural areas houses are generally visible

Neatly designed single-storey extensions at the Railway Cottages, Swindon, Wiltshire.

from all sides, and this is often true also in towns. We should always think of a building in three dimensions; the 'Queen Anne front and Mary Anne back' approach has spoilt many of our old towns and villages. To sum up, even if the design of an addition is not an exact match for the original house (not always desirable in any case), it should surely be a contribution to the development of the building of which we should be proud, both in its design and its workmanship.

ADDING TO AN EXISTING EXTENSION Another way of increasing the accommodation in an old house is by building a second storey on an existing single-storey block, but this is not always as simple as it first appears. The existing walls may not be strong enough to take the extra loading, and professional advice should be obtained. The old ceiling joists are unlikely to be adequate for use as first floor joists. Provided that raising is a practical proposition there will still be questions of design to be considered. Generally it will be best to use matching materials if these are available, and the new roof will need to be carefully designed to blend with that of the main building.

PARTIAL DEMOLITION Alterations to an old house may well involve some partial demolition, either simply to reduce the size of the house, or as a preliminary to building an extension. Several aspects of this will need care. First, it is important to see that no work of historic interest is destroyed in the process. As we have seen, a good historical survey should help to prevent this, but nothing in an old house should be taken for granted, and what appears to be a modern wall may turn out to be a facing on something much older, a fact only revealed after demolition has started. If this happens the work should stop until the wall or other structure has been carefully examined. Even if you ultimately decide that it must be removed it should first be examined and recorded.

Grubbing up old foundations and, indeed, excavations for new ones may reveal evidence of earlier structures, or perhaps artefacts such as pottery. These can all be of value in working out the history of the house and the site, and the opportunity should be given for arch-

175

Improving the accommodation

aeological investigation, as we have already seen in connection with the renewal of ground floors.

It is of course most important to see that partial demolition does not affect the stability of the rest of the building, especially when dealing with houses of cob, flint or rubble stone. It may be necessary to shore up adjoining walls and floors while partial demolition is carried out. Only builders experienced in work of this nature should be employed, and the whole operation must be carefully supervised. Demolition will generally have to be carried out stone by stone. Any builder proposing to call in a demolition contractor, or to use a bulldozer on an old house is probably the wrong person to be employed.

Assertive-looking inserted dormers. LEFT *The large new dormer contrasts unhappily with the older ones higher up the roof.* ABOVE *Even the use of a pitched roof here does not help disguise the sheer bulk of the new dormer.*

BELOW *These small pent-roofed dormers are quite appropriate in design and scale.*

Use of the roof space

Apart from building an extension, it may be possible, more economically, to increase the accommodation in an old house by making more use of the roof space. At times we seem to be bombarded, through our letter boxes, with leaflets from loft conversion firms. There are, however, a number of matters needing careful consideration if you propose to enlarge your house in this way.

First, the structural aspect must be checked. The ceiling joists to the first floor rooms may not have been designed to take the loading required for the floor of a room, and they may need strengthening or replacing. This could cause great problems if the first floor rooms have ornamental, or early ceilings. Then, there may be roof trusses or other timbers which will cause obstructions in the new attic rooms. In the past, main roof timbers such as tie and collar beams have been cut away to form door openings with no regard for the structural

An attempt has been made to break up the scale of this large dormer with the use of traditional leaded casements, but it still destroys the roof line.

consequences, sometimes leading to spreading of the walls, and failure of the roof. Although this work will now be controlled by the Building Regulations it is wise to obtain professional advice before deciding on any alteration to the roof structure.

Next, as already mentioned, the roof may be the earliest and most interesting part of the house, and for this reason too it should not be altered without a full examination. An early crown post roof, hidden away in a loft for generations, can easily be lost in the process of remodelling that loft to form an additional room.

Finally, the conversion of a loft to form living accommodation will almost certainly involve the insertion of additional windows to provide light and ventilation, and a means of escape in the event of fire. This can have a considerable effect on the appearance of the house. The most popular form of attic window is probably the dormer, which, in addition to admitting light, can also help to provide increased headroom. Dormers need not be unsightly, and can sometimes add interest to a roof, but they need very careful design. The large, flat-roofed 'chalet bungalow' type dormers so often inserted today, looking like a large square box pushing through the roof, are most unsightly, especially in old houses where the existing windows are quite different in scale. As a general rule, dormers should not be more than two lights wide, i.e. about 3 foot 6 inches. They usually look best with hipped or gabled pitched roofs, depending on the design of the main roof In some later houses original dormers had segmental curved roofs, lead covered, and these can look quite well, especially on slate roofs. In some areas the dormers were given 'pent' roofs — a continuation of the main roof slope at a slightly flatter pitch. These are particularly suited to pantile roofs, as they involve less cutting of the tiles than other pitched roofs, and they can be adapted for use in mansard roofs. Local traditional practice can often provide useful guidance in the design of dormers. Apart from their size and shape, dormers should not be so numerous as to dominate the roof.

Improving the accommodation

Sometimes it is possible to reduce the number of dormers by inserting small windows in the gable ends of the house. In other instances it may be better to use roof lights, flush with the roof slope, to avoid breaking the line of the roof: several companies now manufacture reproduction traditional cast iron rooflights. In large roof spaces where headroom is not a problem, inset dormers may be preferable to projecting types.

If habitable rooms are being constructed in the roof space for the first time, certain problems could arise under the Building Regulations. While the actual ceiling height is no longer controlled, any new dormers will be required to have a certain size and head height above floor level, and this could affect the appearance of the roof. The work will also, in effect, turn a two-storey house into a three-storey house, requiring higher standards of fire protection. This could involve replacement of or alterations to original doors, and enclosure of the staircase. These matters should be discussed with the Building Control Officer at an early stage, since, as previously mentioned, it may be possible to obtain relaxations of the Regulations to avoid damaging the historic integrity of the house.

An attic conversion, handled in a sensitive and imaginative way, can often produce a very attractive room, exposing and showing to advantage an interesting roof structure which, possibly designed originally to be seen, has been hidden away for generations.

Internal replanning

Having bought an old house, you may well want to alter the internal plan to suit your life-style. In some cases the rooms may be rather small, and you will want to combine two, or three, to make one larger room, although the recent fashion for open-plan living, like that for over-large windows, seems to be declining, perhaps owing to high heating costs. Alternatively, in a later house with large, high rooms, you may want to divide them up, and perhaps insert false ceilings, again to save fuel.

The staircase may be in an inconvenient position; large chimney stacks can take up a considerable amount of floor space, and rooms, particularly bedrooms, leading out of each other in old narrow plan houses, do not accord with modern ideas of privacy. Many old houses have, of course, been altered internally during the course of their history, with varying degrees of sensitivity. If we are really trying to preserve an old house — not merely to adapt it to suit ourselves regardless of the effect on its character and historic value — we shall need to consider any alterations with great care.

First, as I have stressed before, it is important to find out, if we can, the original layout and the sequence of any later alterations. Many people buy a pair or block of cottages to convert them to one house, and may be surprised to discover, following a survey, that the building was originally one house, subdivided at a later date. The

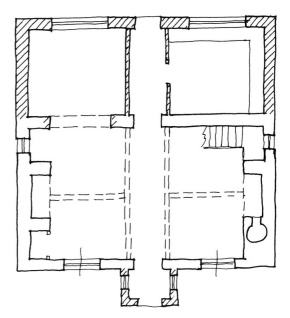

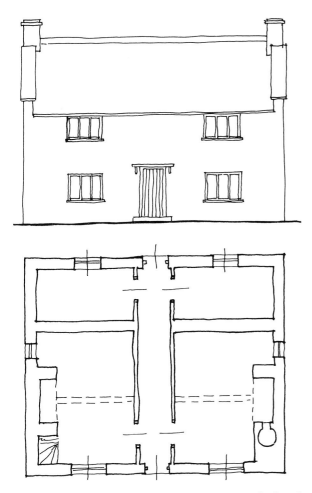

A typical small seventeenth or early eighteenth century house, of symmetrical plan, with rear outshut containing service rooms. The scale of the plan is reflected in the elevation. Such houses are often 'improved' by replacing the outshut with a large rear extension and gutting the original house to form one large room, perhaps with the addition of a porch. The façade is preserved, but the scale and character of the interior is lost, often with some original features. The original is shown LEFT, *the revised form* ABOVE.

original plan form may be largely intact, overlaid by later partitions and possible external additions. In such a case the aim should be to recover the original layout, revealing any early features which may have been covered up during the later alterations. Clearly, it is important to proceed carefully with the work. What may appear to be a modern partition could well be an early one, covered in later plaster or hardboard. A knowledge of the local building style of the period, with its typical plan forms, will be a useful guide to where we may expect to find early features, but every old house is different, and we should never take anything for granted.

It is not always desirable to remove later work, which may be good of its kind, and if we accept that our aim is to preserve the house this will impose some limitations on the extent of any internal alterations. Gutting the whole of the interior of an old house, leaving only the shell, or the main façade in anything like its original form, is *not* conservation, whatever else it may be called.

Clearly, the degree of internal alteration which can be carried out without destroying the interest of the house will depend on a number of things, in particular the age of the house and the extent to which the original layout and features have survived to date. I would, though, suggest two main principles to be followed. First, no original or early features of interest should be *destroyed,* and second, any alterations should be reversible; it should be possible to reinstate the house as we found it without major structural problems. For instance, if you really feel that you must divide up a large room, the new partitions should be cut round any cornice, and not vice versa. If a doorway is no longer needed, and the door and its frame are original, or of a good later design, consideration should be given simply to fixing it shut, rather than removing it and building up the opening. In a timber-framed house, where it is desired to combine two small rooms, it may be possible to remove part or all of the infilling of the partition, leaving the timber studs to form an open screen — always making sure that there are no signs of early paintings on the surface.

STRUCTURAL CONSIDERATIONS Any proposals to remove solid cross-walls or chimney stacks should be very carefully considered, and professional advice obtained. Apart from the risk of destroying features of interest, in an early house this could cause serious structural problems, perhaps leading to a risk of collapse and the need for substantial rebuilding, resulting in the loss of even more original work. All buildings settle to some extent after completion, eventually reaching a state of equilibrium. If after many years this is disturbed, further movement may be set up, the effects of which may not be apparent for some time. Old buildings should be treated like old people — major surgery should be avoided as far as possible.

Furthermore, when planning internal alterations to a semi-detached or terraced house, it must be remembered that the work could affect the stability not only of your house, but also that of whatever is adjoining. This applies particularly to any work affecting the party wall. If this were to be damaged by, for instance, removal of the chimney breasts on one side, the adjoining owner could have a claim for damages against the person carrying out the work. In England and Wales these matters are strictly controlled under the Party Wall Act, which requires a formal Party Structure Notice to be served on all other parties affected. If the adjoining owner objects a suitably qualified surveyor must be appointed to draw up a Party Wall Agreement detailing what work can be done and at whose expense. As such professional fees can be expensive there is a great incentive to try to sort matters out with your neighbours as early as possible, without recourse to the law.

13　Services

Plumbing and sanitation

If you have bought a completely unrestored house these basic services may be lacking, but even if they exist you may well want to alter or renew them. In addition to the principles of good modern practice there are some matters needing particular consideration when you are dealing with an early house.

Plumbing runs should be designed to be as unobtrusive as possible, but if pipes are laid in the thickness of the floors, care should be taken to avoid weakening the joists by notching them any more than is necessary. In some old houses, where the plumbing has been altered several times—perhaps by amateurs—the joists have been cut about to such an extent that there is little strength left in them.

It is of course no longer necessary for soil and waste pipes to be fixed on the exterior of the house, although this disfiguring practice is still common. They can be fixed internally, in ducts if necessary, which can be constructed to minimise sound transmission. Bathrooms should be sited so that the soil stack does not have to pass through the main rooms. In most cases, the main soil stack is carried up as a vent pipe, which has to terminate above any nearby window heads, including dormers. It is not necessary, though, for it to project high above the roof line. It can nearly always be carried up under the roof slope to the required height, and taken through the roof with a lead slate, leaving only the wire balloon guard visible.

Another point to remember is that bathrooms and lavatories can have mechanical ventilation in place of windows, and this can sometimes avoid the need to insert windows where they would be unsightly. While 'mod.cons.' are a necessary fact of life today there is no need to advertise their presence.

In towns, soil drains will almost certainly be connected to a main sewer. Rainwater drainage will also normally go to the main sewer, although in some towns there is a separate rainwater sewer. In rural areas there may be main drainage, but if not, a septic tank will probably be required by the local authority. In addition, if the house is in a catchment area, the scheme will have to be approved by the local water authority. In these cases, rainwater will normally be taken

Unsightly external plumbing of this kind is not necessary under modern Building Regulations.

to one or more soakaways. The only matter needing particular attention when dealing with drainage for old houses is that, as with other excavation work, archaeological evidence may be revealed, and should be recorded.

Most old houses had their own wells, before the days of main water supplies. Sometimes these survive intact, others have been filled in, but occasionally an old well is discovered during repairs and alterations, perhaps covered only by paving slabs. Whether to retain a well, or to fill it in, is a matter for personal choice, but unless the well is in a dangerous or inconvenient position there is much to be said for keeping it as an emergency water supply. In an area with no mains water, if a well is to be used for drinking water, it will have to be tested and approved by the local authority. As some old, comparatively shallow wells are subject to pollution, it may be necessary to sink a new, deeper bore hole. Specialist advice should be sought on this.

Water from a well was first obtained by means of a bucket and winch, but by the eighteenth century lead pumps were being used. Where these survive they should be preserved, and even the later cast iron pumps are now of some historical interest.

Heating and insulation

Domestic heating has evolved from the open hearth, via the smoke bay and fire hood, the large open fireplace and later coal-burning grate, to the various forms of central and individual room heating common today. Your choice of heating system will probably depend on the design and construction of the house and your own requirements, limited mainly by the availability and cost of different fuels.

Domestic 'central' heating systems are of the following main types:

HOT WATER RADIATORS AND PIPES SUPPLIED FROM A BOILER which may be independent, or combined with an open fire or a cooker, and heated by solid fuel, gas, or oil. If this system is adopted in an old house, the radiators and pipes should be carefully sited from the point of view, not only of efficiency, but appearance. Fortunately, modern small-bore systems require much smaller pipes than the older gravity systems, and it is easier to position them unobtrusively. However, in rooms with fine panelling, ornamental plasterwork or other important features it may be difficult to do this. The other point to bear in mind is that if a modern heating appliance is to be connected into an old flue this will almost certainly have to be re-lined.

DUCTED WARM AIR SYSTEMS supplied by a central heating unit, either fan-assisted, or relying on natural convection. These were popular for a time after the Second World War, and were installed both in new and old houses, but on the whole they have not remained in favour. They could, however, be considered in houses where radiators and pipes would be very unsightly.

UNDER-FLOOR HEATING SYSTEMS, either electric or provided by hot water pipes embedded in the floor concrete or screed, were also promoted in the immediate post-war period, but did not prove popular, often being found costly to run and difficult to control. However, modern systems are efficient and controllable and are ideal in ground floor rooms where the floor is being relaid, and where any form of radiator system would be unsightly.

ELECTRIC NIGHT STORAGE HEATERS These can provide useful background heating, but the heaters themselves can be obtrusive. If they are to be used, their siting will need care, and may mean a compromise between efficiency and appearance. The choice of a heating engineer to carry out work in an old house is of course most important. As we have seen with plumbing work, careless installation can damage the structure, as well as fine plasterwork and joinery.

INDIVIDUAL HEATERS are now available in many different forms, starting with the simple open fireplace. We have looked at some of the problems of the large open fireplace in an earlier chapter. Today, wood-burning stoves are popular. These are quite efficient, and their appearance often fits well into an old fireplace. If they are connected to an old chimney it must be remembered that the tarry deposit from a wood fire makes it essential for the chimney to be swept regularly, and probably more often than would be necessary with a coal fire. If this is neglected there could be a serious fire risk – and this also applies if wood is burnt in an open fireplace.

Normal gas and electric fires can fit quite successfully into an old house. It must be a matter for individual choice whether to use those models which attempt to imitate a coal or wood fire. I would, though, like to draw attention to the problems which can be created by the use of flueless gas heaters, whether they use mains or bottled gas, and of free-standing paraffin heaters. With all these, the products of combustion are discharged into the room, and as these contain a high proportion of water vapour they are likely to cause condensation, particularly if the room has been hermetically sealed by double-glazing and draught-proofing. If this type of heater is to be used, it should only be in a *well ventilated* room, and it should if possible stand in a fireplace, where the products of combustion can be discharged up the chimney.

SOLAR POWER is now being promoted commercially to a considerable extent. This is well worth considering, especially if you are installing for the first time or completely renewing the power or hot water system. If solar power is to be used in an old house, great care should be taken not to damage the roof finish or structure, so as not to prejudice the removal of the panels at a later date. They should, so far as possible, be fixed on the less important and visible roof slopes, or even on a nearby outbuilding.

Services

Whatever form of heating you adopt, an old house will probably now be kept warmer, and less well ventilated, than at any previous time in its history. This may be most desirable for the inhabitants, but it can create problems for the building. We should now look at some of these problems, which really fall into two groups: those which affect mainly the aesthetic, architectural and historic character of the house, and those which, more seriously, can affect the structure itself.

ARCHITECTURAL PROBLEMS I suppose that one of the most obvious and common of these is the effect of modern heating systems on the wood-work of old houses. Oak beams and joists may twist and develop shakes. This, though sometimes unsightly, is rarely serious from a structural point of view. Indeed, the frequent use of unseasoned timber in early houses has resulted in this kind of movement over the centuries, and the form of construction, and the high factor of safety provided by the large timbers used in medieval and Tudor houses has generally allowed this movement to take place with little harmful effect.

The problem is more serious in later Stuart, Georgian and Victorian houses, where softwood joinery, and panelling using wider timber members were more common. Here, the shrinking and twisting resulting from the drying effect of modern heating can be most unsightly, and cases have occurred where panelling has been pulled away from the wall, due to shrinkage of the timber grounds and battens as well as of the panels themselves. The introduction of humidifiers may reduce this trouble to some extent, but they should not be used indiscriminately. As we shall see later, increased humidity can produce even more serious problems. In houses containing fine joinery it is important to control the temperature, and to see that it is brought up gradually at the start of the heating season. Sudden changes of temperature and humidity can be most damaging.

Today, of course, there is a great emphasis on saving fuel, with the consequent development of various forms of insulation and draught-proofing. Draught-proofing of doors and windows can reduce the air intake needed for open fires, especially for the large old fireplaces so often being opened up today, and possible ways of dealing with this have been discussed in an earlier chapter. Double glazing is popular now, and is being strongly promoted commercially. In many old houses the original windows are being replaced by new double-glazed units. This is, as we have seen, often damaging to the character of the house, even if the so-called 'period' designs are chosen. Many of these windows are of metal or plastic and may have flat strips imitating glazing bars attached to the face of the glass, or even fitted between the two glass sheets. These are quite unsuitable for old houses. In most cases it is possible to fit internal secondary glazing, leaving the original frames unaltered. In many old houses, the windows were fitted with internal wooden shutters. Sometimes

Installation of double glazing need not involve loss of original windows. In this example internal secondary glazing has left the existing windows intact.

these survive in working order, but often they have been nailed or screwed back to the window jambs, or effectively fixed by layers of paint. It is often worthwhile restoring these shutters to use, or replacing them if they have disappeared, as they can provide very good insulation, especially when combined with thermal lined curtains. These alone, when drawn, can be almost as effective as double-glazing, and are considerably cheaper. Apart from the question of aethetics, the cost-effectiveness of double-glazing is questionable.

Research carried out on behalf of English Heritage has shown that only a small amount of the heat lost from a house is lost via the windows, and of this, most is lost via draughts, not through the glass. So, it makes more sense to tackle loft insulation or draught-proofing than to replace or modify original single-glazed windows.

Old external doors may not fit too well, and this is probably why they are often replaced. If the door is original to the house, or a good later example, it should if possible be kept. As we have seen, modern

'Georgian' type aluminium or UPVC windows with mock glazing bars may look fairly convincing at a distance, but on close inspection their bogus character and lack of depth become all too apparent.

standard doors rarely look right in an old house. Sometimes copper or other draught-stripping can be fitted, or the frame adapted without spoiling its appearance, but it must be admitted that any door opening directly into a room or hall can be a source of considerable heat loss. Depending on the design and character of the house, it may be possible to add an external porch of appropriate type, but this will be less easy in the case of a formal classical building, or of a house in a formal terrace, where the addition of one odd porch, or worse still, of a series of unrelated ones, can spoil the unity of the design. In these cases it would probably be better to form an internal lobby.

STRUCTURAL PROBLEMS One of the most cost-effective improvements to an old house is loft insulation, generally by some material such as fibreglass quilt laid over the ceiling joists, or vermiculite laid loose between them. This can certainly be effective in reducing heat loss, but there are dangers which should not be ignored. By stopping heat from the rooms below from entering the loft the air temperature there is reduced, and, since moisture vapour is not excluded by most insulation materials, there is a real risk of condensation in the roof space, particularly if the roof has been felted or sealed. In extreme conditions this can be sufficient to set up wet rot in the timbers. This trouble is less likely to occur in old roofs which have not been felted, as there will probably be enough natural ventilation to prevent excessive condensation, but if there is any doubt about this, adequate ventilation should, as recommended in an earlier chapter, be provided at the eaves and the ridge. It may sometimes be advisable to insert a vapour barrier to prevent moisture vapour entering the roof space from below. A related problem, as we have seen, is that of the deterioration now found to be occurring in lead roofs, apparently as a result of modern heating and lack of ventilation. This is becoming a serious problem in churches, where lead roofs are more common, and it could affect similar roofs in houses.

In view of the problems of this kind which can arise, and the fact that old houses and their roof spaces differ greatly in their design, professional advice should be obtained before loft insulation is installed in an old house. One hopes that these matters are sufficiently considered when insulation grants are offered by local authorities.

The walls of most early houses are quite thick, and unlikely to require any additional insulation. The only exceptions to this are likely to be in timber-framed houses, and in later cottages with thin brick walls. As far as timber framing is concerned, we have seen that it is rarely practicable to expose the timbers both externally and internally. The old wattle and daub filling had quite a good insulation value, but later brick infilling is less efficient. If an internal wall lining is to be fitted to give additional insulation this can be improved by backing it with a material such as fibreglass or one of the newer types of environmentally friendly, or ecological, insulation products, such as sheeps wool, hemp or cellulose. It is, though, most important not to create conditions which could encourage condensation within the thickness of the wall, and possible timber decay, and professional advice should be obtained. In the case of cottages with thin brick walls, an insulated lining can generally be fitted, but here again professional advice is important.

We all know that an open fireplace in a room assists natural ventilation and regular air changes. This was recognised by the public health authorities in the nineteenth century, most of whom required external air bricks to be fitted in all rooms without fireplaces. Nowadays these vents are often blocked in the interests of fuel saving, as indeed are many unwanted fireplaces. This can result in condensation, as we have seen, and it is aggravated when old absorbent lime plaster is replaced by modern impervious wall and ceiling finishes. More seriously, there have been cases where the introduction of improved heating and draught-proofing has apparently resulted in outbreaks of dry rot and beetle attack, not only in roof spaces but elsewhere in the house. Most wood-boring beetles have a long life cycle, but this seems to be accelerated in warm, moist conditions. The spores of dry rot fungus are always in the air, but can only start to germinate where the temperature and humidity are right. Reduction of ventilation and increased temperature may create ideal conditions for fungus as well as for beetles.

For all these reasons, as I have already emphasised, the installation of modern heating and associated schemes of insulation and draught-proofing should not be carried out in old houses without great care, and in most cases professional advice should be obtained. 'Do-it-yourself' schemes and the activities of 'cowboy' firms may cause serious long-term problems.

To sum up, in the past there is no doubt that our houses were cooler and better ventilated than they are today, and people compensated for this by wearing warmer clothes and, perhaps, taking more exercise. It may be that, with rising fuel costs, and a growing realisation of some of the problems which may be caused by modern developments, we shall see a return to something more like the earlier conditions.

14
Conversions

So far we have been looking at some of the choices to be made when altering an old house for use today. There is also considerable interest in the conversion of non-residential buildings into houses or flats, and this can present a different set of problems. First, perhaps, we should consider why conversions are so popular today. It is not a new idea: buildings of many types have been converted for residential use in the past, but until recently this was generally for utilitarian reasons—it was cheaper to convert an existing building than to put up a new one. This is not necessarily so now. Such work tends to be labour-intensive, and whereas in the past materials accounted for the major cost of building work, labour costs are now usually the higher. It will generally cost more to convert, say, a barn into a house than to improve an existing house; so, what is the advantage of conversion?

One reason may well be that it is sometimes easier to obtain planning permission to convert an old building into a house than to build a new house on a particular site, especially if the building to be converted is of architectural or historic interest, and if conversion appears to be the only way it can be preserved. Another reason may be the desire to own a house of distinctive character. On the other hand, some people may feel that a building like a barn gives more scope for internal replanning than an existing house, particularly one where there are architectural and historical as well as structural restraints.

If we are really trying to preserve an old building of character, whether it is a house or of some other type, then the principles to be followed in conversion will be similar to those we have already considered in connection with alterations. In other words, we should

LEFT Residential conversion of a barn in Hampshire. Although some large windows have been inserted the building still retains something of its agricultural character.

respect the character of the buildings, and not try to transform them into something quite different. Indeed, if you want a conventionally planned house, it will probably be best to give up the idea of converting a non-residential building of any merit. The result may well be rather an unhappy compromise.

Some of the best conversions of non-residential buildings have been carried out by the Landmark Trust who, as we have seen, use them as holiday accommodation. Alterations are kept to a minimum and the buildings retain their integrity. Holiday use facilitates this treatment. One can probably put up with—even enjoy—the experience of living in, say, a Martello tower for one or two weeks. It would be another matter to make it one's permanent home.

Let us look, then, at some of the buildings most often converted to houses, and their particular problems.

Barns

I suppose the most important features of old barns are their large open interiors, unbroken roof slopes and, in some examples, interesting roof structures. These can all be very easily lost in the conversion process. Some of the most successful schemes are based on an 'open plan' interior, with part of the building left open to the roof, perhaps surrounded by galleries, and leaving the roof structure exposed to view. Indeed, if you want an open plan house it is probably better to think in terms of a barn conversion than to buy an old house and proceed to gut the interior. Lighting of the upper rooms can be a problem, as the insertion of many dormers can break up the roof line. As with houses, windows can sometimes be fitted in the gable ends, and inset dormers may be less obtrusive than the normal projecting

Residential conversion of farm buildings in Cornwall. Here again, the agricultural origin of the buildings is still apparent.

Good conversion of a farm building. External alterations have been kept to a minimum, and the skylights are not too obtrusive.

type. Flush roof lights may also be acceptable, particularly on slate or other dark coloured roofs.

New doors and windows should as far as possible be fitted into existing openings, and should be simple in character. Far too many old barns have been transformed by the insertion of a large number of domestic style windows and doors. The typical large cart entrances can provide an opportunity for incorporating glazing, extending the full height of the walls.

Some old barns already have inserted upper floors, often over part of the building only. Where possible these should be retained and used. They may be helping to support the outer walls, and if they are removed structural problems could occur. The trouble is that they may not always be at a convenient height to suit either the ground or the upper storey. It should be remembered that Building Regulations ceiling heights apply only to habitable rooms, and if there are areas with rather low headroom they can sometimes be used for bathrooms, cloakrooms, utility rooms or stores. In the roof space the trusses may present a problem, obstructing headroom. Where possible, any partitions required should be on the line of the trusses, and any disturbance to them kept to a minimum. If the roof structure is interesting it should be exposed as far as possible — another argument for 'open plan' design.

As most barns are large, compared with normal house sizes, it will probably not be necessary to consider additions to them. If these are required, however, they should be of traditional form, simple lean-tos or outshots, continuing the lines of the main roof.

Wind and watermills

A few windmills have been converted to houses, but they present considerable problems, and are probably most suited for holiday use, or for the dedicated enthusiast. Due to the restricted space on each floor, such a conversion will probably involve removal of most of the machinery which, if it has survived to any extent, would be regrettable.

Watermills are easier to convert but, here again, if the machinery

LEFT Thorney Mill, Somerset, sensitively converted to residential use with minimal change to elevations.

survives it should if possible be left in position, a fact which will restrict the planning of the house. There is a growing interest in the revival of milling and the generation of electricity using water turbines, and the aim in any conversion should be to enable the mill to be re-used — if not at once then at a later date. Any alterations should therefore be reversible.

You may be fortunate enough to find a mill with an attached or adjoining mill house, and this simplifies the problem. The living accommodation, particularly the bedrooms and service rooms, can be mainly or totally confined to the house, leaving the mill itself largely unaltered, even if it is used as a living area. Low headrooms on the various floors may present difficulties, but where possible they should be accepted. As with old barns, pulling out upper floors could affect the stability of the building. The old access steps between the floors will not comply with the Building Regulations, but it may be possible to obtain a relaxation to enable them to be retained, particularly if there is another, more conventional staircase within the mill house. The old doors and windows should be retained as far as possible, together with other features, such as sack-hoists. Like barns, many old mills have suffered from over-domestication.

Maltings and Breweries

Residential conversion of a maltings building in Suffolk. The large dormers, although frankly modern features, are perhaps reminiscent of the original kiln projections, typical of such buildings.

These can present great problems if they are to be converted for residential use, as the headrooms on all floors tend to be very low. If

Conversions

these are altered, the window positions are unlikely to be suitable, and all too often one ends up with, in effect, a new building. There have been some successful conversions, but they need an imaginative designer, and a client willing to accept a house with some unconventional features, particularly with regard to floor levels and ceiling heights. For instance, it may be best to use the top floor, extending into the roof space if necessary, for the living accommodation, with the low-ceilinged lower floors for the kitchen, bathroom, etc. If the old kiln and flue survive they should be preserved. On the whole, though, as with windmills, these buildings are best converted for holiday or other specialised use.

Stables and coach houses

In London and other cities and towns, mews conversions have for long been popular and we are now seeing similar developments in rural areas, where the outbuildings of large country houses, no longer needed for their original purposes, are being converted for residential use. These do not normally present any particular problems: headrooms are generally reasonable, and the existing doors and windows can be retained, making use of the large coach house doors for garages, often difficult to incorporate satisfactorily in other buildings.

Sometimes these buildings are a full two storeys in height, but often they are of one storey and an attic, or loft, and it may be necessary to insert additional dormers or rooflights to light the upper floor. As we have seen with old houses, these should be designed in character and scale with the building, and their number kept to a minimum. Sometimes there is an old loft door in a gabled dormer which can be adapted as a window.

If any of the old stable partitions and fittings have survived they should if possible be retained. Indeed, the old harness room may supply some interesting relics and artefacts, which should not be destroyed. If they cannot be kept in the building they should at least be offered to a local museum.

ABOVE *A small coachhouse and loft converted to a maisonette at Newport Pagnell, Buckinghamshire.* RIGHT *Residential conversions of stable buildings in Staffordshire.*

Residential conversion of a village school. The original schoolroom is largely unaltered, but the cross-wing is rather spoilt by the windows, particularly the pseudo-Georgian bow.

Schools

Many village schools are now being closed and sold. Although some date from the eighteenth century or even earlier, most of them are Victorian, often built in a Gothic style. The smaller ones consist of one large room, perhaps divided by a folding screen, and open to the roof, with windows at rather a high level. If these windows are to be kept it may be difficult to insert an intermediate floor, and an 'open hall with gallery' treatment may be appropriate. If the school house forms part of the complex the problem is simplified, as the smaller rooms can be planned within this, leaving the old schoolroom as a large living area.

Inns

Old inns are sometimes sold for residential conversion. Some of these were originally private houses, and these should not present many problems if they revert to this use. The internal fittings may have been removed before the sale, but if they survive, and are of Victorian, or even Edwardian date, they should not be destroyed. If they cannot be kept in the house a local museum may be interested in acquiring them. This also applies to ornamental or engraved glass windows and mirrors, and wall tiling. On the other hand, an old inn may have been subjected to a good deal of fake 'restoration', with the insertion of old oak beams and similar features simply for effect, without structural function, and unrelated to the design of the building. No harm will be done by removing these, but a careful survey will be necessary to differentiate between authentic and bogus features.

Inns of an earlier period occasionally come on the market, dating from Tudor or even medieval times. These will need very careful conversion and a thorough historical survey should be carried out before any alterations are planned. The upper rooms may have been approached by open galleries, filled in at a later period; indeed a

This town house has come full circle. The inserted shop window and door have been redesigned for a restored domestic use.

central courtyard may have been roofed over. Although it may not be practicable to restore the original form of the inn, care should be taken not to *destroy* any early features, and it may be possible at least to reveal them, adding to the interest of the house. Old wine bottles and similar objects may be found in an old inn, particularly in the cellars, and the local museum can probably help in dating these.

Shops in towns

As conditions in towns change, some shopping areas lose their trade and the buildings may revert to residential use. As we have seen in an earlier chapter, in old towns many buildings are older than they appear, having been refaced, perhaps more than once. Here again, a thorough historical survey is called for. In some cases, the ground floor will always have been used as a shop, or for some commercial purpose, but in others the shop was a later insertion. If the ground floor is to be used for living accommodation you may want to alter the façade, to provide more privacy than is afforded by a shop front. On the other hand, a good early shop front should not be destroyed. I think the following points should be considered before a decision is taken on this:

Was the ground floor always a shop, and if not, what was its original form? Sometimes adjoining unaltered buildings can provide the answer to this. If, in a residential terrace, only a few houses have been turned into shops, it may be a good thing to restore the original ground floor design, thus regaining the unity of the terrace, especially if the shop front is recent, and of no particular interest. If, however, the shop front appears original, or a good example of eighteenth- or nineteenth-century design, it is generally best to retain it, accepting some loss of privacy. Indeed, if the building is large enough, it may be possible to arrange the main living accommodation on the first floor where it would probably have been when the shop was first in use.

A former coaching inn, now a private house. Minimal alterations have been carried out to the ground floor.

194

If the shop has escaped recent alterations there may well be some old fittings, tools and containers, etc. Even those of the early twentieth century are now beginning to be of historic interest. If they cannot remain in situ they should be offered to a local museum. Of course, you may want to retain the shop itself for some business use, and to convert the upper floors for living accommodation. In recent years the custom of 'living over the shop' has declined, but as heavy traffic is removed from town centres there are some signs of a return to the older practice — something to be welcomed as a way of bringing more life back to these areas. Such use of the upper floors may involve problems with the Building Regulations; it will probably be necessary to arrange access to the upper floors without passing through the shop. Early consultation with the authorities concerned is essential if the character of the building is not to be spoilt.

Churches and chapels

Churches have been converted to houses from medieval times onwards, particularly at the time of the Reformation and dissolution of the religious houses. Some of these have, in more recent times, been restored to their original form, for instance, Odda's Chapel, Deerhurst, Gloucestershire and the Saxon church at Bradford-on-Avon, Wiltshire. While the domestic or other use might not have been ideal for a historic church it did at least preserve the fabric.

Today, many redundant churches of all denominations are being converted to houses. Generally, the typical eighteenth-century galleried churches and chapels are easier to convert than the more traditional Gothic designs, as the former, externally at least, have the appearance of two-storeyed buildings. If the church is of real historic interest then, remembering the case of Bradford-on-Avon, the conversion should be designed to be reversible, so that the building could be reinstated at some future date without the loss of any original features. It is therefore most important not to destroy any of these features, or the original fabric, or the plan form, but to plan the house to accommodate these. If the interior of the church is well proportioned, part of it might be kept as a full height room — a medieval 'hall'. As with barns and mills, if rooms are wanted in the roof space, over-large dormers should be avoided.

As we have seen in Chapter 2, in the Church of England the procedure for dealing with a redundant church is clearly defined, and any church sold for domestic conversion is likely to be the subject of a number of restrictive covenants and conditions, dealing in particular with the disposal of any monuments and the use of the churchyard. With other denominations these procedures do not apply, but the local church organisation is likely to lay down similar conditions. The conversion of a church to another use, particularly as a house, may arouse strong local concern — even opposition — and any prospective purchaser should be prepared for this.

A former monastic gatehouse now used as a private house. The original archway, now partly built up, can still be seen, and the building retains many medieval features.

Warehouses and other early industrial buildings

These are now being converted both into houses and flats, and this may sometimes be the best way of preserving a class of building which is often much at risk today. They are generally very solidly built, with reasonable headroom, large internal floor areas, and regular ranges of windows, making conversion a relatively simple process. The windows may retain their old cast iron sashes, which should if possible be preserved. There are firms who can repair these, and make replicas if necessary. As with other conversions, the greatest danger is perhaps that of over-domestication.

If an old warehouse is to be converted into flats, the Building Regulations may be more stringent than those applying to a single house, and it may also be necessary to provide adequate parking space, particularly in a town, where this can be difficult on a restricted site. For these reasons, early consultation with the various authorities is advisable.

The conversion of a non-residential building is likely to present more problems than the adaptation of an existing house but, sensitively carried out, it can secure the preservation of a building which might otherwise be lost. The success of a conversion scheme can be gauged by the extent to which the original form and, indeed, the original function of the building are still recognisable after the work has been completed.

Redundant seed merchant's premises in Somerset converted, with a modern infill, to accommodate the offices of the local authority and its planning department.

Part III.   *Some case histories*

1   Cottages in the High Street, Winfrith Newburgh, Dorset

This L-shaped block of four cottages, and the adjoining barn range formed an important feature of the village street. They were included in the original statutory list of historic buildings for the parish in 1959. In their present form, the cottages are mainly of eighteenth-century date, possibly incorporating earlier structures. They are built of brick, with thatched roofs, and are typical cottages of this part of Dorset, at the junction of the chalk downland and the heath. The barn, also of brick and thatch, shows interesting diaper patterning in the gable ends, produced by the use of burnt headers.

Like most of the village originally, these buildings were owned by a local large estate, and the cottages had been let for many years at low rents, insufficient to cover proper maintenance. The conditions of both the cottages and the barn had deteriorated, and other listed barns attached to the cottages on the east had already been demolished by the late 1960s. The estate also owned land at the rear of the cottages, which had become available for development as a result of agricultural reorganisation. In order to obtain a satisfactory vehicular access to this land, partial demolition of the cottages, and of the barn was considered necessary. In 1967, listed building consent was granted for this work, and it was hoped that the surviving cottages would be repaired in conjunction with the development. The scheme was not implemented, and in 1974 an amended scheme was submitted, involving demolition of more of the cottages, but retaining the barn, and this also received approval. This scheme was also abandoned, and in 1976 the whole site was sold to the district council. The council at first applied for consent to demolish all the cottages, using the land at the rear for council housing. Following some local objections, the council withdrew this application, and investigated the possibility of repairing the cottages themselves. This idea in turn was abandoned as being too costly, and in 1978 the council sold the cottages and the northern part of the barn to the Old Buildings Restoration Trust, a preservation trust registered with the Civic Trust, but retaining the southern section of the barn for conversion to garages for their own housing scheme. The architect for the Trust was John Sell.

The problem of vehicular access to the land at the rear—the orig-

The cottages under repair

Cottages in the High Street, Winfrith Newburgh, Dorset

inal reason for the proposed demolition—was eventually resolved by forming a new access to the north of the cottages through land also in the council's ownership, which involved reducing the gardens of some adjoining houses. With this problem out of the way, a scheme was prepared, repairing the four cottages and converting them into three slightly larger ones, installing modern amenities, with the minimum alterations to their structure and design. This scheme received planning and listed building consent, and the necessary waivers of Building Regulations were granted to avoid the need to alter ceiling heights. The roofs were re-thatched and the timbers repaired as necessary. Care was taken to retain existing doors and windows as far as possible, and any replacements were purpose-made to match those existing, avoiding the suburban character which so often results from the use of standard components.

Financial assistance was obtained from the district council in the form of improvement grants. The Historic Buildings Council gave a Section 10 grant, and a loan was obtained from the Architectural Heritage Fund, this being repaid when the cottages were sold. In fact, the Trust made a small profit on the scheme, and did not need to take up the offer of a further loan from the county council.

When the Trust first bought the buildings it was hoped that the barn could be repaired and used either for some community purpose, or as a craft workshop. These uses, however, did not prove viable, and it is being converted to a house. This scheme has secured the preservation of a good group of buildings in the most attractive part of the village. Redundant agricultural cottages and farm buildings are all too easily lost, and the rehabilitation of this group, after so many years of neglect and uncertainty over their future should encourage similar projects in other villages.

View from the east ABOVE *before and* RIGHT *after repair.*

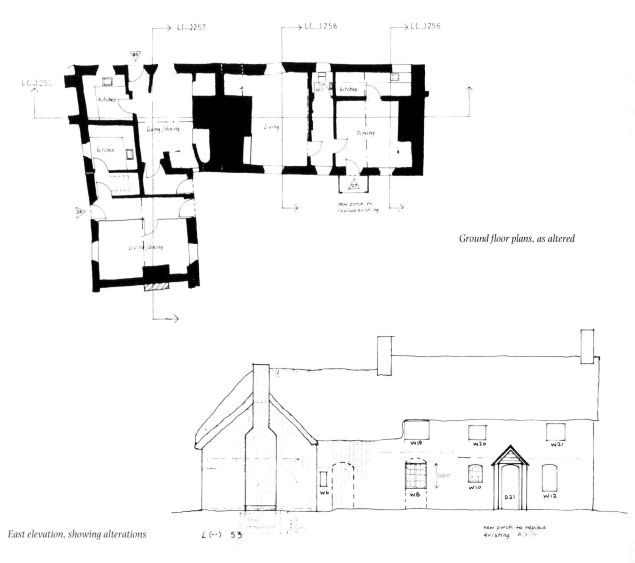

L(--)257 →   L(--)258 →   L(--)256 →

L (--) 255

kitchen

kitchen

Living/dining

Living

Dining

WC   kitchen

Living/dining

new porch to
replace existing

Ground floor plans, as altered

East elevation, showing alterations

L (--) 53

W19   W20   W21

W6

W8   W10   D21   W12

1100

new porch to replace
existing   A(3)01

View from the south-east, after repair

2   Queen Ann Yard, Norwich, Norfolk

This case illustrates some of the problems found in historic town centres. Houses of medieval or Tudor origin, often of timber-framed construction, are altered and sub-divided many times over the centuries, with no consideration for their architectural quality, or even for their structural safety, as when main timbers are cut away for new door and window openings. As the buildings descend in the social scale the standard of maintenance declines: roofs and gutters are neglected, allowing water to penetrate and encouraging fungus and beetle attack particularly in attics and other little-used parts of the building. At the same time, the alterations probably obscure the original character of the houses, so that their interest and value are not appreciated, and all too often they fall victim to schemes of slum-clearance, road-widening or a more profitable redevelopment of the site.

Once a group of early houses reaches this state of disrepair, its rehabilitation may be complicated by the fact that the various buildings may by then be in multiple ownership, involving such problems as flying freeholds. Even if one or two of the owners are anxious to preserve their buildings, this becomes very difficult if not impossible if other owners in the group are unwilling to co-operate.

The group of buildings known as Queen Ann Yard, Norwich, on the corner of Colegate and Saint Miles' Alley, in the historic centre of the city, is an example of this type of problem. The buildings are basically of timber-framed construction, with some later brick repairs. In Saint Miles' Alley, facing the Church of Saint Michael, Coslany, are two houses dating from *c.* 1500, possibly originally church property. No. 1. Saint Miles' Alley, is a narrow-plan house, with a gable end to the road, while the adjoining house, now No. 59b, is of the wider plan form, with its roof parallel to the road, and of jettied construction. On the Colegate frontage, No. 57, a mid-seventeenth-century building, at one time an inn, is also of wide-plan form, with two gables facing the road. The building on the corner site itself was demolished as unsafe *c.* 1950, and the same fate threatened the whole group, which was all in poor repair. Often, when corner buildings are demolished in old city centres, the opportunity is taken to 'improve' the road junction, leaving an ugly gap site, and this could well have happened here.

In 1972, however, the whole site was acquired by the Norwich Preservation Trust, a local society which had already carried out some good rehabilitation schemes in the city. It was decided to repair the surviving buildings and retain them for housing, and to build a new infil block on the corner, maintaining the old street lines.

BELOW *Architect's drawing of the scheme, showing the inner courtyard and the new buildings on the corner.*

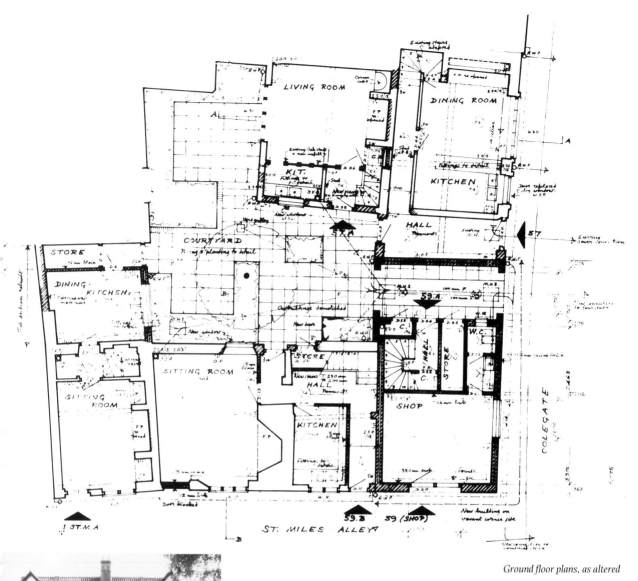

Ground floor plans, as altered

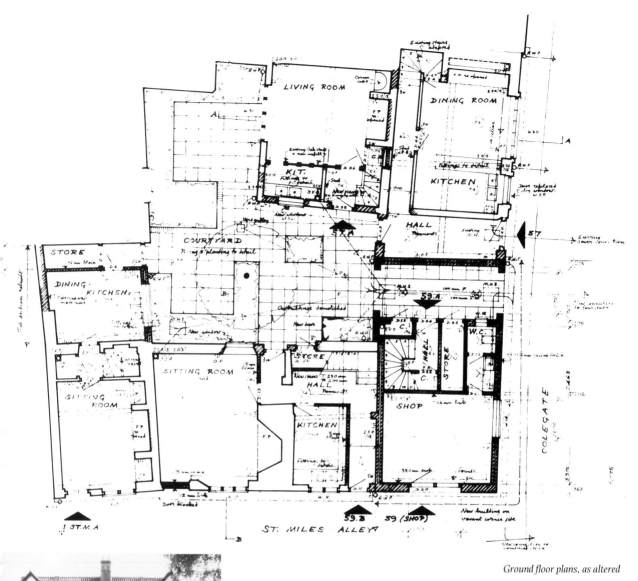

View from Saint Miles' Alley, after repair

The two buildings facing Saint Miles' Alley were adapted as single houses, providing modern amenities, but taking care to retain their character. The external plaster was kept on No. 1 (the gabled house), but on the upper storey of No. 59b it was stripped, exposing the timber framing. The brickwork of the lower storey of this house (a later replacement of the original timber framing) was also stripped. As discussed in an earlier chapter, this is always a difficult decision to make, but in this case it was decided that the condition of the timber frame and its importance to the appearance of the group justified its exposure.

In Colegate, No. 57 was converted into two units, one facing the street and the other, a smaller house, facing the inner courtyard. In the courtyard itself, some later buildings were cleared to provide more light and air at the rear of the houses, and creating a paved and planted area shared by all the residents, entered through an archway in the Colegate frontage.

Queen Ann Yard, Norwich, Norfolk

The most interesting problem in this case was perhaps the design of the new infil building on the corner site. It has been designed to blend with the existing buildings on each side without copying any actual period features. A rectangular building, with a gable end to Saint Miles' Lane, it is built of brick, plastered on the upper storey, and with a steeply pitched pantile roof finished with the typical East Anglian bargeboard at the verge. Windows and doors are of modern design, of stained timber, but in scale with the old windows in the adjoining buildings. This new block was originally designed with a shop on the ground floor, and a maisonette above, extending into the attic, but the shop is now used as an office.

The local authority, Norwich City Council, gave improvement grants for the work, and a conservation area (Section 10) grant was made by the Historic Buildings Council. As is the normal policy of this Trust, the repaired buildings were not sold, but retained for letting. The architects for the work were Michael and Sheila Gooch.

ABOVE *and* BELOW *The completed scheme, showing the new corner building.*

Puddlebrook House from the south-west

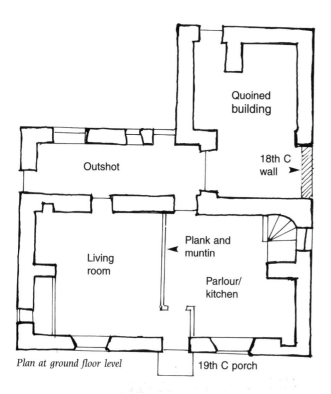

Plan at ground floor level

Quoined building

18th C wall ►

Outshot

Plank and muntin ◄

Living room

Parlour/ kitchen

19th C porch

3 Puddlebrook House, Milborne Port, Somerset

At first sight, this is a small, symmetrical seventeenth-century yeoman farmhouse, surrounded by later buildings. Research and recent restoration has unearthed, as is often the case, interesting material which fills out its history over three centuries.

The authenticity of a datestone marked IC 1672 set in lime mortar into the south façade is supported by documentary evidence which shows that the house was built by, if not for, a local landowner James Carent, who died in 1675. The property became part of the Medlicott Estate at the end of the seventeenth century, and remained so until 1979, and so the estate was responsible for most of its many alterations.

The main house has a typical seventeenth-century plan with two chimney stacks in the gable walls, but immediately to the north of the house is evidence of an earlier, high-grade building with quoins up to first floor level and measuring esternally only 5.5 x 4.6 metres, which was incorporated into the property at a later date. That the quoined building predates the 1672 house is made clear by the construction of the ground floor outshot which was contemporary with the house: its abutment to the quoined building at one corner proves that the quoined building was there first. The use of the two properties must in some way have been related. It is possible that the quoined building was a forge (it has a massive and high-lintelled fireplace, but the quality of the build suggest some superior use). That the building was an external and independent kitchen to the main house is unlikely as it predates the house, though probably by only a few years.

Iron-framed windows with leaded lights, well carpentered, stop-chamfered beams, even in the outshot, reeded plank and muntin to divide the two ground floor rooms, and reeded panelling surrounding the spiral wood stair, as well as a handsome carved fireplace in the first floor 'chamber' bedroom suggest the house of 1672 had social pretensions, although the original doors at the first floor level and their wooden catches are primitive indeed.

An upgrading of the property happened in the early eighteenth century, when the western parlour was panelled, shuttered window cases were provided to the iron-framed window lights, and the quoined building was incorporated into the main house by the building up of the west wall to the roof line, with access between the two at both ground and first floor levels.

Much subdivision of the house took place in the nineteenth and twentieth centuries, as the property descended the social scale and for a long time, according to the census records, had multiple occupancy by a succession of farm workers.

When restoration of the house started in 1998, a second staircase inserted in the late nineteenth century was removed, revealing the untouched seventeenth-century plank and muntin that had been

James Carent's datestone is set under the eaves to the right of the door.

Left: Well-cut quoins are clearly to be seen both internally and externally. The outshot to the main house was built in 1672, and it is notched into the earlier quoined building. Inside the house the external wall of the quoined building is continuous with the internal wall of the outshot.

covered with lath and plaster in the early eighteenth century. Two very large fireplaces were opened up, and a blocked window half way up the spiral stair was restored with an oak frame to match the window at attic level. The top storey of the main house, lit only by this window, had clearly been used as bedrooms because of the design of the trusses to give headroom through the A-frames, and because of the plastering of all internal surfaces. This use as bedrooms was restored. A skylight in the twentieth century asbestos roof was removed to give an unbroken roof line, but attempts to restore the house's original thatch were thwarted because of the council's refusal to allow relaxation of the 12 metre rule, the house being within 3 metres of adjacent property on the west side.

Much of the interest in the substantial and well restored house derives from the authentic original detailing, especially in the carpentry, and it is creditable that the external appearance apart from the roof is now barely altered from its original appearance around 1700. Earth which had accumulated against the south façade to approximately one metre over three centuries was removed to relieve dampness in the absorbent limestone walls. The nineteenth-century slated porch, mentioned in the listing details, has sensibly been left undisturbed, as have the nineteenth-century northern extensions to the quoined buildings which, at some time in the nineteenth century, was a glove workshop, gloving being the principle industry of Milborne Port.

Restoration was undertaken in 1998 and continued in 2002 when the main house and the quoined building were reunited under the same ownership.

A replacement window has been inserted where the original opening was blocked. It matches the window above, which lit the second floor. In the photograph a straight joint can be seen where in the eighteenth century the main house and the quoined building were joined by a new rubble wall.

Distinctive stop chamfers and reeded carpentry on the first floor level (above), around the staircase (left) and elsewhere are evidently the work of a single seventeenth-century carpenter.

4   135–145, Magdalen Road, Norwich

This is a terrace of six early nineteenth-century artisan houses, of simple design, and having no particular outstanding features of interest, but which had survived practically unaltered probably because as tenanted houses, let at low rents, they had not been thought worth the cost of modernisation and 'improvement'. Terraces of this kind are often found just outside the historic cores of old towns, and they are particularly vulnerable to schemes of road-widening and slum clearance.

These Magdalen Road houses are built of brick, with low-pitched pantiled roofs, and have two storeys. In plan they are single-fronted, i.e. one room wide, and two rooms deep, with a third room, the kitchen, in a rear lean-to. The centre rooms on each floor therefore had no natural ventilation, and were lit only by borrowed lights in the partition between them and the rear rooms. The front rooms on the ground floor were entered directly from the street, and the stairs rose from the centre room. In their elevational treatment the houses still showed Georgian influence. They had sash windows, retaining all their glazing bars, and panelled doors with ornamental semi-circular fanlights, all under gauged brick arches. In the centre of the terrace a through-passage, under a similar archway, led to the rear yards.

By the late 1970s the houses had fallen into disrepair and had been classed as unfit by the city council. The accommodation was considered inadequate, particularly in view of the unventilated central rooms. On the first floor, the rear bedroom (in the lean-to) led out of this centre room. In 1980 the council acquired the houses from the landlord, for demolition and redevelopment. The local conservation area advisory committee (the chairman of which was the vice-chairman of the council's planning committee), however, hearing of the proposals, considered that the houses were of some architectural merit and notified the Department of the Environment of the threat. As a result, the terrace was spot-listed just before demolition was due to start.

In the light of this new situation, the city council now decided to consider how the houses could best be preserved. They eventually decided to repair and improve them for subsequent sale to private owners. The original tenants had all by then been re-housed, and did not wish to buy and move into their old homes. The council could perhaps have sold the houses as they were, for improvement, to new owners, but this might have made it more difficult to carry out the work as a unified scheme, essential if the character of the terrace was to be preserved. Work was started in 1981 and completed the following year.

Care was taken to retain the character of the houses, and alterations were kept to a minimum. On the ground floor, the central room

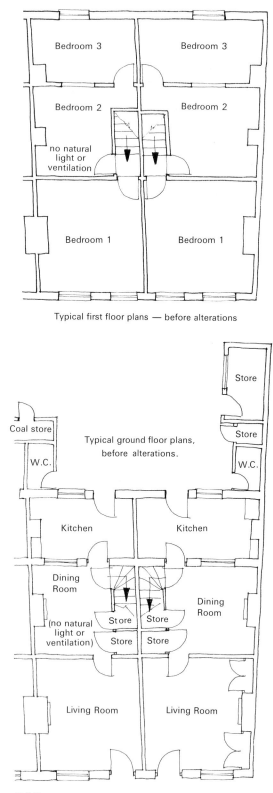

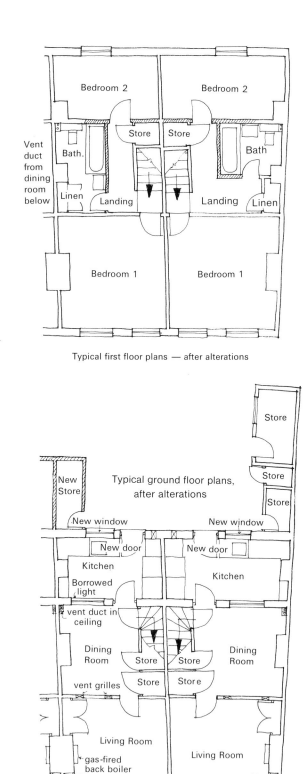

Before alterations (first floor, left):

Bedroom 3   Bedroom 3

Bedroom 2   Bedroom 2

no natural light or ventilation

Bedroom 1   Bedroom 1

Typical first floor plans — before alterations

After alterations (first floor, right):

Bedroom 2   Bedroom 2

Vent duct from dining room below

Bath.   Store   Store   Bath

Linen   Landing   Landing   Linen

Bedroom 1   Bedroom 1

Typical first floor plans — after alterations

Before alterations (ground floor, left):

Store

Store

Coal store

W.C.   W.C.

Typical ground floor plans, before alterations.

Kitchen   Kitchen

Dining Room   Dining Room

(no natural light or ventilation)

Store   Store   Store   Store

Living Room   Living Room

After alterations (ground floor, right):

Store

Store

Store

New Store

Typical ground floor plans, after alterations

New window   New window

New door   New door

Kitchen   Kitchen

Borrowed light

vent duct in ceiling

Dining Room   Dining Room

Store   Store   Store   Store

vent grilles

Living Room   Living Room

gas-fired back boiler

208

ABOVE *View from rear before repair—note assortment of added windows and extensions.*

ABOVE *Section of front elevation, showing passage to rear.*

View from rear after repair, showing restoration of original windows and tidying of extensions.

View from front after repair.

remained as a dining room, still lit only by a borrowed light from the kitchen at the rear, but with supplementary mechanical ventilation. On the first floor, the central room was converted to form a bathroom, with mechanical ventilation and artificial lighting, and a passage giving access to the rear bedroom. The original stairs were retained. The old external wc's at the rear of the houses were rebuilt to form stores.

Although the front elevation of the terrace had survived unaltered, the rear elevation had, over the years, been rather spoiled by the insertion of an assortment of modern windows of inharmonious type—a very common occurrence. As part of the improvement scheme these intrusive windows have been replaced by new ones in scale with the building. As a result of this, and of the building of the new stores with matching bricks and pantiled roofs, the rear elevations of the houses are now almost as attractive as the fronts, something all too rare in schemes of this kind.

The houses have now been sold, and the fact that they are listed should protect them from undesirable alterations. With their simple dignity they may indeed be contrasted with other terraced houses of similar date in the same road which have been 'modernised' by individual owner-occupiers with little regard for the effect on the terrace as a whole. It is perhaps rather ironic that the reason for the survival of Nos. 135 to 145 in their original state—their continuation in one ownership, let at low rents for many years—was also very nearly the cause of their demolition.

The farmhouse and entrance arch before restoration.

5   Bineham Court, Somerset

Delamination of one of the walls in the south range indicates imminent collapse.

Bineham Farm was built in the early nineteenth century as a model farm for the Duke of Devonshire on estate land in Somerset near Somerton. It can be precisely dated to the time of the demolition of the Ilchester Gaol, as the Blue Lias stone from this building was hauled from Ilchester about three miles distant and used for part of the farmhouse and outbuildings, supplementing stone from blue lias quarries to the north. It was, therefore, an early example of architectural recycling.

The property later fell into private hands, and by the 1990s, although the farmhouse was sound, the west, north and south ranges around the courtyard were in severe disrepair, and the courtyard itself contained several unsightly metal buildings, agricultural stores and debris. Planning permission was sought and obtained for conversion to fourteen dwellings of which three were to be subdivisions of the house. This building, a very large farmhouse, retained all its original Georgian details. Alongside, a stone archway built of Ham stone and blue lias, and capped with a steep-pitched gable with hamstone coping stones formed the rather grand original entrance to the farmyard, and was sound, whereas the walls and roofs of the courtyard ranges were not.

Work was begun in 1998. The architectural concept is that of the architect Charles Louwerse, of Sherborne, Dorset, who proposed the reduction of the number of residential units to eleven, creating eight substantial living spaces in the courtyard flanks. The intention was to retain an agricultural feel to the façades and the courtyard whilst providing maximum flexibility internally.

The cleared courtyard is now a level square measuring 40 metres by 40, with a central square laid to lawn, as in a university college court. There is a wide walkway around the perimeter laid with reconstructed stone flags with a textured surface. In an area famous for its blue lias flagstones from nearby Keinton Mandeville, the decision to use concrete was probably a financial one, but the result is very satisfactory, thanks to close supervision of both colour and laying patterns. The project, completed in 2001, initially had a somewhat bare appearance which will be softened as the controlled tree planting scheme matures. Residents have communal rights over the courtyard land.

The buildings were not listed, but close interest was taken by South Somerset District Council, which meant that the development was treated as if the buildings were protected and permitted development rights were withdrawn. The fenestration pattern was carefully retained, even in the rebuilt North range, and external staircases in the West 'Barn' range were retained and repaired, and taken into use in two of the properties where living levels were inverted, with bedrooms on ground floor and living /dining/kitchens above. Roof and other timbers were retained or re-used where possible, and the main 'barn' ridge line untouched, though it is somewhat undulating with the sagging of the ridge pieces.

No chimney stacks have been inserted, in spite of some of the purchasers' requirements to have fireplaces - the flues are vented unob-trusively in the pitches of the slated roofs, which are the original slates, re-used throughout. The roof of the south range is carried on a steel frame with some RSJs exposed. To simplify reconstruction and to avoid additional loading on the original walls, which have shallow footings, this steel frame renders the walls structurally redundant. The span of the agricultural outbuildings was a standard 7 metres, and the architect has used some ingenuity in varying and increasing the width

The central courtyard, showing the original fenestration patterns retained and the formal lawns.

Right: the slit windows in the south gable are new, as are the 'conservatories' which extend the ground floor living space.

by adding new conservatories at the rear. The result is an impressively widened open living space. The single low-pitched glazed roof illuminates an extended open-space ground floor as well as a loft space over an extended ceiling which has provision for heat recovery units.

Ceiling glazing is also used in the north-facing aspect of the north range to admit important sunlight.

Two corners of the courtyard, which were open cart stores when the project was started in the 1990s, could have been left open to increase access and 'airiness', but instead were built up with timber frame construction and oak cladding to give variety and to lighten up the corners of what could have been a rather formidable aspect if built entirely of stone.

The success of a project of this kind depends heavily in the long term on maintaining the unity of the concept. When multiple ownership takes place there is always the danger of this unity being destroyed as owners express their indiviuality. At Bineham Court the inventiveness of the interiors, belied by the elevations, may be a sufficient substitute.

Ground floor plan showing relative size of the eleven units.

Left: Timber frame and oak cladding closes the north-west corner of the court-yard. External staircases are retained in the west range, ex-grain store.

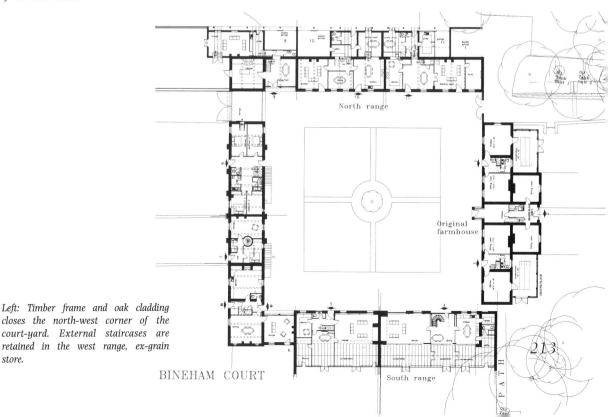

North range

Original farmhouse

BINEHAM COURT

South range

213

6 Southfield Square, Manningham, West Yorkshire

This case illustrates some of the problems of old houses in run-down inner city areas. Southfield Square was built between 1851 and 1864, by two local Building Societies, as a 'middle class' development of seventy-five two-storeyed terrace houses, with basements and attics, planned round three sides of a square—a late survival of a common eighteenth- and early nineteenth-century form of urban development. The houses were built of the local sandstone, with slate roofs, and in their architectural style they retained elements of the Greek Revival. The plans were generally of the typical urban form; a narrow entrance hall leading to a rear staircase, and two main rooms on each floor. They were not, however, identical, some being larger, with rear extensions, and the standard of the internal finishes also varied. This was probably due to the fact that several local architects were involved in the development.

The central area is now divided to form individual gardens, for the various houses, but this sub-division does not appear to have been the original design, as it first appears on an Ordnance Survey Map of 1908. Before then the Square was open, like most town squares of this type.

When first built, the houses would have been occupied as single family dwellings, and represented a good standard of accommodation for their time and class. As often happened, however, as the original owners moved out to the suburbs, the Southfield Square houses became unfashionable, and most of their later owners and occupiers had neither the means nor the interest to maintain them adequately, or to install modern amenities, so that the houses began to deteriorate rapidly. In addition, although they had generally been well and substantially built, certain structural problems had arisen, owing partly to the original design and partly to lack of maintenance, resulting in the buckling of some of the front walls.

ABOVE *Some of the houses after repair*

RIGHT *Rear view of repaired houses, showing small roof lights to attics.*

214

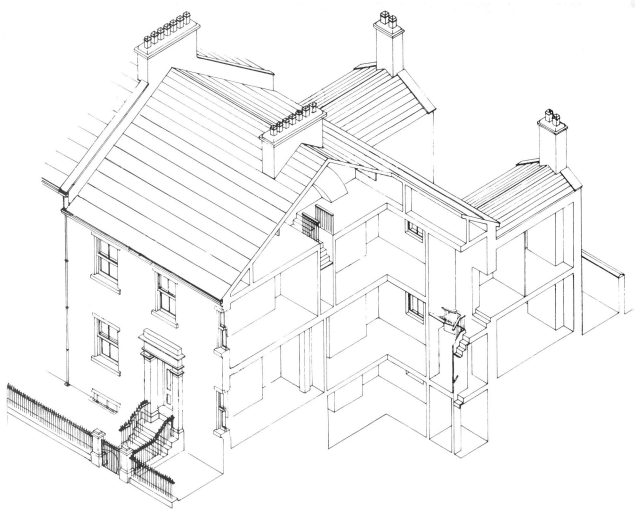

Sectional drawing of a typical house.

By the late 1960s, the local council had decided that the Southfield Square houses were unfit, and had included them in a clearance programme. By about 1978 the council had acquired twenty-three of the houses and were seeking a compulsory purchase order for the rest of the Square. In 1976, however, the Department of the Environment had listed seventy-three of the seventy-five houses, and opposition to the proposed clearance was growing, particularly among the residents, who had formed the Southfield Square Action Group. In 1978, the Civic Trust, supported by the Monument Trust (a preservation trust), became interested and tried to persuade the council to think in terms of rehabilitation, rather than clearance, suggesting that the Square should be designated both as a conservation area, and as a housing action area, thus becoming eligible for the maximum grant aid. Following an approach to the Department of the Environment, the public inquiry into the council's application for listed building consent for the demolition of the houses was postponed, and the comparative costs of rehabilitation and of demolition and redevelopment were worked out. These indicated that rehabilitation would be cheaper, taking into account the likely available grants.

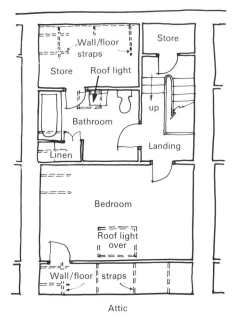

Typical first-floor and attic plans, showing method of repair, and planning of internal bathroom.

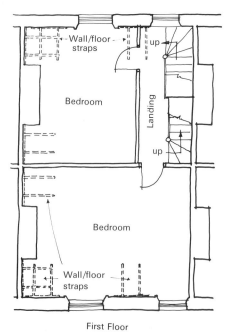

Southfield Square, Manningham, West Yorkshire

Although the inquiry was eventually held, the council offered no evidence in favour of demolition, and indicated that they now wished to see the Square rehabilitated. Soon after this, Southfield Square was designated as a conservation area, and as a housing action area, as had been previously suggested. The Monument Trust agreed to purchase the council-owned houses for repair and re-sale, while the various individual owners were offered advice and financial aid. Repairs are now in hand, and a very useful guidance leaflet has been prepared by the council, setting out the standard of repairs required. These are designed to secure the retention of the character of the houses; windows, doors and other features, both external and internal, have to be repaired or replaced in replica.

Most of the repairs needed were quite straightforward, the kind of thing to be expected in houses of this date and type. Roof slating, and in some cases roof timbers, needed repair, as did doors and windows. Internally, because of damage from water penetration, plaster and joinery needed varying amounts of renewal. Care has been taken to retain, and where necessary match, the original details. The main problems, as previously stated, were caused by the bulging front walls of some of the houses. These walls had been built up with a double skin of stone, and in some cases the outer skin had pulled away from the inner one. In addition, since the first floor joists frequently ran between the party walls (i.e. parallel to the front and back walls), they did not help to stiffen the front walls, so that in some cases the whole wall, not simply the outer leaf, was bowing. The conventional treatment for all this would have been to rebuild the front walls completely, but this, as well as being very costly, could have initiated further movement in the structure. For this reason, a system was devised by the consulting engineer for tying together the two skins of the walls with stainless steel bolts, and for restraining these strengthened walls by tying them back to the floors at both ground and first floor level.

As had been the case when the Square was first built, several firms of architects have been involved in the restoration work. Messrs Anthony Short and Partners were initially engaged by the Civic Trust to advise on the possibility of saving the houses, and have since acted for the Monument Trust and for some of the private owners. Messrs Geoffrey Lee Associates, Messrs Michael Lyall Associates, and Messrs Nuttall, Yarwood and Partners have acted for other private owners.

This cannot yet be called a complete success story. Of the seventy-five houses, in 1982 forty-eight still awaited repair. In the case of the privately owned houses, the initiative must come from the owners, and inevitably some will be more interested in repairing and improving their property than others. The important thing, however, is that Southfield Square has been saved from demolition, and that the local authority, originally interested mainly in clearance and rebuilding, is now actively encouraging a sympathetic rehabilitation of the Square.

7   Newton Hall, Hyde, Greater Manchester

This is an example of a rather specialised 'museum piece' restoration. It also illustrates how an early building can, in effect, be 'lost' for centuries, and only be rediscovered by accident. All too often such buildings disappear, demolished before their significance has been appreciated.

In 1967 a piece of land on which stood a group of redundant farm buildings was bought by a local firm, Messrs William Kenyon and Sons Ltd, who were building a new factory on the adjoining site. It was known that one of the barns, a brick and slate building, contained some 'old beams' believed to be of some interest, which the Hyde Corporation, the former owners of the site, wished to see preserved, though not necessarily in their original position.

The then chairman of the firm, Sir George Kenyon, called in a local historian, Dr Marsden, of Manchester University, who made a full inspection of the building and found that it had originated as a fourteenth-century timber-framed building, of cruck construction, its framing concealed and partly replaced by brickwork. Although it had been used as a barn for centuries, it is believed to have been a house, consisting of a single open hall, belonging to the de Newton family, who had owned the land in the medieval period. The building had not been included in the original statutory list of buildings of special architectural or historic interest for the borough of Hyde, but it was spot-listed in 1969, and described as 'cruck frame building formerly part of Newton Hall'.

Having realised and appreciated the interest of the building, the owners decided to preserve it. This necessitated complete reconstruction, and the replacement of much material, but enough of the original framing had survived to enable an accurate reconstruction to be made. The framing of the west wall had disappeared completely

Interior view as reconstructed, showing cruck truss and inserted fireplace.

Newton Hall, Hyde, Greater Manchester

Re-thatching of the Hall in progress

and has not been replaced, and neither has that of the north gable. In the south gable, sufficient of the framing had survived to justify reconstruction, but new cruck blades had to be formed, and the difficulty in finding timbers of sufficient size to cut these illustrates the limitations of this form of construction, and the restraints it imposes on the span and height of the building, as compared with post and truss or box-frame construction, which eventually superseded cruck building.

In the reconstruction of Newton Hall care was taken to copy the original methods of framing, jointing, and indeed of rearing the crucks and the previously assembled wall frames, providing an interesting practical exercise, and throwing some light on the problems of the medieval builders, although in this case a crane was used to raise the cruck-framed south gable into position.

The building has been left as a large open hall, paved in stone, and lit by windows with diagonally set timber mullions (these would originally have been unglazed, and shuttered). A hearth, with stone jambs and plastered fire hood, has been constructed against the north gable wall. In order to provide more light in the hall, and to display some of the original framing to better advantage, a large glazed bay window has been constructed in the reconstructed east wall. This frankly modern feature does destroy the original profile of the building which, in spite of the care taken with the restoration, cannot be said to have retained much of the atmosphere of a medieval hall. It does, however, provide an excellent text-book example of the fourteenth-century timber-framed construction of the area, and demonstrates the scale and grandeur of the open halls of that period.

The Hall after reconstruction, showing the large inserted window.

218

8   Albion Street and Albion Place, Chester

These two parallel streets lie in the south-east corner of Chester, just within the medieval city walls. The area was developed, or redeveloped, as artisan housing in the second half of the nineteenth century. The houses are typical of their date and class, single-fronted and two rooms deep, some with rear extensions. The small rear gardens or yards of the houses on the south side of Albion Street and on the north side of Albion Place abut each other, providing no separate rear access to the houses, and parts of these yards have been built over with an assortment of additions and extensions. At the front, the houses are entered directly from the street.

The houses are built of red brick, with slate roofs, and have sash windows and panelled doors with plain fanlights. The terraces are given some additional character by the use of ornamental brickwork, around door and window openings, and in the form of horizontal string courses. The chimneys have terra-cotta pots of a decorative design.

A few of the houses are owner-occupied, but most are tenanted. The area is surrounded by land in commercial use, producing noise and traffic problems. Most of the houses lack basic amenities and are in need of repair, some having structural problems. They are not listed, and are not likely to be considered of listable standard by present criteria. They are, however, largely unaltered examples of their type. Until a few years ago, such houses, classified as unfit, would almost certainly have been recommended for clearance by the local authority. Indeed, in the excellent conservation report on Chester, prepared by Donald Insall in 1968 — a document which marked

ABOVE *Detail of front elevation of Albion Street houses. The left-hand house had had a modern door inserted before the start of the scheme.*

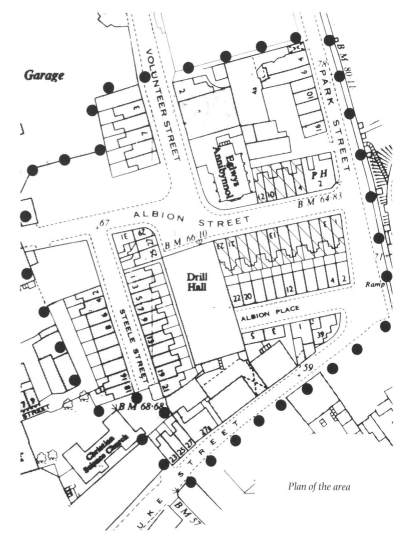

Plan of the area

View of the rear yards

the beginning of a serious approach to conservation in the city—it was suggested that the Albion Street area was suitable for redevelopment.

Since 1979, however, the city council has been turning away from the idea of wholesale clearance and redevelopment in favour of setting up housing action areas, to promote schemes of rehabilitation and environmental improvement in streets and areas of this type. The Albion Street houses had been included in a clearance area, but were removed from this when the housing action area was set up. It is interesting to note that in the first housing action area to be implemented, in another part of the city, it was found that clearance and redevelopment would have cost about 60 per cent more than the adopted scheme of rehabilitation.

The setting up of the housing action area meant that improvement and repair grants could be made available under the Housing Acts, for owners of individual buildings, and that in addition, environmental grants could be given for certain external works, to improve the amenities of the area. Loans could also be offered to help owners meet the balance of the costs, and mortgages offered to help sitting tenants buy their houses if they so wished.

These housing action areas are now being set up in many towns and cities, often in areas of nineteenth-century terraced housing. What makes the Albion Street scheme of particular interest is the concern of the city council for the architectural aspect of the work. In many areas where improvements have been grant-aided, the living conditions have been improved with little regard for the visual consequences. Sash windows have been replaced by single-pane, louvred, or various types of aluminium or plastic frames. Panelled doors have given way to various modern or pseudo-'period' designs. Natural slate roofs have been replaced by concrete tiles of varying colours and

Houses in Albion Place

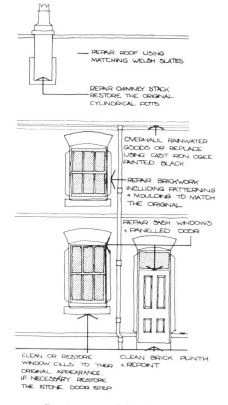

REPAIR ROOF USING
MATCHING WELSH SLATES.

REPAIR CHIMNEY STACK
RESTORE THE ORIGINAL
CYLINDRICAL POTS

OVERHAUL RAINWATER
GOODS OR REPLACE
USING CAST IRON OGEE
PAINTED BLACK.

REPAIR BRICKWORK
INCLUDING PATTERNING
+ MOULDING TO MATCH
THE ORIGINAL.

REPAIR SASH WINDOWS
+ PANELLED DOOR

CLEAN OR RESTORE
WINDOW CILLS TO THEIR
ORIGINAL APPEARANCE.
IF NECESSARY RESTORE
THE STONE DOOR STEP

CLEAN BRICK PLINTH
+ REPOINT

Drawing prepared by the City Council showing required standards of repair.

Albion Street and Albion Place, Chester

styles, or, at best, by asbestos cement. Chimneys have been removed, and the external brick walls colourwashed, rendered, or stone-clad. With unlisted buildings, most if not all of this work is permitted development, not requiring planning permission, even in a conservation area. When grants are offered under the Housing Acts most local authorities do not lay down conditions regarding the architectural qualities of the work on unlisted buildings. In the case of the mandatory intermediate grants they would have no right to do so, and even in the case of discretionary grants, most councils would probably be unwilling to refuse a grant on these grounds.

Albion Street, however, lies within the important Chester City Conservation Area, and although some of its immediate surroundings are rather unprepossessing, it is clearly visible from the city walls, a popular walk and amenity area. The council therefore decided that the improvements to the houses must respect their architectural character. Three steps were taken to achieve this. First, the Department of the Environment were asked to make Section 10 grants available to help cover the additional costs involved in, for instance, repairing or replacing in replica the original doors and windows, rather than replacing them with standard components. Second, an 'Article 4' direction was made by the council, and confirmed by the Department of the Environment, bringing under planning control the alterations which would normally be permitted development. Third, a design guide was prepared by the council and circulated to the house owners, drawing their attention to the character of the houses and setting out in detail how the improvements and repairs should be carried out. Matters given particular attention were the use of natural slates in re-roofing, the retention of chimney stacks and pots, maintenance of the original door and window designs, maintenance of the original brickwork, including ornamental work, use of traditional pattern cast iron for rainwater goods, and the design of any new rear extensions. Work is now in hand, and is helping to give the owners a new appreciation of, and sense of pride in their houses.

In some cases, alterations had already been carried out before the scheme started, and a few unsuitable doors and windows have appeared, as well as unsatisfactory rear extensions. The council has no power to insist on their removal, but it is hoped in the end to achieve this by persuasion, and the offer of grants.

This scheme is of particular interest in that it demonstrates how, given the will, a council can secure the preservation and enhancement of unlisted buildings where they have sufficient character to merit this, and particularly if they are in a conservation area. Even where, as in Chester, the historic buildings lists have been revised fairly recently, there are still many nineteenth century streets, terraces and squares which are not accepted as listable by the Department of the Environment, but which are important in the townscape. All too often these are spoilt by well-meant but insensitive 'improvements', and their value is only just beginning to be appreciated.

222

9   45–67, Cherville Street, Romsey, Hants

One of the most common threats to old buildings in town centres arises from local authority road schemes. A new road is planned, or it is decided to widen an existing one, often many years before the work can be put in hand. As properties on the 'reserved' line come on to the market they are acquired by the council and often little or no maintenance is carried out on them. If the buildings are left empty they will probably be vandalised, and in order to prevent danger to the public and possible insurance claims it is usual for the doors and windows to be boarded up, creating conditions favouring fungus and beetle attack. If the road scheme eventually goes ahead the buildings will be demolished, but if, as sometimes happens, there is a change of plan and the scheme is abandoned—perhaps for political or financial reasons—the buildings, no longer required, are generally offered for sale on the open market. Unfortunately, by this time they will probably be in far worse condition than when the council acquired them, and they may still be demolished!

This is a depressingly familiar story, and it could well have been the fate of an informal terrace of houses in Romsey, Nos. 45 to 67 Cherville Street. These are mainly of eighteenth-century date, although No. 55 includes the core of an earlier timber-framed building. The terrace was not complete, a gap site between Nos. 51 and 55 had resulted from an earlier demolition. The whole terrace had been blighted by a road scheme for about twenty years. The houses had few modern amenities, and were falling into disrepair, as the various owners had little incentive to maintain them. As they fell vacant they were gradually acquired by the Romsey Borough (later the district) council, the last private owner moving out in 1975. In the meantime, however, the road scheme had been made obsolete

Nos. 45-67, Cherville St. Romsey. Main elevation before renovation.

65 63 61 59 57 55

Parking area

New infil building

67

59 & 61

65 63 57 55 passage 53 51 49 47 45

Cherville Street

Scale 1:500

Key plan, showing the new infil building

as a result of a new Town Plan in 1968, and in 1972 the whole terrace had been listed Grade II, by the Department of the Environment, following the resurvey of the Borough.

Having acquired all the houses, the district council considered that they were not worth repairing, and proposed to demolish and replace them with new council housing. Their listed building application for demolition was, however, strongly opposed by the Hampshire County Council, and by the Romsey and District Preservation Trust, and it

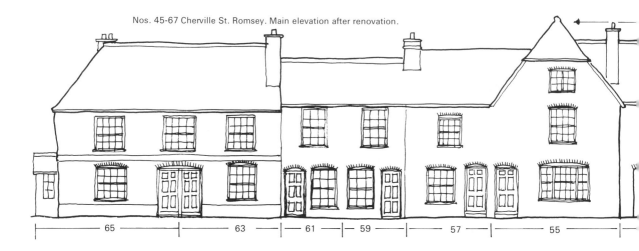

Nos. 45-67 Cherville St. Romsey. Main elevation after renovation.

65 63 61 59 57 55

Rear view of new infil building

was 'called in' for a public inquiry in 1976. At the inquiry the Trust, with the backing of the Hampshire Buildings Preservation Trust, offered to buy and renovate the houses, and produced plans prepared to show how this could be done. Consent for demolition was refused by the Secretary of State, and after two more years of negotiations, during which the houses stood empty, the district council eventually agreed to sell them to the Trust. Since a higher offer for the houses had been made by a private developer, it was necessary for the council to obtain the sanction of the Department of the Environment to sell at the lower figure. Purchase was completed in 1978, and the work of repair started the following year under a Southampton architect, Mr J. Trowbridge.

Substantial repairs were necessary, including stripping and re-tiling the roofs, repairing and partially rebuilding the walls, and renewal of much of the joinery. The ground floor of No. 47 had in the past been turned into a shop. This was restored to domestic use, with a new door and windows similar to those in the adjoining houses. Apart from this, and the replacement of a few later windows, external alterations were kept to a minimum, particularly at the front. At the rear some later additions were removed. Internally, a considerable amount of replanning has taken place, to provide modern amenities and produce more viable units. Nos. 59 and 61, two very small

ilding

45–67 Cherville Street, Romsey, Hants

houses which needed partial rebuilding, have been combined to form one house.

It was decided to insert a new building, with flats on the ground and first floors to fill the gap site, incorporating an arched opening on the ground floor, giving access to the back of the site. This building has been designed to blend with the rest of the terrace, but has been set back slightly from the main building line.

Grants for the work were obtained from the Department of the Environment under Section 10 of the Town and Country Planning (Amendment) Act, 1972, from the Hampshire County Council under the Historic Buildings Acts, and from the district council under the Housing Acts. The Romsey Conservation Area was in fact extended in order to enable the scheme to qualify for the Section 10 grants. At first, work proceeded on the houses in groups of four at a time, but it was then decided to reduce the amount of capital tied up at any one time by repairing the houses and selling them singly. In 1983 work was in its final stages.

Since the Trust operates on a 'revolving fund' basis the houses have been sold on completion of the repairs. This enables a Trust to recover its costs, but it is not without its problems. In spite of covenants designed to control future alterations one of the first houses in the terrace to be completed and sold subsequently acquired mock-Georgian UPVC windows! The Trust has secured the replacement of these with timber sashes matching those which were illegally removed, and is initiating an improved public relations scheme with all the owners to avoid a repetition of this occurrence.

This scheme illustrates the value of a preservation trust in a historic town, particularly when it receives local authority backing. It would have been far more difficult to carry out a scheme of this kind had all the houses been individually owned and occupied.

ABOVE *Part of the terrace before repair, showing the gap site adjoining No 55 and* RIGHT *Nos 57–65 showing repairs in progress.*

Epilogue: The Barchester Inquiry

Grantly Terrace, Hogglestock Road, Barchester, was built in the early nineteenth century, on the outskirts of the old city. It consists of ten superior artisan cottages, still in the Georgian tradition, and designed as a symmetrical composition. At the rear of the terrace is a triangular area of waste ground, the site of an old railway siding and workshops, which was bought by the Barchester City Council some years ago, when the railway closed down, with the aim of using it as a car park. The only access to this site at present is a pedestrian way adjoining the old railway line, entered from Puddingdale Lane, a narrow cul-de-sac, lined with small shops. Even if properties here could be acquired, Puddingdale Lane is not considered to be suitable for access to the car park by the Highway Authority, Barsetshire County Council. The only access considered suitable would be from Hogglestock Road, but this would involve the demolition of part of Grantly Terrace, destroying the symmetry of the design.

Until recently, Grantly Terrace had belonged to an elderly lady, a Miss Thorne, the last representative of the family who had owned it for several generations. The cottages had been let at low rents to long-standing tenants, and although some maintenance work had been carried out, there had been few improvements. Miss Thorne had not applied for improvement grants, being reluctant to get involved with the council or disturb the tenants, and the council had not pressed for action on this, since they were hoping eventually to acquire and demolish the cottages, which were not listed, and were considered to be sub standard. On Miss Thorne's death, the terrace was put up for sale by her heir, a distant relative. Because of financial restraints, the city council were unable to buy, and Grantly Terrace was bought by a development company who had discussed with the council officers a scheme for redeveloping the site for shops and offices, and incorporating a multi-storey car park. This scheme was encouraged by the council officers, and the company completed purchase on the understanding that it was likely to receive planning permission. After the purchase a few of the cottages fell vacant and were left empty, encouraging vandalism, and the whole terrace began to take on a run-down appearance.

Epilogue: The Barchester Inquiry

At this stage the newly formed Barchester Civic Society began to be anxious, believing that Grantly Terrace was of some architectural merit. Letters to the development company asking about their proposals met with no satisfactory reply, and when the Society approached the city council they were told that no decision had been taken. This was strictly true; the matter had not been placed before any council committee, and both the council officers and the developers were anxious to avoid publicity at that stage. The Civic Society, concerned at the continuing deterioration of the cottages, then approached the conservation officer of Barsetshire County Council, who, they knew, was carrying out a re-survey of the city on behalf of the Department of the Environment in connection with the revision of the list of buildings of special architectural or historic interest. Since his recommendations had to be confidential at that stage he could tell them nothing about Grantly Terrace, but he did remind them that they, or anyone else, could ask the Department of the Environment to consider listing buidings which appeared to be of merit, and were under threat. The Society approached the Department, informing them of the situation, with the result that an inspector was sent to the city, and Grantly Terrace was spot-listed.

In view of this development, the city council officers advised the development company to submit a listed building application for the demolition of the terrace, with a planning application for the new development of the whole site, including the car park. When these proposals were advertised the Civic Society formally objected to them, and further representations were received from two national amenity societies, from the Barsetshire Historic Buildings Trust, and from a number of local residents. As a result, the applications were 'called in' for public inquiry by the Secretary of State for the Environment.

The Inquiry

The Inquiry was held at the Barchester City Hall, and was taken by an inspector from the Department of the Environment. The developers, who stood to lose financially if consent was refused, had briefed Counsel to appear for them. The city council were represented by their Chief Executive, while the Civic Society were represented by one of their members, a local solicitor who was giving his services free. It was agreed that he should also represent the national amenity societies. At the request of the Civic Society, the Barsetshire Conservation Officer attended, although it was made clear that he was not representing the county council. The Barsetshire County Surveyor was, however, called by the city council, since his advice on the car park access, a county council matter, as Highway Authority, was an important aspect of the application. Those individuals who had submitted representations on the applications were invited to attend and give evidence if they wished, and in addition the local press and several other members of the public were in attendance.

The case for demolition

After the Inspector had taken the names of all those present, he invited Counsel for the applicants to open their case. He recounted the history of the application at some length, emphasising the problem that had been created by the spot-listing of the terrace. 'My clients had gone to considerable trouble to co-operate with the city council, and to comply with their requirements. They consider it most unfair that this listing should have been carried out without consultation with them or the council, and whatever the outcome of this Inquiry they will suffer financial loss due to delays in starting the work.' He then called as witness the architect for the scheme, and in his initial questioning elucidated the fact that the architect had carried out two similar projects for the company. Asked by Counsel for his opinion on Grantly Terrace and the desirability of its preservation, the architect replied that in his opinion the cottages were of mediocre design and construction, had suffered from lack of maintenance for many years and that their repair and improvement would be extremely costly, quite uneconomic in terms of any rent they might produce.

Invited by the Inspector to cross-examine, the solicitor for the Civic Society asked whether the architect had had any experience in the repair and improvement of cottages of this type. 'I have prepared specifications for the work needed to these cottages, and they were priced by a quantity surveyor; his figures, which are available, proved to my satisfaction that this would not be an economic exercise.' 'But have you actually carried out any similar schemes yourself?' 'Not on properties as sub-standard as these.' 'Did you consider asking for a second opinion, from one of the national amenity societies specialising in this type of work?' 'I did not consider it to be necessary.' Counsel for the applicants (re-examining): 'Did you consider that the specification you prepared and the prices obtained provided a realistic assessment of the work necessary to preserve these cottages?' 'Yes, I have every confidence in those figures.' 'Thank you, that concludes my client's case.'

The Inspector then invited the city council to put their case, and the Chief Executive began. He explained how the council had bought the land at the rear of Grantly Terrace after the railway closed, with a view to turning it into a car park when the opportunity arose. In the opinion of his council, particularly of their technical officers, Grantly Terrace was sub-standard and due for demolition. No move had been made in Miss Thorne's lifetime, as she was a respected local resident and a kindly if somewhat inefficient landlord. Financial constraints had prevented the council from buying the terrace themselves when it was offered for sale, but the developers had been fully prepared to co-operate with the council over the redevelopment of the site. Plans had been well advanced, although no planning application had been submitted, when the terrace was spot-listed. This had put the council into a difficult position. It fully appreciated its responsibility to secure the preservation of historic buildings as far as possible, but in the opinion of the council these cottages were not of sufficient merit to justify the abandonment or substantial modification of a scheme which they considered to be for the benefit of the city as a whole. 'My council would strongly refute any suggestion that they do not care about their historic buildings. All applications for listed building consent are given careful consideration—ample proof of that is provided by the favourable comments of visitors to Barchester on the way the city and its old buildings are maintained.' For his first witness the Chief Executive called the City Planning Officer, who confirmed the Chief Executive's account of the purchase of the railway land, and the negotiations with the developers about the redevelopment of the site. 'Although Grantly Terrace is of some architectural interest I consider that it is not outstanding, and its retention not justified in the present circumstances. Repairs and improvements would be costly, and the council's limited resources for conservation work had to be concentrated on the historic core of the city.'

Cross-examining for the objectors, the Civic Society solicitor asked, 'You have said that Grantly Terrace is not worthy of preservation. Is it not true that a terrace of very similar design in another part of the city is illustrated on page 10 of the city guide book recently published by your council, as an example of the Regency period expansion of the city?' 'The terrace illustrated has been well maintained, and is in far better condition than Grantly Terrace.' 'But the design is very similar—they were probably by the same builder?' 'Probably, yes.'

As his next witness the Chief Executive called the council's Environmental Health Officer. He described the condition of the cottages, their lack of modern amenities and dilapidated condition. Several of the cottages were now empty and the council, having declared the terrace unfit, were in the process of re-housing the remaining tenants, although a few of them were not anxious to leave. Invited to cross-examine, the Civic Society solicitor asked whether the late owner had been approached by the council with a view to improving the cottages with the aid of grants. 'Miss Thorne knew about the availability of grants, but did not wish to apply for them.' 'Would it be fair to say that, although Miss Thorne knew about grants, no great effort was made by the council to persuade her to take advantage of them because it was the ultimate aim of the council to demolish the terrace?' 'I think that is a fair comment, although if Miss Thorne had applied for grants the matter would have been carefully considered.' 'You have spoken of the dilapidated state of the cottages today, and I do not think anyone would disagree with this. Do you agree that their condition has deteriorated sharply since they were bought by the applicants and left empty as they fell vacant?' 'There has been trouble from vandalism. I understand that it was necessary to board up the doors and windows of the empty cottages to keep out squatters.'

Re-examining, the Chief Executive asked, 'Is it fair to say that most of the tenants were elderly people who did not want to be disturbed, and that this may have been the reason for Miss Thorne's failure to carry out improvements?' 'That was certainly my opinion.'

For his next witness the Chief Executive called the Barsetshire County Surveyor. 'Quite apart from the proposed redevelopment of the site, do you consider that a satisfactory access to the car park could be formed without demolishing a considerable part of Grantly Terrace?' 'No.' 'Do you consider that a satisfactory access could be provided off Puddingdale Lane, assuming that the necessary land could be acquired?' 'No. Puddingdale Lane is a narrow cul-de-sac, terminating at the industrial site on part of the old railway land. It is already congested, particularly at the morning and evening rush hours, and any additional traffic turning in and out of the car park would create a dangerous situation.' 'Would you say that the only possible access to the car park would be from Hogglestock Road?' 'Yes, unless Puddingdale Lane could be widened, which is not a practical proposition in the foreseeable future.'

The Civic Society solicitor, cross-examining, 'Do you not consider it was rather improvident for the city council to buy land for a car park to which there was no access apart from a footpath?' 'If the council had not bought the land at that time they would probably have had no other opportunity to do so. A car park is needed in the area, and there was no prospect of any other suitable land becoming available.'

The case for preservation

At the conclusion of the city council's case, the Civic Society solicitor was invited to put the case for the objectors. He began straight away by calling on the Secretary of the Barchester Civic Society to explain the Society's position. He began by giving a brief description of the development of the city, from an early medieval market town, its prosperity in the later middle ages as a cathedral city, a period of semi-stagnation following the Reformation and the Civil War, and a further period of growth in the later eighteenth and early nineteenth centuries. It was to this period that Grantly Terrace belonged, one of a number of modest but attractive developments on the outskirts of the old city, several of which had been demolished in recent years. It was for this reason that the Society considered that Grantly Terrace should be preserved. Hogglestock Road was probably the most attractive road into the city. Proceeding along it from the country to the south you passed first a series of detached Victorian and Edwardian villas, standing in their own grounds, then past terraces of smaller Victorian houses until you came to Puddingdale Lane, with its small shops. Immediately past this was Grantly Terrace, designed as a unit, with its slightly larger projecting houses at each end. Beyond this again was the site of the old level crossing, now part of the industrial area—an eyesore which would benefit from a suitable infil building—and past this you were in the old city with its medieval and Tudor buildings, some with Georgian façades. Grantly Terrace played an important part in the street. It was unfortunate that the similar terrace on the opposite side of Hogglestock Road had been demolished in the later nineteenth century, but at least the replacement houses were similar in scale, and not unattractive in design.

The Society had been concerned about Grantly Terrace for some time, even before Miss Thorne's death. It was obvious that the low rents of the houses did not allow for more than minimum maintenance. The Society had indeed suggested to Miss Thorne that she might be able to improve the cottages, and had offered to help her prepare a scheme, but she had been reluctant to do this, and most of the tenants seemed quite happy to go on living in the houses as they were. Miss Thorne's death and the sale of the terrace made the Society realise that it could be in danger. Grantly Terrace was not listed, and the Barchester Conservation Area included only the medieval core of the city. The Society had several times asked the council to extend the conservation area to include the Regency developments, but without success.

Approaches to the developers and to the city council about the future of the terrace had produced no satisfactory reply, and for this reason the Society had asked the Department of the Environment if it could be listed. They fully appreciated the problems this had created for the developers and for the city council, but in the circumstances they felt they had no alternative but to take this action, and that the council at least should have been aware of the value of the houses. The Society were convinced that, given the will, Grantly Terrace could be saved and the houses reconditioned without loss of character. The opportunity to create a car park, however desirable, should not be considered sufficient justification for the demolition of these buildings.

Cross-examining for the applicants, Counsel asked 'You have described the approach to Barchester along Hogglestock Road, and it would appear that it contains buildings of various dates and styles; is this correct?' 'Yes, the later buildings are on the outskirts of the city, and the earlier ones near the centre.' 'Do you agree that this mixture of styles and dates in its buildings contributes to the character of Barchester?' 'Yes.' 'Do you not feel then that there is a place for modern buildings, that they too can add to the character of the city?' 'Good modern buildings in the right place, yes, but it should not be necessary to destroy good older buildings to make way for them.' 'But, surely, this is what happened in the past. Barchester, we understand, was founded in the thirteenth century when the cathedral was built, but even in the historic centre we find buildings of many different dates—indeed the cathedral itself has been altered and enlarged many times during its history, do you not agree?' 'Yes, that is true, and some of these changes are to be regretted. The important thing though is that the rate of change is so much greater now; in many historic towns the whole centre has been rebuilt in recent years. We are beginning to appreciate the need for a more careful approach.' 'But you do agree that there can be a place for modern building in an old town?' 'In the right place, and the right circumstances, yes, but we do not consider that the case for demolishing Grantly Terrace has been proved.'

The next witness called by the objectors was the Barsetshire County Council Conservation Officer. It was made clear to the Inspector that he was present with the permission of the county council, but that he was not appearing on behalf of that council. The only reason for his attendance was that he had been involved indirectly in the listing of Grantly Terrace. He would be speaking solely on the architectural and historic interest of the terrace, and not commenting on the applicants' scheme, the determination of which was the responsibility of the city, not the county council, who were only involved with the highway aspect of the proposals. 'I understand that you have been carrying out a re-survey of Barchester on behalf of the Department of the Environment, in connection with the revision of the statutory list of buildings of special architectural or historic interest?' 'That is true.' 'Is it also true that in selecting buildings for listing you have to be guided entirely by criteria laid down by the Department, and cannot take into consideration any other matters such as the condition of the buildings or any proposals for their demolition?' 'That is also true.' 'Did you consider that Grantly Terrace met the criteria for listing?' 'I did, yes, and that view has now been confirmed by the Department of the Environment.' 'If buildings are considered worthy of listing, does that mean that they are worthy of preservation?' 'In the words of the Department of the Environment's own circular, "They merit every effort being made for their preservation"'. 'I realise that you cannot comment on the redevelopment scheme as such, but do you consider that every effort should be made to preserve Grantly Terrace?' 'Yes, I do.'

Counsel for the applicants, cross-examining, asked, 'You have said that Grantly Terrace merits every effort being made to preserve it. Is it true that, a few years ago, the Barsetshire County Council demolished a very similar terrace to enlarge a school site?' 'Yes, they did.' 'Did the Barchester Civic Society try to get that terrace listed?' 'I understand that the Society had not then been formed.' 'That was very fortunate for the County Council.' Re-examining, the Civic Society solicitor asked, 'At the time the County Council demolished the terrace referred to, were you employed by them?' 'No.' 'If you had been, and had been consulted, what advice would you have given?' 'The terrace had been demolished before I came to Barchester, but if it was similar to Grantly Terrace, I would probably have recommended its retention.'

The next witness for the objectors was a well-known architect specialising in historic building repairs, who had been asked by the two national amenity societies to report on the application. In his initial questioning, the Civic Society solicitor elicited that this architect had had considerable experience in repairing buildings of the late eighteenth and early nineteenth centuries, and that he had won three national awards for schemes of this kind. 'Have you inspected the houses in Grantly Terrace?' 'Yes, with the permission of the owners I was able to gain access to all the houses.' 'We all know that they need a considerable amount of repair, but do you consider that this is feasible, and could be carried out economically?' 'Yes, provided that improvement grants were made available; these can be increased above the normal level for listed buildings.' 'The houses are modest in scale; do you consider that, architecturally, they would justify this expenditure on their preservation?' 'Yes, although modest as you say, they are good examples of their type. As we have heard, Barchester has lost other similar buildings. In my view the great merit of Grantly Terrace is that it is largely unaltered. The windows all retain their glazing bars, the original panelled doors and fanlights survive, even the interiors are largely unaltered, retaining their original joinery, fireplaces, staircases, etc. It is rarely that one finds so much original work intact.'

Cross examining, Counsel for the applicants: 'We all acknowledge your experience in this field, but do you not consider that there are more important buildings in Barchester in need of repair, and that any funds available should be concentrated on these, rather than on what you agree is a "modest" terrace on the outskirts of the city?' 'I think we have to consider each case as it arises. I do not know of any more "important" building in the city which is at present under threat.' 'You have said that Grantly Terrace is largely unaltered. Is this not simply because so little has been done in the way of repairs and improvements for many years?' 'That is probably true. All too often improvements to old houses are not carried out sympathetically and result in the loss of original features, particularly in the interiors.' 'Do you not agree that, even if they are repaired at considerable expense, these cottages would still provide sub-standard accommodation, that it would be difficult if not impossible to bring them up to modern standards without destroying the "unaltered" character by which you set so much store?' 'No, not if the work is sympathetically carried out; it has been proved that there is a great demand for small houses of this type within easy reach of a city centre.' 'But, if the work is carried out in a way of which you would approve, would you agree that the people who would live in them, who could indeed afford them, would be of a very different class from the present occupants?' 'That may well be so.' 'Thank you.'

The next witness was the secretary of the Barsetshire Historic Buildings Trust. The Trust had just completed a scheme, which had won a national award, for the repair and conversion to flats of the former vicarage at Plumstead Episcopi. This scheme had presented many of the problems which would be met in Grantly Terrace, lack of maintenance over a long period, rising damp, dry rot attack and defective roofs. The flats had now been sold on long leases, making a modest profit for the Trust, and they were anxious to proceed with a further scheme. They would be very interested in taking on Grantly Terrace, and hoped they would be able to buy it by agreement, at a figure reflecting the present condition of the cottages, or, if the city council were to serve a repairs notice, followed by compulsory purchase, the Trust would be willing to take the terrace for the price paid by the council, which would presumably be fixed by the district valuer. The Trust would also be prepared to buy the council-owned land at the rear of the houses, at the original purchase price and to keep it, either as public open space, or as allotments, for which there was some local demand.

Other representations

The Inspector now invited members of the public who had sent in representations to speak if they wished. The first to do so was the Secretary of the Barsetshire Branch of the Royal Institute of British Architects. His branch had considered the scheme, and while they would not necessarily oppose the demolition of Grantly Terrace, provided that it was replaced by a building of quality, they wished to raise strong objections to the proposed redevelopment, which they considered to be insensitive and out of scale with its surroundings. 'The building is quite unrelated to its setting; it appears to have been designed solely to make the most profitable use of the site, regardless of the aesthetic consequences. The site is one of great importance at the approach to the city centre, and we consider that the council should hold an architectural competition, with an assessor appointed by the President of the Royal Institute of British Architects. Much of the recent development in Barchester has been mediocre, quite unworthy of its setting. Here is an opportunity to provide a fine building, and the council should accept the challenge.'

Next came the secretary of a local Residents' Association, who produced a petition with five hundred signatures protesting about the proposed use of the site. 'Barchester has enough shops and offices, several are standing empty. What is urgently needed is more public open space. We would prefer to see Grantly Terrace repaired, with the old railway land at the back laid out as an open space, with access from the footpath in Puddingdale Lane. If the cottages cannot be kept their sites should be added to the open space. The industrial site to the rear should be screened by tree planting. This would be a real asset to the city.'

The next speaker was a city councillor who emphasised that he was speaking in a personal capacity, as a long-standing resident. 'I have lived in Barchester all my life, and I know Grantly Terrace well. It is no better than a slum, and should be pulled down. It is nonsense listing buildings like these. I would not support spending any public money on them. Barchester cannot go on living in the past; it must move with the times!'

Finally, one of the Grantly Terrace tenants, who had lived there most of her life. 'We were happy there, Miss Thorne took an interest in us. It is different now: these new people don't care about us; they just want us out so they can pull the place down. The empty cottages are getting into a dreadful state, full of rats. I suppose we shall all have to go and live in council houses, but it's all wrong!'

Summing up

Summing up for the objectors, the Civic Society solicitor again stressed the importance of Grantly Terrace in its setting, and the concern that had been voiced by the national amenity societies over its threatened demolition. He reminded the Inspector of its particular value as an unspoiled example of its period, of the noted architect's opinion that repair and improvements were feasible, and, above all, that the Barsetshire Historic Buildings Trust were willing to acquire and renovate it. If the council were prepared to purchase the cottages they need suffer no financial loss, since the Trust were also willing to buy the land at the rear at the original price. The demolition of Grantly Terrace would not only be most regrettable, but unnecessary. Repaired by the Trust, to the high standards for which it was known, Grantly Terrace would be a credit to Barchester. He hoped very much that consent for the demolition would be refused.

Summing up for the council, the Chief Executive said he wanted to refer to certain statements made by the objectors and others. The question of extending the Barchester Conservation Area had been raised. The council had considered this, but had felt that the historic centre of the city was of such outstanding importance that it would be devalued by including the outer areas. By keeping the Conservation Area relatively small, the council could concentrate their attention on it, ensuring a high standard of development control, and offering financial aid in appropriate cases.

The local branch of the Royal Institute of British Architects had suggested holding an architectural competition for the redevelopment of the Grantly Terrace site. This was not, however, a practical possibility, as the council did not own the whole site, and a scheme could only be produced in co-operation with the developers, who wished to use their own architect. The suggested use of the site as a public open space might appear attractive, but would produce no financial return on the cost of purchase. In the present financial situation this was quite impossible to consider, and, in any case, the council considered that the car park was needed.

The council had every respect for the work of the Barsetshire Historic Buildings Trust. The conversion of the old vicarage at Plumstead Episcopi had received encouragement and financial aid from the council. The suggestion, however, that the council should acquire

Grantly Terrace by compulsory purchase and sell it to the Trust, with the land at the rear, would have to be considered by the council members. In view of their support for the developers' scheme he did not want to predict their reaction to this suggestion. In any case, this solution would not provide a car park. While appreciating the motives of the Trust and of the other objectors, he considered that the application should be approved.

Summing up for the applicants, Counsel also paid tribute to the work of the Trust, but thought that it was unfortunate that it should have tried to intervene in this case. 'In view of the support my clients have all along received from the council, it would be a most serious breach of faith if the council were now to consider serving a repairs notice in respect of Grantly Terrace, and to proceed with compulsory purchase if the notice was not complied with.' Commenting on the evidence of the objectors, he agreed that the cottages could be repaired, but the cost would be high, out of all proportion to the architectural value of the buildings. He regretted the criticism of his clients' scheme by the local branch of the Royal Institute of British Architects, pointing out that it had been prepared by a competent architect, and approved by the council's Planning Committee. He considered that the listing of this rather ordinary terrace had been most unfortunate, and had already cost his clients a considerable sum. In spite of this, they were still anxious to proceed with the scheme, and he hoped that consent would be granted with a minimum of delay.

The site inspection

Thanking all those who had attended, the Inspector closed the Inquiry, and proceeded to inspect the site, with a representative from the applicants, from the council, and from the objectors. The picture was depressingly familiar; a simple but attractive terrace which, not so long before, had been reasonably well maintained and fully occupied. Now nearly half the houses were empty, some boarded up, some with broken windows, and the walls covered with graffiti. Those houses still occupied were run down in appearance and the whole terrace bore the 'ripe for development' stamp. However, the Inspector was used to seeing buildings in this state, as he was to hearing evidence of the kind submitted earlier in the day. He could tell that the basic structure was sound and that in the right circumstances Grantly Terrace could live again. The question was: could these circumstances arise? If the Secretary of State decided to allow the demolition, and redevelopment, that would be the end of the story. If, however, he were to refuse consent, it would only be the end of a chapter. The developers might do nothing for a time, leaving the houses to deteriorate, trusting that the council would take no action, and, eventually, submit another application with evidence that the houses were now beyond repair. The council might even be forced to declare the houses unsafe. If, as a result of continued neglect, a serious outbreak of dry rot were to occur (assisted perhaps by the removal of some roof slates), even the Barsetshire Historic Buildings Trust might be discouraged from taking over the terrace. Alternatively, the developers might put the terrace up for sale at a price high enough to cover not only the original purchase price but the cost of their, so far, abortive work. This could also discourage the Trust. The terrace might be bought by another developer, and the whole process repeated, the cottages continuing to deteriorate. Alternatively, if no purchaser could be found willing to pay their price, the developers might submit a further application, stating in support that they had tried without success to sell the cottages. Without the goodwill of the council, the chances of Grantly Terrace being saved looked bleak.

On the other hand, the council's attitude might change in the face of strong public opinion, particularly if an election were imminent. Building preservation is not normally a party political issue, but in local politics a case like this, possibly taken up in the press, could become an election issue. As the Inspector drove away from Barchester all these things must have been passing through his mind, and we must leave him to write his report.

Appendix 1: Fire precautions for thatched properties

Whilst there are many thousands of thatched properties in the British Isles, very few are damaged or destroyed by fire. However, since such buildings are very often several miles from a fire station it is inevitable that there will be some delay in appliances reaching the scene. Adequate supplies of water to enable the firemen to fight the fire with all speed is vital. It is essential that firemen have easy access to the roof space and that they have adequate room in which to work.

The following will affect the outcome of any fire:

> Time taken to discover it.
> Time taken to call the fire service and for the firemen to arrive.
> Accessibility for fire appliances and men.
> Adequate supply of water.

Electric cables Where the supply cables for electricity are above the ceiling joists and under the rafters in the loft they should comply with BS 6207 Part 1 'Wiring system using Mineral Insulated Cables', or alternatively BS 31 or BS 4568 Parts 1 and 2 'Wiring system using PVC Insulated Cables enclosed in a conduit'.

If the thatched roof is covered with protective wire netting this must not come within 12 inches (300 mm) of an electric cable unless adequate insulation is provided.

Electric fittings Electric light fittings in the roof space should be enclosed in a bulkhead or well-glass fitting.

Television aerials Television aerials should not pass over or under the thatch. Aerials should be fittcd to a free-standing pole at least 20 feet 7m) from the roof. Where this is not possible, aerials can be fixed to a gable end chimney and the lead taken down the wall, avoiding any contact with the thatch.

Draughts Close all gaps from inside the loft, at eaves, wall plate, gable ends and chimneys with a cement/lime/sand fillet mix in the proportion of one of cement, two of lime and four of sand by volume. Make the trapdoor to the loft as airtight as possible.

Appendix 1 : Fire precautions for thatched properties

Open fires and chimneys The height of the chimneys should conform to local council recommendations. Avoid fuels which emit sparks and those which make a lot of soot. Log wood should not be used. Chimneys must be swept regularly. Chimney breasts and flues should conform to the Building Regulations, particularly with regard to the proximity of combustible or conducting materials. As a general principle these materials should not be within 2 inches (50 mm) of a chimney breast. In the case of flue pipes the distances are much greater and expert advice should be sought.

Storage Do not store combustible materials in the roof space.

Smoking No naked lights or smoking should be permitted in the roof space.

Restricting the spread of fire All thatched roofs should have Masterboarding or Supalux insulation board attached as a fire retardant. The retardant board is fixed and made as airtight as possible by sealing all joints between it and the adjacent surfaces with good quality plaster. The sealing of the Masterboarding or Supalux insulation board lining, and the rendering at the edges of the thatched roof, must be maintained in good condition.

To ensure that the roof supports hold for the maximum amount of time in the event of fire, all timbers should be treated with fire-retardant paint or solution in accordance with the manufacturer's instructions.

Structural aid to fire fighting Ceilings beneath a thatched roof need to be sufficiently strong to support firemen and their equipment (approximately 500 lb (227 kg). A large roof would require appropriately greater support. Access to the roof should be from inside with a hatch of not less than 3×2 feet (900×600 mm) serving each space. The hatch should have a cover or doors which would resist fire for at least half an hour.

Should fire occur
Call the Fire Brigade immediately, give the precise address and nearest main thoroughfare or landmark and tell them that the property is thatched.

A garden hose connected to a water supply of sufficient pressure can be used to dampen the thatch if it is on fire externally and can be reached without endangering personal safety. An adequate length of non-kink hose permanently attached to an outside supply is a wise precaution.

If possible remove furniture from the upper floors, as this will help arrest the spread of fire.

Do nothing which will increase draught inside the roof space or the building. Keep all doors and hatches closed. *On no account remove thatch from the roof* as this will create an aperture through which draught will rush to fan the fire.

Fixing methods for wire-netting on thatch

Main roof Netting is laid vertically from ridge to eaves, with seams side by side and not overlapping, and using a metal hook designed for the purpose, the two edges are twisted together at 9 inch (228 mm) intervals.

Apex Netting is joined at the apex where it meets at the ridge centre.

Under eaves The netting is secured to the eaves timber with clenched 1.5 inch (approximately 40 mm) galvanised wire nails (not staples).

Gables Netting is carried round thatched gables or secured to gable boards or rafters with clenched 1.5 inch (approximately 40 mm) galvanised wire nails.

Hips/Valleys Netting is cut to fit and closely joined along the angle of hip or valley.

Windows Netting is secured to the window frame with clenched 1.5 inch (approximately 40 mm) galvanised wire nails.

Chimneys Fixing is made by plugging mortar joints in brickwork or stonework to enable the netting to be nailed to the stack. Finally, weak mortar fillet can be applied to the stack, which further secures the netting. Netting is secured under lead flashing.

Removal of wire netting

If the above recommendations are carried out, wire netting can be easily stripped from a thatched roof. First, pull the netting apart at the point where it is joined at the apex, the vertical seams are then separated by pulling each scction apart. Finally, the netting will be released by pulling it away from the nails at gables and under-eaves.

The Dorset Model

Dorset has a thatch heritage of particular value. There are well over 5000 thatched buildings in the county, about half of which are listed.

The Building Regulations have for many years enforced strict separation requirements on all new build. Local planning demands frequently fell foul of the regulations, so the thatching industry set about finding ways around the problem, but with limited success. Some authorities, particularly in Dorset, also considered the separation requirements were inappropriate because there was no evidence to show that the occupant's safety was being jeopardised.

A major initiative by all local authority building control across Dorset was unertaken to find an acceptable solution. This resulted in the 'Dorset Model' which represents an important step forward allowing more freedom to construct thatched buildings in a responsible way. National Building Regulations now make reference to the 'Dorset Model', and increasingly the main elements are incorporated in repair and renovation of existing old and listed buildings.

Details of the Dorset Model can be sourced from any Local Authority or www.dorset-technical-committee.org.uk

Appendix 2: List of useful organisations

Central Government organisations in Britain

DEPARTMENT OF CULTURE, MEDIA AND SPORT, 2-4 Cockspur Street, London SW1Y 5DH. 020 7211 6000. The Department issues the statutory Lists of Buildings of Special Architectural and Historic Interest, which are prepared on the advice of English Heritage. Requests for permission to alter or demolish listed buildings are determined by local planning authorities, and any resulting appeals by the Department of the Environment.

ENGLISH HERITAGE, 23 Savile Row, London W1X 2HA 020 7973 3000. English Heritage is the Government's statutory adviser on all aspects of the historic environment. In 1999 it was amalgamated with the Royal Commission on the Historical Monuments of England, which has to be given the opportunity to inspect and record any listed building in advance of its demolition.

HISTORIC SCOTLAND, Longmore House, Salisbury Place, Edinburgh EH9 1SH 0131 668 8600. CADW:WELSH HISTORIC MONUMENTS, Crown Building, Cathays Park, Cardiff CF1 3NQ. 02920 500200. DEPARTMENT OF THE ENVIRONMENT FOR NORTHERN IRELAND, Environment and Heritage Service, Commonwealth House, 35 Castle Street, Belfast BT1 1GU. 02890 251477. These bodies provide advice on the giving of financial assistance for the repair of historic buildings, including houses. Normally only Grade I and Grade II* buildings are eligible for assitance, but Grade II buildings may receive help under town schemes, or in Conservation Areas.

HERITAGE LOTTERY FUND, 7 Holbein Place, London SW1W 8NR. 020 7591 6000. The HLF operates through the National Heritage Memorial fund. It provides grants from the National Lottery which can include assistance with the restoration of historic buildings.

NATIONAL MONUMENTS RECORDS FOR ENGLAND, SCOTLAND AND WALES. The following hold large publically accessible databases and archives of the historic buildings (and archaeological sites) of their respective countries. England: National Monumnets Record Centre, Kemble Drive, Swindon, SN2 2GZ, 01793 414600. Scotland: John Sinclair House, 16 Bernard Terrace, Edinburgh, EDH8 9NX, 0131 662 1456. Wales: Cathays Park, Cardiff, CF10 3N, 02920 823819.

Voluntary organisations

ANCIENT MONUMENTS SOCIETY, St Ann's Vestry Hall, 2 Church Entry, London EC4V 5HB. 020 7236 3934. An organisation with similar aims and objectives to those of the Society for the Protection of Ancient Buildings (see below). Publishes annual transactions concerned with architectural history.

ARCHITECTS ACCREDITED IN BUILDING CONSERVATION REGISTER 33 Macclesfield Road, Wilmslow, Cheshire SK9 2AF. 01625 523784. Scheme of conservation accreditation for architects.

ARCHITECTURAL HERITAGE FUND, Clareville House, 26-27 Oxendon Street, London SW1Y 4EL. 020 7925 0199. Provides loans to building preservation trusts and guidance on sources of grant aid for repair of historic buildings.

BRITISH WATERWAYS, The Locks, Hillmorton, Rugby, Warwickshire CV21 4PP. 01788 566030

BRITISH WOOD-PRESERVING AND DAMP-PROOFING ASSOCIATION, 1 Gleneagles House, Vernon Gate, South Street, Derby DE1 1UP. 01332 225100. Produces code of conduct and training standards for member damp-proofing and timber treatment firms, and provides advice.

CHARITIES AID FOUNDATION, Kings Hill, West Malling, Kent ME19 4TA. 01732 520000. Publishes an annual *Directory of Grant-making Trusts*

CHARLESTOWN WORKSHIPS AT THE SCOTTISH LIME CENTRE, The School House, 4 Rocks Road, Charlestown, Fife, KY11 3EN. 01383 872722 Runs programmes of training courses in the use of lime.

CHURCHES CONSERVATION TRUST, 89 Fleet Street, London EC4Y 1DH 020 7936 2258. Holds and maintains, for the benefit of the nation and church, redundant churches of major architectural or historic interest.

CIVIC TRUST, 17 Carlton House Terrace, London SW1Y 5AW 020 7930 0914. Is concerned with all aspects of civic design. Advises and coordinates the work of affiliated local civic and amenity societies. Prepares and issues booklets, exhibitions and films. Has advised the Department of the Environment Regions and Transport on the drafting of conservation legislation. Gives awards for good design, including work on historic buildings.

COUNCIL FOR BRITISH ARCHAEOLOGY, Bowes Morrell House, 111 Walmgate, York YO1 2UA. 01904 671417. Acts as a link between local archaeological societies and the relevant government organisations, and provides information on all aspects of British archeaology.

COUNCIL FOR THE PROTECTION OF RURAL ENGLAND, Warwick House, 25 Buckingham Palace Road, London SW1W 0PP. 020 7976 6433, and COUNCIL FOR THE PROTECTION OF RURAL WALES, Ty Gwyn, 31 High Street, Welshpool, Powys SG21 7GD. 01938 552525 (Both have branches in all parts of the country.) Concerned with all aspects of the countryside, including rural housing.

CRAFTS COUNCIL, 44A Pentonville Road, London N1 9BY. 020 7806 2500. Maintains a register of craftsmen and suppliers of traditional building materials on a county basis.

Appendix 2: list of useful organisations

FRIENDS OF FRIENDLESS CHURCHES, St Ann's Vestry Hall, 2 Church Entry, London EC4V 5HB. 020 7236 3934. Campaigns to save redundant churches, and owns several.

GEORGIAN GROUP, 6 Fitzroy Square, London W1P 6DX. 020 7387 1720 Originally a sub-committee of the Society for the Protection of Ancient Builldings, now a separate body doing similar work in respect of Georgian buildings.

HISTORIC CHURCHES PRESERVATION TRUST, Fulham Place, London SW6 6EA. 020 7736 3054. Offers grants for repair to churches of all denominations.

HISTORIC HOUSES ASSOCIATION 2 Chester Street, London SW1X 7BB. 020 7259 5688. An association of owners of historic houses, with the aim of preserving such houses, gardens and parks.

INSTITUTE OF HISTORIC BUILDING CONSERVATION, Jubilee House, High Street, Tisbury, Wiltshire SP3 6HA. 01747 873133. Organisation for conservation professionals.

INSTITUTE OF HISTORIC BUILDING CONSERVATION (SCOTLAND), The Glasite Meeting House, 33 Barony Street, Edinburgh EH3 6NX. 0131 529 3919

LANDMARK TRUST, Shottesbrook, Maidenhead, Berkshire SL6 3SW. 01628 825920. Aims to save smaller historic buildings by acquiring and repairing them. Most of the Trust's properties are let as holiday accommodation.

LEAD SHEET ASSOCIATION, Hawkwell Business Centre, Maidstone Road, Pembury, Tunbridge Wells, Kent TN2 4AH. 01892 822773. Trade association providing advice and best-practice guidance notes on the use of lead sheet.

THE NATIONAL TRUST, 36 Queen Anne's Gate, London SW1H 9AS.
020 7222 9251 and
THE NATIONAL TRUST FOR SCOTLAND, 28 Charlotte Square, Edinburgh EH2 4DU. 0131 243 9300,
Own a large number of properties, mostly larger houses but including a number of smaller houses, particularly those with historic interest.

NEWCOMEN SOCIETY, Science Musueum, Exhibition Road, London SW7 2DD 020 7371 4445. May assist in the preservation of industrial monuments.

ROYAL INSTITUTION OF CHARTERED SURVEYORS, BUILDING CONSERVATION GROUP, 12 Great George Street, Parliament Square, London SW1P 3AD 020 7222 7000. The RICS runs a scheme of conservation accreditation for surveyors.

SAVE BRITAIN'S HERITAGE, 70 Cowcross Street, London EC1M 6EJ. 020 7253 3500. A pressure group campaigning against the neglect and needless loss of historic buildings. Compiles registers of buildings at risk.

SCOTTISH CONSERVATION BUREAU, Historic Scotland, Longmore House, Salisbury Place, Edinburgh EH9 1SH. 0131 668 8668. Provides advice to owners of listed buildings.

SOCIETY FOR THE PROTECTION OF ANCIENT BUILDINGS, 37 Spital Square, London E1 6DY. 020 7377 1644. Provides technical advice on repairs and alterations to historic buildings. Organises conferences and courses on this subject, and awards an annual scholarship. May adivse on sources of financial help. Issues lists of threatened buildings for sale or lease (to members only).

TWENTIETH CENTURY SOCIETY, 70 Cowcross Street, London EC1M 6EJ. 020 7250 3857. Campaigns for understanding and protection of twentieth century buildings.

VERNACULAR ARCHITECTURE GROUP, Asheigh, Willows Green, Great Leighs, Chelmsford Esex. 01245 361408. Promotes the study of smaller houses and cottages, as well as farm and early industrial buildings.

VICTORIAN SOCIETY, 1 Priory Gardens, Bedford Park, London W4 1TT. 020 8994 1019. Also originally a sub-committee of the Society for the Protection of Ancient Buildings, now a separate body doing similar work in respect of nineteenth and twentieth century buildings.

THE VIVAT TRUST, 61 Pall Mall, London SW1Y 5HZ. 020 7930 2212. Buys unusual buildings at risk and restores them for use as holiday accommodation.

WEALD AND DOWNLAND OPEN AIR MUSEUM, Singleton, Chichester, West Sussex PO18 0EU. 01243 811475. Runs regular courses and events about traditional construction.

In addition to the national organisations, local historical, civic and amenity societies may provide help and advice for owners of old buildings. Their addresses are usually available at the local public library. Local museums may also provide information.

The Lists of Buildings of Special Architectural and Historic Interest, compiled by the Department of the Environment, may be inspected at the county and district council offices.

Appendix 3: Glossary

Adze An early tool for finishing the surface of timber, pre-dating the plane. Use of the adze gives a characteristic slightly undulating face to the work.

Aisled hall A hall, the main living area of a house, divided into three (or occasionally two) aisles by arcades (lines of posts and arches supporting the roof). The arcades in houses are generally of timber, but are occasionally of stone, as in a church.

Almshouse A house, or a building divided into units, for the accommodation of elderly or poor people, generally provided by a religious or other charitable organisation, or by a private benefactor.

Apron A panel of raised brickwork under the sill of a window, typical of the early eighteenth century.

Architrave In Classical architecture, the lowest member of the entablature, immediately above the columns. In domestic building, the moulding covering the joint between a door or window frame and the adjoining wall face.

Ashlar *a.* Stone cut into smooth rectangular blocks and laid with fine joints in regular

courses. *b.* In an attic room, timber studding, normally plastered, cutting off the angle between roof line and floor.

Baluster A vertical or stone timber member, often turned, supporting a handrail or capping, as on a staircase or balustrade.

Bargeboard (or verge board) A timber board, often moulded or carved, fixed to the verge of a roof. Originating in timber-framed construction, where it covered the exposed ends of the purlins and wall plates, it was later used also on brick and stone buildings, particularly in the nineteenth century.

Bay The space between two roof trusses, or between the truss and end wall of a building or room. Also used to describe the vertical divisions of a façade, by pilasters or windows.

Bond The pattern of laying bricks in walling. English Bond consists of alternate courses of headers (bricks laid at right angles to the wall line) and stretchers (bricks laid parallel to the wall line). Flemish Bond consists of alternate stretchers and headers in each course.

Box-frame construction Timber-framed construction in which

the walls support the roof and the upper floors, the whole being framed together.

Braces Timber members, often curved, linking horizontal and

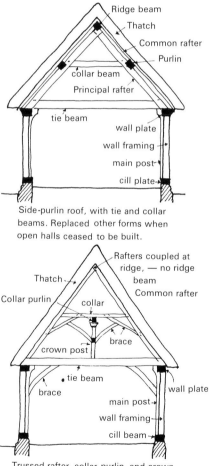

Side-purlin roof, with tie and collar beams. Replaced other forms when open halls ceased to be built.

Trussed rafter, collar purlin, and crown post roof. Typical of southern and eastern areas.

Roof construction in box-framed buildings

vertical members in a roof or wall, to strengthen the joint between them and prevent distortion of the framing.

Burgage plot A house site in a medieval town, generally long and narrow, held by a burgher or freeman of the town.

Buttery A service room for the storage of drink.

Byre A building to house animals, either a separate building or the lower end of a long-house.

Chamfer A splay, cutting off the outer angles of a beam, a door or window jamb, or a window mullion.

Closed string stair A stair in which the treads and risers are framed into the string and their ends concealed by it.

Closing Order An order placed on a house by the local authority, preventing it from being occupied as a dwelling until certain specified works have been carried out.

Clunch A soft, chalky limestone sometimes used in building, particularly in Chilterns and parts of East Anglia.

Cob A primitive form of concrete made of chalk, mud and chopped straw.

Collar beam A beam connecting a pair of principal or common rafters at some distance above their feet.

Collar purlin A longitudinal timber joining a series of collars at their centres in a trussed rafter roof.

Common rafters Pairs of rafters forming a pitched roof, either supported on purlins and trusses, or framed in a trussed rafter roof.

Console A carved or moulded bracket supporting a door hood or canopy.

Coping The capping, of stone or brick, to a parapet or free-standing wall.

Cornice In Classical architecture, the top member of the entablature. In domestic building, a moulding at the junction of the wall and the ceiling in a room, or a moulding on an external wall at the eaves line.

Crown glass Early blown glass cut from a disc and having a slightly uneven texture.

Crown post A vertical post rising from a tie-beam in a roof to support a collar purlin.

Crucks Large curved timbers supporting a roof from the ground, without the need for load-bearing walls.

Curing chamber A space generally of circular plan, leading off an early fireplace, where meat was hung to cure in the smoke from the fire.

Cut string stair A stair in which the string is cut away to allow the ends of the treads and risers to be seen. The nosing of the tread is generally returned round its ends as a capping to the string at tread level.

Cutwater An angled projection to the piers supporting a bridge.

Dado Panelling on the lower part of an internal wall, usually extending to about three feet above floor level.

Dais A raised platform, particularly at the upper end of a hall.

Dog-leg stair A stair formed in two flights, the upper flight returned alongside the lower flight, with a half-space landing at the junction of the flights.

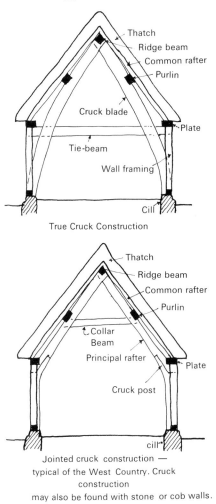

True Cruck Construction

Jointed cruck construction — typical of the West Country. Cruck construction may also be found with stone or cob walls.

Double-hung sash window A timber window consisting of two vertical sliding sashes, operated by counter-weights concealed in a boxed frame.

Double-pile plan A plan of a house two rooms deep under a single-span roof.

Down barn A barn, sometimes incorporating a cottage, built on downland away from the main farm complex. Typical of the late eighteenth and early nineteenth centuries when downland was enclosed for grazing.

247

Dripping eaves Eaves of a roof with a wide overhang and without gutters. Almost universal with thatch, dripping eaves are sometimes found on stone-slated and occasionally on tiled roofs.

Duck boards Slatted wooden boards laid in lead parapet and valley gutters to protect the lead from damage.

End-hall house A house with a hall and one two-storeyed block only, containing service rooms on the ground floor and a solar on the first floor.

Entablature The structure supported by a column or collonade, divided in Classical architecture and most Classical reconstructions into three horizontal bands, architrave, frieze and cornice.

Façade The main external elevation of a building.

Fire hood A hood, generally of lath and plaster, formed over an open hearth to direct the smoke to the louvre or smoke-hole in the roof of an open hall. A forerunner of the chimney.

Firring Levelling up uneven joists or rafters with tapered timbers fixed on top of them.

First-floor hall house A house where the main living area, the hall, is on the first floor and is often approached by an external stair.

Four-centred arch An arch struck from four centres, in use from the later fifteenth to the mid-seventeenth centuries, sometimes called a Tudor arch.

Frieze In Classical architecture, the centre member of an entablature. In domestic building a band, sometimes ornamen-ted, at the top of a wall, below the ceiling or cornice.

Glazing bars The bars dividing window sashes into smaller panes.

Hall In early houses, the main living area. In later periods the hall declined in importance and eventually became the entrance vestibule.

Hardwood A term used to describe timber from deciduous trees.

Heartwood Wood cut from the centre of the log which was no longer growing when the tree was cut. Generally durable and resistant to beetle attack.

Hipped roof A roof in which the slopes rise from the eaves on all sides of the building, that is, without gables; the hip being the junction between two adjoining slopes.

Hood mould (weather mould) A projecting moulding over the head of a door or window opening, designed to protect the opening from rainwater running down the wall face.

Hydraulic lime Lime containing a proportion of clay and other minerals, the effect of which increases its strength and ability to harden while still drying out.

Hygroscopic salts Salts which will absorb moisture from the atmosphere.

Jamb The side of a door or window opening.

Jetty An overhanging wall in timber-framed construction. Usually an external feature, it is occasionally found internally in open hall houses.

Jointed cruck truss A roof truss in which the crucks are formed in two sections, jointed at or near the eaves line.

Joists The smaller of the timber beams carrying a floor or ceiling. In small rooms they may span between the walls, but in larger rooms they are carried on main beams.

Keystone The central stone or brick in an arch, sometimes treated decoratively.

King post A vertical timber member rising from a tie beam in a roof to support the ridge piece.

Knapping (of flint) Cutting of flints to show the dark, shiny interior.

Laithe house A later development of the long-house where the byre, or the barn, still attached to the house, is not connected with it internally.

Lintel A beam spanning an opening of a doorway, window or a fireplace.

Listed building A building included in the Statutory Lists of Buildings of Special Architectural or Historic Interest.

Long-house An early type of house, divided into a living area and a byre for animals, usually with opposed doors and sometimes with a through-passage between the sections.

Louvre *a.* A horizontal slat inserted at an angle in an unglazed window to prevent the entry of driving rain. *b.* A turret in the roof of an open hall, sited above the hearth, to allow smoke to escape.

Mansard roof A roof having two pitches, that of the lower part of the roof being steeper than that of the upper slope.

Matchboarding Timber boarding, grooved and tongued at the edges to fit together as a covering for walls and, less often, for ceilings.

Mathematical tiling Special tiles used for vertical cladding, made to resemble brickwork and pointed as for brickwork after fixing.

Mortice A rectangular recess cut in a timber framing member, to take a tenon (q.v.).

Mullion A vertical member of stone or timber which divides a window into sections known as lights.

Muntin A vertical intermediate framing member in a door, or in panelling.

Newel post *a.* The central post of a spiral or newel stair. *b.* The main vertical framing member in a straight-flight, dog-leg or open-well stair. Newel posts are often finished with ornamental caps and pendants.

Ogee arch An arch formed with a reversed curve, giving an S-shaped profile.

Open hall The hall or living area of a medieval or early Tudor house, open to the roof and generally extending through two storeys.

Oriel A projecting bay window at ground or an upper floor level. In the later medieval manor house, the oriel at the upper end of the hall eventually developed into a small projecting room or alcove.

Pantile A single-lap tile with an S-shaped profile.

Pantry A service room for the storage of food (originally bread).

Parapet A wall extending above a roof, at the eaves or at a gable.

Pargetting An early term for any plastering; now generally restricted to ornamental external plastering, typical of the sixteenth and seventeenth century timber-framed buildings.

Parlour A 'withdrawing' room leading off the hall. In early houses it was generally used for sleeping, and later it became a private living room.

Party wall An internal wall dividing two properties.

Pediment A shallow and triangular, or occasionally arched, head to a door or window opening, derived from the shallow pitched gable end of the classical temple.

Pentice A lean-to open shelter, or a porch of similar design.

Pilaster A half-column fixed against a wall, often framing a door opening.

Pitch (roof) The angle of the roof slope.

Plank and muntin An early form of timber partition consisting of vertical members (muntins) linked by thinner planks slotted into the grooved edges of the muntins.

Plinth A projecting moulding at the base of an external wall, column or pier.

Principal rafters The main rafters in a roof truss, supporting the purlins and the ridge piece.

Purlin A principal horizontal member in a roof, supporting the common rafters and carried on the principal rafters of the trusses.

Queen post roof A roof where the trusses have two vertical members which support the principal rafters, rising from the tie-beam and generally tied at their heads by a collar beam.

Quoin *a.* The corner of a building. *b.* The stones forming the corner of a building, often larger than those in the rest of the wall and also sometimes ornamented or raised.

Rail A horizontal framing member in panelling or a door.

Reveal The side of an opening in a wall for a window or door.

Ridge The upper intersection of the main slopes of a roof.

Ridge piece or beam A beam forming the ridge of the roof, supporting the tops of the common rafters and itself supported on the main trusses.

Rubble Roughly cut stone in a wall. It may be laid in courses or completely random laid. The joints are thicker than those in ashlar work and the whole effect coarser and less regular.

Sapwood The outer part of the log, which was still growing when the tree was cut. More susceptible to fungus and beetle attack than the heartwood (q.v.).

Scheduled Ancient Monument A building, monument or an earthwork which may not be altered or demolished without the consent of the Department of the Environment. Inhabited houses and churches do not qualify for this kind of scheduling.

Screens passage The passage at the lower end of a hall, separated from the hall by a screen rather than a solid wall.

Shingles Thin slabs of timber, usually oak, used for roofing, similarly to slates or tiles. In modern work cedar is often used.

Shouldered arch A mock arch formed by shaped timber posts or stone jambs supporting a lintel.

Single-pile plan The plan of a house one room deep.

Skirting A moulding at the base of an internal wall.

Sleeper walls Dwarf walls, generally built honeycomb-fashion to provide ventilation, supporting timber suspended floors.

Smoke bay The first improvement to the open hearth in an open hall. The upper part of the central truss in a two-bay hall or, in a larger hall, the truss nearest one end wall, was filled in to channel the smoke towards the louvre.

Softwood A term used to describe timber from coniferous trees. Some 'softwoods' are in fact harder than some 'hardwoods' (q.v.).

Solar A private withdrawing room, used for sleeping or as a living room, at first floor level. (Literally, 'The room above the floor'.)

Soldier arch A course of bricks laid vertically above a door or window opening. Is intended to give the appearance of an arch, but has no structural value.

Spere truss The truss at the lower end of a hall, retaining aisle posts and framing the screen.

Stile The outer vertical framing member in a door.

String The outer member of a staircase, into which the treads and risers are framed.

String course A continuous moulding on an external wall, often at an upper floor level, dividing the façade into storey heights.

Strut An alternative name for a brace (q.v.), but generally used of straight timbers.

Stucco A term used to describe a hard plaster finish, often incorporating mouldings and ornament in classical style, popular in the late eighteenth and early nineteenth centuries.

Studs, studding Vertical timber members in a wall or partition.

Tenon A projection on a timber member, formed by cutting away the surrounding timber, to fit into a mortice (q.v.). Generally used for jointing timbers at right angles to each other.

Tie-beam A beam joining the feet of a pair of principal rafters in a roof truss.

Torching Pointing the underside of a tiled or slated roof with mortar, to improve weather and wind resistance. It is not needed when a roof is felted, and little used today.

Truss A framed structure supporting a roof, consisting of a pair of principal rafters, secured by a tie-beam or a collar-beam, supporting purlins which in turn support the common rafters.

Trussed rafter roof A roof without main trusses but generally having tie-beams at intervals. Each pair of rafters is joined by a collar. Sometimes there are struts between the collar and the rafters.

Two-centred arch A Gothic arch struck from two centres.

Underpinning Strengthening a wall by inserting new foundations without disturbing the wall itself.

Valley The internal junction between two roof slopes.

Valley gutter A horizontal gutter between two parallel pitched roofs.

Vault *a.* An underground chamber, also one used for burials. *b.* An arched ceiling constructed of stone or, less often, of brick, found in some cellars and the undercrofts of some first-floor hall houses.

Verges see Bargeboard.

Voussoirs Tapered stones, forming an arch.

Wattle and daub The earliest form of infilling to timber-framed walls and partitions. Vertical timber rods were inserted into holes and grooves in the horizontal framing members. Willow or hazel withies were woven around these, basket-fashion, and the whole finished with a 'daub' of clay, chalk and mud, with a final coat of lime plaster.

Wealden house A late medieval and Tudor form of open-hall house of small or medium size, based on the plan of the larger house. The name is derived from the Weald of Kent and Sussex, where some of the best examples are found.

Weather boarding Overlapping timber boards laid horizontally, to clad a wall (generally used externally).

Weather mould see Hood mould.

Wind bracing Curved braces in the plane of the sloping faces of a roof, linking the trusses and the purlins.

Bibliography

General
Cunnington, P. *How Old is Your House?* Yeovil 1999
Godfrey, W. H. *Our Building Inheritance*. London 1954
Marshall, J. & I. Williams, *The Victorian House*. London 1986
Wright, A. *Craft Techniques for Traditional Buildings*. London 1991

Chapter 1
Briggs, M.S. *Goths & Vandals*. London 1952
Fawcett, J. (Ed.) *The future of the past*. London 1976
Ministry of Housing and Local Government, *Historic towns: Preservation and change*. London 1967

Chapter 2
Cambridgeshire County Council. *Guide to Historic Buildings Law*. 1995
Department of the Environment/Department of National Heritage. *Planning Policy Guidance 15: Planning and the Historic Environment*. HMSO 1994
Mynors, C. *Listed Buildings, Conservation Areas and Monuments*: 3rd edition. London 1999
Parnell, A. *Building Legislation and Historic Buildings*, London, 1987
Sparrow, C. & D. Pearce, *Public Inquiries - Presenting the Conservation Case*. Council for British Archaeology and Civic Trust, London 1971
Suddards. R. W. *Listed Buildings - the Law and Practice*. London, 1982

Chapter 3
Aldous, T. *Goodbye Britain*. London, 1975
Binney, M. and K. Martin. *The Country House, To Be or Not To Be*. London, 1982
Cantacuzino, S. and S, Brandt. *Saving Old Buildings*. London, 1981
Christian, R. *Vanishing Britain*. Newton Abbot, 1977
Darley, G. A. *A Future for Farm Buildings* (SAVE) London, 1988
Department of the Environment. *New Life for Old Buildings*. HMSO 1971
English Heritage *Register of Buildings at Risk*. Published annually
Lowenthal, D. and M. Binney (eds). *Our Past Before Us—why do we save it?* London, 1982
Mitchell, E. *Emergency Repairs for Historic Buildings*. English Heritage 1988
SAVE *Silent Mansions—more Country Houses at Risk*. London, 1981
- - - *The Fall of Zion—Northern Chapel Architecture and its Future*. London, 1980
- - - *Vanishing Houses of England*. London, 1982
Shillingford, A. E. P. *England's Vanishing Windmills*. London, 1979
Society for the Protection of Ancient Buildings. *The SPAB Barns Book*. London, 1982
Strong, R., J, Harris and M. Binney (eds). *The Destruction of the Country House*. London, 1974
Williams, B. *The Under-use of Upper Floors in Historic Town Centres*. York, 1978

Chapter 4
Architectural Heritage Fund *Funds for Historic Buildings in England and Wales - A Directory of Sources*. 2001
Architectural Heritage Fund *How to Rescue a Ruin - by setting up a local Buildings Preservation Trust*. 1999
Charities Aid Foundation *Directory of Grant-Making Trusts*. Published annually
English Heritage. *Directory of public sources of grants for the repair and conversion of historic buildings*. London, 1988

Bibliography

Chapters 5 and 6

Benson, Evans, Colomb and Jones. *The Housing Rehabilitation Handbook*. London, 1982

Bowyer, J. *Vernacular Building Conservation*. London, 1980

Braun, H. *The Restoration of Old Houses*. London, 1954

Brereton, C. *The Repair of Historic Buildings: Advice on principles and methods*. English Heritage 1991

British Standard BS 7913 *Guide to the principles of conservation of historic buildings*. 1998

Cathedral Communications *The Building Conservation Directory*. Tisbury. Published annually

Davey, A., B. Heath, D. Hodges, R. Milne and M. Palmer, *The Care and Conservation of Georgian Houses - a maintenance manual*. Edinburgh, 1978

Department of the Environment, *Notes on the Repair and Preservation of Historic Buildings - Timberwork*. HMSO 1965

Edmonds, R. C. *Your Country Cottage*. Newton Abbot, 1971

Fielden, B. M, *Conservation of Historic Buildings*, Oxford, 1998

Insall, D. W. *The Care of Old Buildings*. London, 1958

Lander, H. *The House Restorer's Guide*. Newton Abbot

Pike, B. *The Good Looking House*. Bristol, 1980

Oliver, A. *Dampness in Buildings*. Oxford, 1997

Powys, A. K. *The Repair of Ancient Buildings*. SPAB, London, 1929 facsimile reprint with notes, 1981

Saunders, M. T*he Historic House Owner's Companion*. London, 1987

Thomas, A. *Treatment of Damp in Old Buildings*, SPAB Technical Pamphlet, London

Chapter 7

Billett, M. *Thatching and Thatched Buildings*, London, 1979

Brockett, P and A. Wright, *The care and repair of thatched roofs*. SPAB Technical Pamphlet 1986

Building Research Establishment Digests: *Recovering old timber roofs*, 1990; *Condensation in roofs*, 1975

Council for Small Industries in Rural Areas *The Thatcher's Craft*. 1961

Council for the Care of Churches *Church Roof Coverings*. London 1952

Cox, J and Letts, J. English Heritage Research Transactions Vol. 6 *Thatch: Thatching in England 1940–94*. London 2000

Moir, J, and J. Letts, English Heritage Research Transactions Vol. 5. *Thatch: Thatching in England 1790–1940*. London 1999.

Ridout, B. *An Introduction to Timber Decay and its Treatment*. Stourbridge, 1992

Ridout, B. *Timber Decay in Buildings: The conservation approach to treatment*.London, 2000

Williams, G. *Chimneys in Old Buildings*. SPAB Technical Pamphlet, London.

Chapter 8

Ashurst, J. & N. English Heritage Technical Handbook Series. London, 1988; Vol. 1, *Stone Masonry*; Vol. 2, *Terracotta, Brick and Earth*; Vol. 3, *Mortars, Plasters and Renders*; Vol. 4, *Metals*; Vol. 5, *Wood, Glass and Resins*

Brunskill, R. and A. Clifton-Taylor *English Brickwork*. London, 1978

Clarke, Martin and A. Townsend, *The Repair of Wood Windows*. SPAB Technical Pamphlet 13

The Georgian Group Guide No.1. *Windows*. London

Historic Scotland Technical Advice Notes: No. 3, *Performance Standards for Timber Sash and Case Windows*. 1994; No. 1, *Preparation and Use of Lime Mortars*. 1995

Holmes, S. and M. Wingate, *Building with Lime: A practical introduction*. London, 1997

Hughes, P. *The need for old buildings to breathe*. SPAB Information Sheet

Locke, Peter. *Timber treatment - a warning about the de-frassing of timber and the surface treatment of timber-framed houses*. SPAB Information Sheet

Martin, D. G. *Maintenance and Repair of Stone Buildings*. Council for the Care of Churches. London, 1970

Schofield, J. *Basic Limewash.* SPAB Information Sheet

Townsend, A. *Rough-Cast for Historic Buildings.* SPAB Information Sheet

Williams-Ellis, C, and J. E. Eastwick-Field. *Buildings in Cob, Pisé and Stabilised Earth.* London, 1919

Building Research Establishment Digests: *Cleaning exterior masonry,* Parts 1 & 2, 2000; *Clay bricks and clay brick masonry,* Parts 1 & 2, 1999; *Rising Damp in Walls, Diagnosis and Treatment,* 1989; *Painting Exterior Wood.,* 1997

SPAB Technical Pamphlets, London: J. Ashurst. *Cleaning of Stone and Brick;* J. Macgregor. *Outward Leaning Walls;* K. Reid. *Panel lnfilling to Timber-framed Buildings;* G. Williams. *Pointing of Stone and Brick Walling.*

Chapter 9

Historic Scotland Technical Advice Note 2: *Conservation of Plasterwork.* 1994

Hughes, P. *Patching Old Floorboards.* SPAB Information Sheet

SPAB Technical Pamphlet: *Strengthening Timber Floors.* London

Chapter 10

Council for the Care of Churches. *The Conservation of English Wall Paintings.* London, 1959

Lander, H. *The Do's and Don'ts of House and Cottage Restoration.* Redruth, 1999

Chapter 11

Clark, K. *Informed Conservation: Understanding Historic Buildings and their landscapes for conservation.* English Heritage. 2001

Lander, H. *The Do's and Don'ts of House and Cottage Restoration.* Redruth, 1999

Chapter 13

Building Research Establishment Digests, *Soakaways.* 1991

Williams, G. *Chimneys in Old Buildings.* SPAB Technical Pamphlet. London

Chapter 14

Building Research Establishment Digests: *Increasing the Fire-resistance of Existing Timber Floors.* 1988;

Department of the Environment. *New Life for Old Churches.* HMSO, 1978

de la Hey, C. and K. Powell, *Churches: A Question of Conversion.* SAVE Britain's Heritage. 1987

Latham, D. *Creative Re-use of Buildings.* Shaftesbury 2000

SPAB Technical Pamphlet *Electrical Installations*

Index

Page numbers in *italic* refer to illustrations